PULLING NO

PUNCHES

PULLING NO PUNCHES

*Memoirs Of
A Woman In Politics*

By India Edwards

*G.P. Putnam's Sons
New York*

SBN: 399-11574-9

Library of Congress Cataloging in Publication Data

Edwards, India.
  Pulling no punches.

  1. Edwards, India. 2. Politicians—Biography.
I. Title.
HQ1413.E48A33   1977   329   76-56223

PRINTED IN THE UNITED STATES OF AMERICA

Dedication

To Herbert, my dear husband, a mature man whose loving understanding and cooperation made possible my activity in politics and so this book. And to my courageous, liberated mother, India Thomas Gillespie, whose self-reliance, compassion and tolerance have been my constant inspiration. Also to my beloved daughter, India Moffett Williams, who with her fine husband, John Williams, have given me five lovely granddaughters: Challen, India, Pamela, Andrea and Eugenie, members of the current honest, conservation-minded generation: the hope of the world.

Introduction

In the autumn of 1948, while traveling aboard the Whistle Stop Campaign Train, I was having breakfast with President and Mrs. Truman. Since their dining room was small and there usually were local leaders aboard who were honored with invitations to have a meal with the President and Mrs. Truman—known as "the Boss" to her husband—my being the only breakfast guest was a special event.

Their daughter, Margaret, never appeared at the breakfast table, for she was a late riser but she gave her father valuable help later in the day when at every stop the crowd would yell "We want Marg'ret, we want Marg'ret" if she did not appear the moment the President finished speaking. The introduction of the Boss, and their daughter was the finale of every whistle stop and a grand finale it was.

Near the end of the meal, the President confided in me, "India, sometimes I think there are only two people in the whole United States who really believe I am going to be elected and both of them are at this table. But the Boss is not one of them."

I am not writing my memoirs simply to record moments as unique as that memorable one in 1948, though the eight years I spent work-

ing for and with the thirty-third President of the United States were
the highlight of my career. I am following President Truman's
advice to "tell the truth and pull no punches" when I asked him in
1957 whether he would have any objection to my writing about my
life. I want to remind women who today are working for equal rights
and seeking to have more women in elective and appointee offices
that Presidents Franklin D. Roosevelt and Truman were actively involving women in government years ago. Eleanor Roosevelt and
Mary W. Dewson, the head of Democratic women in New York
State and then vice chairman of the Democratic National Committee, never let FDR forget that women are first-class citizens and
should be given a voice in government.

Roosevelt appointed the first woman to serve in the cabinet.
Frances Perkins served as Secretary of Labor during all of the years
of FDR's administration. Two women represented him as ministers
to foreign nations: Mrs. J. Borden Harriman to Norway and Mrs.
Ruth Bryan Owen to Denmark. He included at least one woman on
almost every one of the commissions established to advance his
New Deal and to lay the foundation for the new world organization
of which he dreamed. Mrs. Charles W. Tillett took Molly Dewson's
place as vice chairman of the Democratic National Committee during the latter part of the Roosevelt Administration and with Mrs.
Roosevelt carried on the support of women.

When Harry S. Truman became President, he could have had no
one nudging his elbow and saying "don't forget the women." He
and his estimable wife, Bess Wallace Truman, did not number career women among their friends. It was not difficult for me to persuade President Truman that he should give consideration to wom-
en. His wife was an astute politician, albeit not a vocal one. My
campaign was to get a lot of jobs for a lot of women instead of a
Cabinet post or an ambassadorship for myself, though such a position was offered to me in 1948.

While working for the Chicago *Tribune* during World War I, I discovered that I could tell exactly what sort of woman a man had as a
wife after I had dealt with him a short time. His attitude toward the
women with whom he worked was conditioned by his mental image
of his wife. If Mrs. Truman had not been the Boss in her husband's
estimation, he might not have been so willing to give consideration

to women whose names I presented as possible high officeholders. Helping to elect Democrats was my chief occupation during the years I worked with the Democratic National Committee, but I determined early that helping to raise the status of women in our party was an important part of my duty.

As a woman with very little ambition but with a vast concern for and interest in people, I think I made a success of being a wife, mother, newspaper-woman and politician. I hope these memoirs will encourage more women into political life and to participate in government on every level.

After serving as vice chairman of the Democratic National Committee and director of the women's division of the Democratic Party, my name was presented to the Democratic convention for the Vice Presidential nomination in 1952. I knew it was an idle gesture. I told a male reporter, who couldn't believe I really didn't expect to be nominated, "Since I'm on the national committee I can't campaign for anybody, least of all myself. But there's no denying that the mere gesture is in the right direction. Just getting such a thing talked about may one day—who knows how soon—make it easier for it to happen. In other words, although I see no reason whatsoever why a woman shouldn't be Vice President, I feel sure that woman won't be me."

My meaning was clear, even to the male reporters and most of the male politicians. There were some, however, who really feared that the work of valiant women would make it possible to have me nominated.

Speaker of the House of Representatives Sam Rayburn, a staunch friend and one of the finest men I ever knew, was the chairman of the 1952 convention. My sponsors had to obtain his permission to present my name for nomination. Shortly before the morning session at which my name was put into nomination, one of my strong Texas supporters said to the Speaker tearfully, "Mr. Sam, is it true that India is going to withdraw her name after it is presented?"

"You're damn right it is," Mr. Sam answered. "Otherwise I wouldn't let any lady's name be put into nomination."

The Chicago *Tribune,* where I had spent over twenty years as an editor, ran a delightful editorial entitled "We Rise to Defend a Friend":

Mrs. India Edwards . . . still holds a warm spot in our hearts in spite of the fact that in recent years she has frequently been seen in the disreputable company of Democrats. For old times' sake we feel it our duty to denounce those low, scheming characters who are talking of nominating her for Vice President.

Mrs. Edwards has opinions on virtually every subject, which she delights in expressing, sometimes at length. The principal duty of the Vice President is to preside over the Senate, and the Senators have jealously seen to it that the Vice President only presides. He may speak only when spoken to. It's a mousetrap, India. Two months of such inhibitions and the men in the white coats would be closing in on you.

In 1965, the Women's National Democratic Club threw a seventieth birthday party for me, and brought together such old friends as Averell Harriman, Willard Wirtz, Oscar L. Chapman, Leon Keyserling, Anna Roosevelt Halsted and scores of others.

President and Mrs. Johnson sent me a beautifully framed picture of their family with the inscription, "Congratulations to you, India, on a milestone that truly represents as many good *deeds* as it does good *days*."

Harry Truman wired, "Having just breezed by my 81st, what can be exciting about a mere 70? I am glad for you that it has given many of us an occasion to greet you and to thank you and to wish you a long, happy and useful life."

My old friend Adlai Stevenson, then U.S. ambassador to the United Nations, wrote, "There must have been an error in the number of your birthday. Nobody is older than I am. And few are younger than you are in spirit, in the love of life, and in the understanding of humanity. I would add my gratitude for the political advice and assistance you have given me over the years, but I would not want to remind you of one of your few unsuccessful causes! So instead I send you all my best wishes for a busy and happy future."

Emma Guffey Miller of Slippery Rock, Pennsylvania, Democratic national committeewoman for Pennsylvania from 1932 until her death in 1970 at the age of ninety-five, wrote, "I never have known a more astute and able politician than India, who I believe had as much to do with the election of President Truman in 1948 as our beloved Harry himself."

I cannot agree with Emma that I had as much to do with electing

Truman as he did himself but I know there was no one who worked harder to help President Truman in the campaign of 1948. As a result of that work I had the good fortune to be associated for eight years with the thirty-third President of the United States, a thoroughly ethical man in his private and public life.

I have now reached the time of life when, as Montaigne wrote, "I speak truth, not so much as I would but as much as I dare; and I dare a little the more, as I grow older."

Chapter 1

To start, I should go back almost eighty years to the first summer I remember. That summer we spent the warm weather months in Waukesha, Wisconsin. My mother, India Thomas Walker, my baby sister Virginia, our nurse Babby, and I, three years old on June 16, 1898, stayed at the Fountain House, which my uncle managed. It was a fashionable resort frequented by Midwesterners and Southerners. We were among the latter, for we came from Nashville, Tennessee. We could not have afforded to be there, but Uncle Jim was a bachelor and wanted some of his family with him. Though I cannot remember his being with us, Mother told me my father came several times that summer. It was not until the next year that my parents were divorced. My father, Archibald Walker, had a fondness for the bottle, a fact that accounted, no doubt, for Mother's abomination of hard liquor.

My most vivid memory of that summer was watching a group of ladies and gentlemen ride away in a tallyho, a high coach drawn by four horses. Babby was holding baby Virginia in her arms and struggling to keep me from running after the tallyho. I wanted more than anything in the world to be up there with my beautiful, red-haired mother in her green silk suit and big hat with a green plume flowing

13

over one shoulder. Ladies cared nothing for comfort in those days.
The more inappropriate their costumes, the more chic and proper
they were. I remember my mother and her friends in their tennis and
golfing outfits: long, white skirts that touched the ground, long-
sleeved, high-collared blouses and sailor hats pinned atop their
bouffant coiffures, hats which almost made them fly in high winds.

I've retained such clear images from that summer because it was
so different from our everyday life.

Actually, I never had the joy of riding in a tallyho, despite Babby's promise that when I was a lady I could ride in one every day.
Dear Babby, who could neither read nor write but who cared for us
wisely and lovingly and for whom we had an affection second to
none, was as homely as she was black.

I was a most unattractive-looking baby, judging by my pictures
and from the way I remember myself when I was old enough to be
conscious of my looks, especially of the difference between my pic-
ture-book pretty sister and my own plucked-chicken appearance.
When Uncle Jim, who adored me from the very first, brought his
dear friend, the Shakespearean actress, Viola Allen, to see me, she
admired the lacy bassinette in which I was being displayed and then,
struggling for something nice to say about the skinny bit of humanity
within, uttered these words: "She has such pretty little ears." Mother, who like mothers the world over, thought her first-born was a
thing of beauty, was infuriated.

Babby was a snob of the first order, and although I am sure she
knew we were far from wealthy she considered us "quality folk,"
and she was not bashful in telling the German or French governess
of two children of a very wealthy family from Chicago summering at
the Fountain House that "my chillun don't have real lace on their
underwear like yours do but yours won't never move in the same society that mine will." I heard about this in later years from Mother,
and I often remembered it when I was society editor of the Chicago
Tribune and sometimes wrote about those two girls who had had real
lace on their underwear. They were about my age, perhaps a little
younger. I occasionally met one of them after I moved to Washington, Mrs. Raymond F. Tartiere, the owner of the house in nearby
Virginia that President and Mrs. John F. Kennedy rented.

I had a happy childhood in Nashville and never missed not having
a father in the house because we were a large close family. My

mother's brother lived next door, and his three sons were like my brothers. We made our home with our maternal grandmother. Our paternal grandparents, aunts, uncles and cousins lived in the same neighborhood.

Mother was the beauty of both families. We were delighted with her many beaux, who brought us candy and often took us riding in their runabouts (light, one-seated open carriages) behind high-stepping horses. Grandmother's surrey, pulled by a steady horse, seemed very unexciting when she took us to market after these drives with our make-believe uncles. If, however, Millard, our black houseman, had several live chickens on the front seat when we left the market, the drive was more exciting.

I was "l'enfant terrible," always blamed for everything naughty my sister and my cousins did. I was not the only one punished, but I was always scolded and made to feel responsible—which I may have been. Spanking was not the Thomas family method of punishing children. Instead, we girls were made to wear our boy cousins' clothing, and they had to wear our dresses. We would be so ashamed that we would remain indoors. Actually, the boys' short, tight pants with wide-collared blouses, often edged with embroidery, were far prettier than our dresses, but girls then did not want to wear pants. William, John Thomas, Virginia and I were punished in this way when we had a funeral for our live white rabbits. I have always thought the punishment was most unfair, for we had no way of knowing that a funeral should only follow death. We had been fascinated by the funeral of the man who lived next door to Grandmother, so we decided to have one of our own. Following Babby's description of an actual funeral, Virginia and I took some black veils from Grandma's closet and draped them over our heads. William and John dug the holes, and then we put the four rabbits into four shoe boxes. We put flowers from the garden on the graves after we had shoveled dirt over the boxes. While we were mourning loudly, someone in the house heard us and came to see what the matter was. By the time the rabbits were dug up they were dead, and then we had a real burial for them, and our weeping was real, too.

The first and only automobile I ever rode in as a little girl was my uncle's White Steamer, which had the words "The Yellow Bird" on both sides of the tonneau. Those privileged to ride in the vehicle entered it from steps at the rear and sat along the sides, facing each other. When President Teddy Roosevelt came to Nashville, he was driven in this automobile from the railroad station to wherever he spoke. The entire family was very proud of this distinction and perhaps that is why most of my relatives were Republicans! My mother always was a Democrat and many years later she became very angry when one of her sisters pleaded, "Don't say anything at the country club today about little India working for the Democrats." To Mother I was solely responsible for our party's victories.

I have always been considered honest and forthright. If I have been exceedingly honest—an impossibility, I believe—a punishment inflicted on me by my grandmother is responsible. The terrible lie that brought about the punishment concerned my unusual first name. It was my mother's name and also a great aunt's, and I hated it. Why couldn't I have been named Mary Lou or Lucy Lee or something equally familiar? I became so bored of responding with the truth when people asked me why I was named India that, when a new Sunday school teacher asked the question, I answered, "Because I was born in India." Then I went on to tell about our life there. I knew nothing of that far-off country, but neither did she, apparently. I told her about the monkey and parrot we had brought home with us. I described some of their antics, no doubt calling on memories of stories that had been read to me or that I had read myself. When the Sunday school teacher met my mother a short time later she suggested that it would be nice if the class could visit me some day to see the monkey and the parrot.

Mother understood that I wasn't lying, but simply trying to be interesting. Grandmother took another point of view, for she was a strict Presbyterian who insisted that my sister and I go to church three times each Sunday: to morning school, then to the deadly long morning service, and later in the day to Christian Endeavor. Grandmother's punishment for lying was to wash my mouth with kitchen soap and then to cleanse the rest of my insides with a large dose of castor oil. The thought of it still makes me ill.

My memories of our move to Chicago are jumbled, and there is no one left of Mother's generation to ask for details. There was a fire at grandmother's house one night. Although it was almost destroyed, everyone escaped safely—that is, everyone but the big, walking doll which had belonged to an aunt and was my most prized possession.

After the fire Mother went to Chicago to work, and my sister and I were temporarily parceled out to aunts. I started school in Nashville, but by second grade we were in Chicago. A few years later, Mother married John Alexander Gillespie, a Canadian. He was truly a father to Virginia and me until he died in the late thirties.

I do not think there was such a thing as a ready-made dress in those days, at least not in Nashville or St. Louis, where we later moved. All our clothes were made by a seamstress who seemed to spend her life in our house. Annie, a young black woman, came once a week and spent the day washing the hair of all the females in the household. Living in a matriarchy, with a grandmother, two great-grandmothers, a mother and two young unmarried aunts, it was quite a task. Annie used rainwater which had been collected in a huge barrel out by the kitchen stoop to wash our hair. She brushed us dry in the sun. If there were no sun we sat in front of a fireplace, which was very uncomfortable in summer.

I remember the first evening gown I persuaded Miss Tommy, our seamstress, to make for me, with nothing but straps over the shoulders. "Don't deliver it until about 8 o'clock Saturday night," I told her, figuring that if I put it on at the last minute before the boy who was taking me to the fraternity dance arrived I could leave the house without Father seeing me.

The plan did not succeed. My father called me into the room and said, "Nindy, take off your cape and let us see your new dress." There was nothing I could do but slip off the wrap and let Father see my bare shoulders and arms. Miss Tommy, who had followed me downstairs, was standing there and Father, after taking one look at me, told her to take me upstairs and put some short sleeves into my dress if she had any more material. I almost died with embarrassment that my young beau should see me treated like a child, but, anticipating my father's reaction, Miss Tommy had some material.

Although he was my stepfather, Jack Gillespie was a real father to Virginia and me and we felt as if he loved us as dearly as he did his own two daughters, Grace and Helen. Brought up in a Baptist household in a small town in Ontario, he was much more strict than mother. He never would allow us to have bicycles, for he considered them unladylike. He did not approve of our playing card games, although we did so except when his mother visited us. Then the cards were hidden and we had morning and evening prayers, which I dreaded, for as the eldest daughter I had to read aloud from the Bible. My difficulties with the long Biblical names made Grandmother Gillespie aware that I was not accustomed to pronouncing them. Father also disapproved of the popular songs we sang with our friends as I banged on the piano. He embarrassed us by snatching the music from the piano, tearing it into pieces and forbidding us to sing "such trash." "Everybody's Doing It" elicited his worst wrath.

We had moved to St. Louis after a year in Detroit. One day in high school, I played hookey to go riding in a new Ford that an eighteen-year-old boyfriend had just received as a birthday present. He was waiting in the little car outside the school when I arrived, and the combination of the glorious spring day and puppy love made me an easy victim to his suggestion that we drive out in the country for the day. We crossed the Mississippi River and drove to Belleville, Illinois, where we had hot dogs and Cokes and banana splits.

Leaving the lunchroom, my young hero suggested that we get a marriage license and be married by the justice of the peace whose sign we could see across the street. I acquiesced enough to cross the street, but I was reluctant to enter the office of the j.p. to find out where we could obtain a license. The boy (I cannot even remember his name) went in while I waited outside. The j.p. asked the boy my age, which was sixteen, and then walked to the window and shook his head at me with such a nice, fatherly smile that I came to my senses. When the boy rejoined me I insisted that we go home immediately. He was probably as glad as I that we were not so foolish as to attempt to be married.

In spite of our series of moves around the country, Virginia and I never considered any place but Nashville home. We spent every vacation—short and long—with various members of Mother's large family there. Life for a teenage girl in those days was very different in the South than it was in the North, and we thoroughly enjoyed being Southern belles. The days and evenings were filled with pleasure, all of it involving the other sex. Unpopular indeed was the girl who did not have five or six boys "crazy" about her.

I do not know why there were more boys than girls in Nashville, but there must have been, for at every dance there were at least four boys to every girl. Program dances were unknown, and cut-ins by the stag line were in order, except for the first and last dances, when a girl danced wth the boy who had brought her to the party. There were many picnics, some of them out at the Hermitage, Andrew

Jackson's beautiful and romantic old home, still a cherished show-place, and others at Centennial Park in town, where a replica of the Parthenon had been erected. On dates, we would take walks, holding hands if it were dark enough, or sit in swings on wide verandas where occasionally a courageous and aggressive lad might put an arm across the back of the swing or sofa on which he and his girl were sitting. Or, we might go down to the vaudeville show, but that, of course, depended upon the condition of the boys' wallets. So did visits to the "dog wagon," which were considered special treats after dances.

Being in Nashville only during vacations made my sister and me sort of special, so we had more beaux than most of the other girls we knew. Coming from the North, we were more dashing, more up-to-date, why, we even smoked cigarettes occasionally when our aunts were not around. Two girls with indulgent aunts who always had plenty of goodies to eat could not fail to be popular.

One summer I had to do a lot of fast talking to keep my coterie of beaux intact, for several of them went on a camping trip, and I wrote each the same letter. It never occurred to me that they would show each other letters, but of course they were only on their way to becoming gentlemen.

I created a sensation at a house party we attended at a camp on the Cumberland River by appearing for our first swim in an Annette Kellerman, a one-piece knit suit, which I had bought while on a visit to Chicago. The hostess took one look at me and said, "India, have Dick give you his raincoat to wear into the river." I was about as voluptous looking as an angleworm, but an Annette Kellerman was a shocking outfit compared with the long-sleeved, high-necked, long-skirted bathing suits females wore in the early days of this century. I had left off stockings, too, which would have contributed to the delinquency of the boys present, since none of them had ever seen a teenaged girl's legs without hose. Actually, they had not seen very much of a girl's legs *with* hose, for our skirts were long. Long skirts and hair-up marked the ascension from childhood to being a young lady, and Southern girls became young ladies at about fourteen.

My mother was more liberal than the mothers of many of my friends, as evidenced by the time the mother of twin girls in St. Louis came to Mother to tell her with horror that she had discovered that the twins had not been wearing underdrawers for several weeks. "Think of it, Mrs. Gillespie," the woman said. "They have been going out with boys without their drawers. I thought you would want to find out if India and Virginia had been doing the same." Mother assured her that she did not think it mattered whether we had been with boys or girls without underwear, but that she would find out why we had left them off, if we had. We readily confessed that we had not been wearing the usual bulky, flounced, starched muslin drawers, for they kept our long, white piqué skirts from fitting the way we wanted them to. Mother agreed that we could have more form-fitting panties, so she bought us some silk tricot ones, but the other mother was adamant that her daughters wear the drawers they had been wearing since they were little girls.

My mother was a remarkable woman and quite a liberated one for her time. She was puritanically strict as to her daughters' behavior with the other sex, but she had a delicious sense of humor and was very popular with Virginia's and my peers. Our home always was a gathering place for our friends and I shudder now to think of how much expense our constant informal entertaining when we lived in St. Louis must have been to our parents. We held open house every Sunday afternoon, just as Mother and her sisters had done in Nashville a generation earlier, and we felt free to invite up to a dozen or more to stay for supper.

From the time we were about ten and eleven Virginia and I always cooked dinners on Thursday nights and very proud we were of the popovers, pies, cornbread, etc. we would make. Father was so enthusiastic about our prowess as cooks that he often would suggest (jokingly, I am sure but we took him seriously) to Mother that we do all the cooking and housecleaning. We were appalled at the idea, especially at the thought of having to clean the house more than once a week. Mother believed every girl should know how to cook and clean and sew, so Virginia and I had to spend every Saturday morning helping the second maid clean the house. Before the days of vacuum cleaners, we soaked newspapers in buckets of water, then scattered the wet paper, torn into small pieces, over the carpets and swept paper and dust up together.

During my three and one-half years at Central High in St. Louis, inspired by my English teacher, Clarence Stratton, I dreamed of being a writer. I was looking forward to going to the school of journalism at Columbia University, which was then an undergraduate school. There were no college board examinations, so one could enter college with a high school diploma and a letter from the principal detailing one's ability and attesting to one's good character. I knew I would have no trouble getting this from the principal, and I fully expected that Father would agree to my course of action. He didn't. I learned later that things were not going well financially for him when I finished high school, but at the time the only reason he gave for not letting me apply to Columbia was that I was too young to go to New York City, and that, if I wanted to attend college, I could go to Washington University and live at home. Nothing could have induced me to do that, so for two years I just played, golfing and going to luncheons and teas during the days and dancing and partying at nights. I was a poor golfer, but I was a good dancer, so I was offered a job as a teacher in a dance studio. Irene and Vernon Castle were at the peak of their fame, and for a while a friend, Robert Carter, and I dreamed of becoming a popular ballroom dancing couple. We even appeared once for a week as the main attraction at a new ballroom that opened in the West End, St. Louis' best residential section then. Though we did win some contest prizes, I decided that I would become a newspaper writer, even without going to journalism school.

Father lost his job about that time. When I announced I was going to Chicago to get a job, Father and Mother decided to move the whole family there so that I would not live alone. We lived in an apartment on Sheridan Road, near enough to Lake Michigan that Virginia and I could put on our suits at home and take a dip.

Today, the building in which we lived is still standing, but it is many blocks from the lake because of the vast amounts of filling that have been done.

Chapter 2

Not knowing anyone who worked on a newspaper, I could not determine how to get a job on the Chicago *Tribune*, the city's biggest paper and the one I wanted to work for. I needed money, though, for Father was not making much, so when George Hogan, the president of the Heco Envelope Company, whom I had met through a friend, asked if I would like to be his private secretary, I accepted with alacrity. I never had seen a typewriter except at my father's office, and I knew no shorthand. I asked Mr. Hogan how much typing and shorthand his secretary would have to know and was reassured to hear there was a secretarial pool. "The main thing is to have a lady who is nice-looking and has a pleasant voice," he said. Apparently, he thought I qualified. I told him I knew a little about typing and taking dictation—I did not say how little—and that I would like to try it out for a week or two. I felt certain I could learn enough in business school during the next week to be adequate. By the end of the week I realized why the woman who took my money for one-half of a ten-month course had looked at me pityingly when I had said I only had one week in which to go to school.

So, bright and early on a Monday morning, I appeared at Mr. Hogan's office with the typewriter keyboard firmly in mind and an ability to take down one-syllable words. Mr. Hogan's notion of a few letters was fifteen. Fortunately they were all fairly short, but there were few one-syllable words in them. I held my notebook so that he could not see it, for I could write just the first letter of each two- or multisyllable word. When I tried to transcribe my notes, I was horrified at the number of words I could think of that began with the letters I had written. When I put the letters on his desk to sign after a full day of work, I told him I feared I was not experienced enough for the job. Patiently, he suggested that I work a few days longer. Good luck brought a dictaphone salesman into the office the next day. It was a miraculous machine to me. I did such a good selling job on Mr. Hogan that we had a machine delivered the next day. From then on, it was duck soup, for my typing improved rapidly and I did not have to worry about those strange curlicues and signs that Mr. Gregg had developed into shorthand. I can still write many one-syllable words, but I never have found them of much use, either in my newspaper work or in politics.

When I became a private secretary (majestic words), I got $15 a week. That wasn't too bad for a beginner in those days, but it wasn't enough for a silly girl who often spent that much on a hat.

Shortly after going to work, a visiting friend from St. Louis introduced me to a woman with whom he had gone to college. She was society editor of the *Tribune*. When she found the height of my ambition was to work on a newspaper, she began using me as a reporter for night assignments. I was paid $5 an assignment. I would have covered them for nothing, though, since the assignments took me to the opera, theater openings and concerts, and introduced me to a glamorous world.

The Chicago Opera Company, subsidized then by Edith Rockefeller McCormick and her ex-husband, Harold Fowler McCormick, had a ten-week season. A report of who was in the golden horsehoe of boxes of the auditorium and what the most socially prominent wore on the three subscription nights of each week always appeared in the society columns of the *Tribune*. Since the society editor's husband did not like opera, she was delighted to have me cover the opera Mondays, Tuesdays and Wednesdays. On Thursday nights the symphony audience also was given social and musical coverage, so the social reporting fell to me. It was hard work at first because I did not know Chicago society. But more often than not, important-looking people whose names I asked were gracious.

There were so many Armour women that they posed real trouble for me. Once, as I inquired about full names, one of the younger Mrs. Armours replied in a bored tone of voice, "You are so stupid, I am THE Mrs. Armour." "The only rude one I have encountered," I responded. After that, I never included the name of Mrs. Philip D. Armour, III in a *Tribune* society column unless it was absolutely unavoidable, which was very seldom, since her great interest was the Moody Bible Institute, not precisely a center of social activity. The Mrs. Armour III whom I knew was succeeded by another Mrs. Armour III after I had left Chicago.

Captain Joseph Medill Patterson and Colonel Robert R. McCormick, cousins who were grandsons of Joseph Medill, an early owner of the paper, took turns publishing the *Tribune* before they left Chicago to "make the world safe for democracy" in World War I. When they returned from the war, they resumed their alternating publishing, which made for much confusion among editors and reporters, for they had very different philosophies. It must have been unsatisfactory to both the Captain and the Colonel, for in 1919 Captain Patterson went to New York to start the tabloid *Daily News,* leaving the management of the *Trib* to the Colonel. The *Tribune* was such a big moneymaker that the company risked losing money by starting a new paper, and a tabloid at that, but the *News* became an instant success. Another way had to be found to keep surplus profits from the hands of the government. The magazine *Liberty* took care of that nicely.

My mother used to tell me that I never would live to a very old age, considering the life I was leading during those early years in Chicago. I had to be at the Heco Envelope Company office at 9 a.m., and I worked there until 5:30, with an hour off for lunch. I usually took a sandwich from home. After eating it hurriedly in the women's lounge, I would go into the big storeroom, where tremendous stacks of paper were waiting to be made into envelopes. I would take a nap curled up on a stack. I always arranged with one of the girls in the typists' pool to awaken me so that I could be back at my desk on time, but those forty or fifty minutes of sleep each day probably helped me to live to the old age I have now attained.

I needed a daily nap because I often went tea-dancing when I left work, usually at the Blackstone Hotel, but sometimes at the Stratford Hotel (torn down, long, long ago). The latter was a rather more risqué place of which my mother did not approve. Tea, finger sandwiches, raspberry ice and petit fours were my regular order; I ate so much raspberry ice in those years that I never have been able to enjoy it since. About 7: 30 or 8 P.M., I would start my assignment for the *Trib*. My escort would often accompany me if I were going to the opera, symphony, or the theater. At the opera I could write my copy in the press room and send it to the paper by messenger, but for other affairs I had to go to the *Trib* newsroom and write my story there. The beau of the evening would sit in the waiting room and read an evening paper while I worked. When I finished, off we would go for more dancing at one of the many places that featured good bands. The Bismarck Gardens was not far from my home, so it was my favorite place. Going there meant I would get home around midnight. There were not many taxicabs and few buses, so, unless my beau had an automobile (and few did in those days), we had to use streetcars, for the elevated did not go anywhere near my home.

Through some newspaper people I met the publisher of a local magazine, *Fashion Art*. He offered me a job as associate editor, which I accepted and so terminated my employment with Mr. Hogan, who had put up with my lack of expertise as a secretary for about ten months and really seemed sorry to have me leave.

As I remember, I got a three-dollar increase in salary by moving to the magazine, which must have been about the worst ever published, although at the time I was enormously proud to be its associate editor. Subscribers actually paid cold, hard cash for the joint efforts of Rose Segal, the fashion editor, and myself, but I have no idea how many subscribers there were. Rose arranged for the fashion pictures or sketches, and I did all the writing. I wrote about fashion, drama, music, interior decorating, the new books, and everything that had the slightest flavor of belonging in a magazine entitled *Fashion Art*. I continued working for the *Tribune* after 5 p.m., so my daily schedule was about the same as when I was a secretary, with two exceptions: it was more fun to work for the magazine than to type Mr. Hogan's all-the-same letters and pay his bills, and I had nowhere for a noon nap at the magazine office!

I did not work at *Fashion Art* too long. The *Tribune* city editor offered me so many assignments I found I could earn more in a week by working only for the paper. Since there were no female reporters on the paper then, except in the Sunday room, I was given all sorts of things to cover. Most of them were interesting and fun, but a few convinced me that I preferred to be a society reporter, rather than a general one, a feeling that I found later was not shared by many females. It was my love for music that brought about my strange taste, strange that is, for an aspiring newspaper reporter.

Interviewing a woman who was suspected of murdering her husband or covering police courts held no appeal for me. I liked much better listening to Geraldine Farrar, Mary Garden, Lucien Muratore, and the other opera stars of that period and interviewing the visiting artists, musicians, and noted authors to whom I was assigned.

Not every interview was pleasant, but most were. The most unpleasant was with Mary MacLane, who had just written a best-seller, *I, Mary MacLane*. She was staying at the Blackstone, so I called for an appointment and was invited to tea. When I got there, I was surprised to find her in a single bedroom, not a suite. Her secretary, to whom she was dictating, was dismissed, and a sumptuous tea table soon was wheeled in. We sat in chairs while we had tea, and then she suggested we move to the sofa. I found it difficult to get her to talk about herself and her writing. She kept asking me questions about myself and I was too inexperienced to manage the interview properly. "I suppose you have a lot of beaux?" she asked. I smirked and said I had enough to always have a good time. "Have you ever had an assignation?" was the next question, to which I replied, "Well, I don't know. I don't think so. But perhaps I have," not having the faintest idea what she was talking about.

"You would know if you had had one," she said severely. Then she moved closer to me and, patting my leg, said, "Stay and have dinner with me, and we'll have a cozy time." I welcomed her hand on my leg about as much as I would have welcomed the touch of a snake. I jumped up and said I must go. When I got back to the *Trib*, Frank Carson was on the desk, and I went up to him and in an apologetic voice said, "I have fallen down on a story. I just could not get any sort of interview out of Mary MacLane." Frank shouted, "Who in hell sent you to interview the most noted lesbian in the United States? Are you all right?"

"Yes, of course, I am all right," I replied, "but what is a lesbian?"

"Ask your mother," Frank said.

"And what is an assignation?" I asked; "she wanted to know if I ever had had one and I don't know what it is. What is it?"

"Ask your mother that too," Frank replied.

Frank Carson, a well-known newspaperman in Chicago, once did something for me that became the talk and joke of Chicago journalism. Frank told me they wanted me to go to Camp Grant, near Rockford, Illinois, to cover some prizefights between our soldiers and some Canadian ones. I remonstrated that I knew nothing about prizefighting, and he said that was exactly why they wanted me to go. When I asked if I would have to spend the night in a hotel in Rockford, he said that of course I would. "Then I definitely cannot do it," I told him. "My mother never would allow me to stay alone in a hotel overnight. I'd have to have a chaperone."

"My God," Frank bellowed, "then get a chaperone."

So I asked a widow friend of Mother's to go with me. I wasn't sure whether or not I could put her expenses on my expense account, but Frank assured me that would be OK. I was the first and only *Trib* reporter ever to have a chaperone on a story.

I loved the fights, even though one of the bloody-nosed boys was knocked out of the ring into my lap. The fighters were like dancers, I thought, and I became almost as great a fan of prizefights as I was of the Russian ballet. I had made arrangements with Western Union to let me use the typewriter in its office to write my story. It was the first time I ever had filed a story by wire, so after writing the first page, I carefully went through it and cut out all the unnecessary words, just as I would have done in a personal wire. The telegrapher started sending it to the *Trib*, while I proceeded to write the second page. In a few minutes the wire editor at the paper sent this message to the telegrapher for me. "Tell that idiotic girl to stop trying to save the *Trib* money and write so she makes sense."

Chapter 3

On December 22, 1917, I was married to Second Lieutenant Daniel Sharp. He had gone to the second officer's training camp at Fort Sheridan and was ordered to go overseas very soon after receiving his commission. He had asked me to marry him even before America entered the war. We were tentatively engaged but had no definite plans as to when we would be married.

When he had learned late in 1917 that he would be ordered to report in Hoboken early in January, 1918, we began several weeks of "Should we?"—"We should not"—"Yes, we should" conversations. One night he would say, "You must marry me before I go," and I would say, "No, we will wait until you come home." The next night I would have decided that I wanted to marry him before he left, and he would have come to the conclusion that it would be unfair to me to do so. This went on until about December 19, when we both said, "We'll do it, whether it is wise or not. We'll have a little time together and, please God, we will have many years together after the war." It took several days for blood tests and so on, so we were married in my home on December 22 by Horace J. Bridges, the leader of the Chicago Ethical Society, the only religious organization of which I ever have been a member.

Dan, who was born in Boston into a distinguished old family, was one of the most attractive men I ever have known. He was in the real estate business in Chicago. He was seven years older than I and far more sophisticated. We stayed at the Edgewater Beach Hotel in Chicago for a few days in order to have Christmas with my family, and then we went to New York where we stayed at the old Brevoort Hotel. It was my first visit to New York City; like any bride, I looked at everything through rose-colored glasses, misted now and then by the thought that Dan would soon be leaving.

Uncle Jim Walker and his wife Florence lived in an apartment on Central Park South, and they saw to it that we had the gayest and most entertaining honeymoon a poor young couple could have had in that city, which had so much to offer if one could pay for it. We visited all the restaurants and hotels I had heard and read about, many theaters, and all the famous nightclubs. Uncle Jim ordered nothing but the best in food and drink. Dan, in uniform, had to drink his champagne out of a teacup.

After about ten days, Dan had to leave early to report to a pier in Hoboken, not expecting to see me again until war had ended. Imagine my joy when he appeared about 10 o'clock, saying their departure was postponed a day. This happened every day for about eight days. These extra days were like gifts from heaven, but it became increasingly hard for me to see him leave at 6 a.m. and then wonder for the next four hours whether he really was gone for good. When the morning came that he did not return, I broke down entirely and sobbed so loudly that the man in the next room finally telephoned to ask if there were something he could do to help me. This brought me to my senses. I telephoned Uncle Jim, who bundled me up and took me to their apartment, where I stayed for several weeks.

I began seeing some old Chicago friends who lived in Greenwich Village, so I saw a different side of New York life than I had been enjoying with the Walkers. My Chicago friends introduced me to many of their Bohemian acquaintances, including Edna St. Vincent Millay, Augusta and Lucian Cary, Floyd Dell, Max Eastman, Eugene O'Neill, and many other Village writers and artists. It was such a fascinating experience I decided to live in New York while Dan was in France.

My uncle was a friend of Frank Crowninshield, editor of *Vanity Fair*, so it was fairly easy for me to apply for a job there—and to get it. I called my mother to tell her of my plans. She did not voice an opinion, but when Frank Carson called me a few hours later to ask me to return to Chicago as soon as possible and become society editor of the *Tribune,* I detected Mother's Scotch-Irish hand in the offer. I said I appreciated the offer but that I was going to stay in New York to work for *Vanity Fair.* "Girl, are you crazy?" asked Frank. "Every newspaperwoman in Chicago is after this job, knowing the society editor is leaving, and here I am offering it to you on a silver platter, and you are stupid enough to tell me you prefer to be a hack reporter for *Vanity Fair.* You'd better come home and start to work next Monday." I asked him how he could be sure I'd be only a hack reporter on the magazine—I might be a great success. "You might," he said, "but you'll have plenty of competition there, and you will have none as society editor of the *Trib.* Use your head, girl."

So I told Mr. Crowninshield I had decided I would go back to Chicago, and he did not seem to feel he was losing anyone who gave promise of being *Vanity Fair*'s star.

Before returning to Chicago I went to Worcester, Mass. to meet and spend a few days with Dan's only sister, Eleanor Colvin. She took me into Boston to meet an elderly aunt who had never married and who was the wealthy member of the family. The aunt lived in one of those narrow, high houses on Beacon Street. Since she was bedridden, we had to climb several flights of stairs to her bedroom. The room was rather dark so I could see little of her face and apparently she could not see as much of mine as she wished for when I started to sit in a chair several feet away from the bed, she said, "Child, come closer. I want to look at you." After a good, close look she patted my head and said "Humph, I never thought Dan would have sense enough to marry a smart one instead of a pretty one." My same old *bete noire!* And she did not even have my sister, Virginia, for comparison.

Eleanor took me sight-seeing in Boston, pointing with pride to the portraits of four Daniel Sharps in the old State House. Later when I told Mother about this she asked if I had told Eleanor that I was descended from Governor William Bradford, the second governor of Plymouth Colony. I had never thought to brag about my ancestry, I was so impressed with Dan's. Actually, none of my family ever seemed to be impressed with ancestors, our own or anyone else's.

When I went home and started work as society editor of the *Trib*, Frank Carson told me it would not be necessary for me to tell Edward S. Beck, the managing editor, my age. Frank said, "He does not like women on the paper, especially young ones."

The first evening I was there, Mr. Beck stopped at my desk and said, "Hm, so you're the new society editor. Well, I hope you will be all right, but I doubt it. You're too young. What do you mean, Frank," turning toward Frank at his desk, "telling me she is about thirty? She looks about twenty."

Actually, I was twenty-three. I did not know what to do or say, but since Mr. Beck hurriedly went on to his office, I did and said nothing, just went on with my typing until Frank called me to his desk and said, "Don't worry. If you will keep the men from hanging around your desk and show the old man you are serious you'll get by."

This imposed quite a hardship on me, for some of the reporters were the most fascinating men I'd ever encountered. Charlie MacArthur, Ring Lardner, Morrow Krum, Gordon Seagrove, and Bob Lee and Fred Pasley, both rewrite men (Bob later was to be city editor and then managing editor), to mention a few of the outstanding ones. Charlie and I became great friends, but we barely spoke in the office. Gordon and I discovered that we lived across the street from each other, and I spent many an evening and Sunday on his sailboat on Lake Michigan, but in the office we acted as if we were almost strangers. It was on a sail with him one evening that Charlie and his older brother Alfred regaled me with stories about Chicago's underworld, including the careers of the Everleigh sisters, famous madams.

The MacArthur brothers also added to my fund of knowledge about Chicago and some of its leading citizens. Most I have forgotten and what I remember is not printable. Those early Chicagoans certainly led racy lives and some died under peculiar circumstances, to say the least, if what Charlie and Alfred told me was true. Their father was an itinerant minister and the boys' tales about him and their childhood were fascinating. Charlie and Ben Hecht did not exaggerate too much when they wrote *Front Page*. City or local rooms, some editors, and most reporters in my early newspaper days were just about the way Charlie and Ben described them.

Alfred and Charlie had a terrible argument one Sunday that al-

most degenerated into a fist fight that was as funny as anything I
ever saw on a vaudeville stage. Alfred, who was married to Mary
Sheldon, the sister of Ned Sheldon, a well-known playwright, had a
farm northwest of Chicago in Libertyville. At that time the old farm-
house had no running water nor indoor toilet facilities, but groups of
Alfred's friends often had picnics or barbecues at the farm. Once
Charlie invited some friends to a party for Beatrice Lillie, whom he
adored—as did we all. Being the host, he arrived there ahead of the
others. It was a bitterly cold day, so in order to have everything as
comfortable as possible for Bea, he put a ring of soft warm fur
around one of the holes in the two-holer in back of the house. That
was fine until Alfred discovered that Charlie had cut up Alfred's one
and only hunting cap in order to give Bea a warm seat. Alfred liked
and appreciated Bea's brilliance as a comedian but not enough to
give up his warm hunting cap.

I saw Ring Lardner often during my first few years on the *Trib* and
his last ones in Chicago. He was married to a charming young woman, Ellis. In those days the deadline for the morning *Trib* was about
11 p.m., so the editorial staff seldom managed to have dinner at their
homes. Ring hated to eat dinner alone, so if Katie Webber, my assistant, and I were around the local room at dinner time, Ring often
asked us to have dinner with him. On occasion others would join us,
but more often just the three of us would go some place. Ring would
keep us in such gales of laughter that Katie and I could hardly eat.
Several times Ellis invited us to their home, but she was so busy
with young Lardners that she did not have much time for her husband's *Trib* friends. Ring wrote a column "In the Wake of the
News," which ran on the sports page but was not confined to sports.
I have a dim recollection of our persuading him to do several stories
on grand opera, which were excruciatingly funny.

I had a guest from the South who said the one person in the city
she would like to meet was Ring Lardner. I asked Ring if he would
meet us after the opera some night when he was working late and
take us to supper. He met us at the Auditorium Hotel, said how-do-
you-do when I introduced him to Luella, and contributed nothing to
the conversation the entire hour we were having supper. When I
would try to draw him into the conversation he would say yes or no
or huh, but there was no sign of his inimitable dry wit. When I chid-
ed him for behaving in such a churlish manner the next time I saw

him, he said he did not like being put on exhibition like a mynah bird or a talking horse.

Sometimes Frank Carson would join Katie, Ring and me for dinner. One night, after much urging on our part, they took us on a tour of the nightspots that neither of us had visited before. First we went to Chinatown, where the mayor (of Chinatown, not Chicago) took us to see the below-ground opium dens and fan-tan rooms which we found a little frightening. Frieberg's, the most disreputable place in the city we were told, seemed to us a very dull and dreary place. No doubt the upstairs rooms were the setting for the wicked behavior.

Colosimo's, which rivaled Frieberg's in reputation, and where we had a really good Italian supper, appeared as middle-class and respectable as the Greek restaurant where Dan and I often ate a seventy-five cent table d'hote dinner when he wasn't "feeling flush." Katie and I were terribly disappointed not to be having some excitement on our night on the town, until, at the next table at Colosimo's, a man slowly arose from his chair and, leaning across the table, punched a girl in the face. She fell backward with her feet in the air and her underclothes in full view. No one but Katie and I seemed to pay any attention to this, although a waiter and "Big Jim" Colosimo himself quietly picked her and the chair up and pushed her back to her place at the table. Then, in loud tones, she said, "Jeez, I know he loves me or he wouldn't treat me so rough." The evening was made for Katie and me!

During Dan's eight months with the British army in Belgium, I received fascinating letters, in spite of the fact that they had to be censored and many things were half-told. Dan had been one of the Americans assigned to be liaison officers with the British. One of the most amusing letters contained a description of messages his unit received from headquarters while a visiting East Indian maharaja was being entertained at dinner. The final message was that, if His Highness wanted to go to the bathroom, he was to be supplied with a basin of warm water and cotton balls. The soldiers so near the front were glad to have even toilet tissue!

I did not hear from Dan for quite a long time after early autumn in 1918 but did not allow myself to worry. Everyone kept telling me how people often went months without hearing, then suddenly received a large batch of letters. I celebrated both the false armistice day and the real one with joy and the hope that Dan would be coming home soon. On January 16, 1919, I received a wire from the War Department, informing me of his death on December 20. He had been gassed in October, just days before the Armistice, and had been in the hospital since then. It was a stunning blow, for I had thought no news was good news. I never understood why it took so long for me to be notified, but this would not have changed the tragic outcome. I later learned that because he was the first American soldier to enter Belgium King Albert himself decorated him.

The *Tribune* gave me a leave of absence. I went to Florida to visit Dan's uncle and his wife at their winter home in Cocoa, then a sleepy town on the Indian River and the Atlantic, very different from the busy place it became when our space program went into action. The Sharps had a little citrus grove on Indian River.

While I was with the Sharps, Aunt Stella and I took a motor trip down the east coast as far as Miami, stopping in Palm Beach for several days on the way south. In 1919, there was nothing at Miami Beach but a hot dog stand, a few dingy bath houses, and some beach shacks, reached by crossing a long wooden causeway from Miami.

When I returned to Chicago in 1919 from my first trip to Florida, I resumed my work as society editor of the *Trib* and soon found that hard work was the best possible panacea for grief. As a young widow I seemed to be more attractive to men than I had been before I was married. Having had experience as both a sod and a grass widow, I am an authority on man's altruism when it comes to looking after the physical well-being of widows.

In a rather romantic way in July of 1919, I met an attractive, sweet young man who had served in the Air Force during the war, and he wooed me so successfully that we were married in March of the next year. Bastille Day, I had covered a benefit for some French cause at the Onwentsia Club in Lake Forest, and was returning to Chicago alone on a late train. I was wearing one of my most expensive hats, a large black taffeta that dipped down, shading my face. As I stood on the platform, I noticed a young man at a little distance looking at me with more than passing interest. When I climbed aboard the train, he followed me and sat in the seat just opposite. I kept looking out the window, but I was aware that he was staring at me intently. I moved to a seat several rows ahead, and this time he took the seat right beside me, but because I kept looking out into the darkness he did not say a word until the train pulled into the Northwestern Station, and then he said, "May I take you home? It's very late for you to be out alone."

"Thank you, no," I snapped and stalked out ahead of him, almost running to the taxi stand.

The next morning, Sunday, I went to a large brunch given by one of Chicago's noted hostesses. She introduced me to a young Italian officer who was in Chicago with an Italian war mission, an English officer who was serving his country in the same way, and a French officer, almost too stunning to be real in his sky-blue uniform. Then she said, "And this is Jack Moffett, recently with the Air Force." He kept the hand I extended and pulled me over to a corner of the room and said, "Don't you recognize me? We came in from Lake Forest on the same train last night. I never saw under that hat you were wearing, but you have it on today, so I know it was you." I would not have recognized him, for I had never really looked at him. But I saw a great deal of him in the months that followed. I had been leading a quiet personal life after learning of Dan's death, but from the time I met the three foreign officers and Jack I began to have a gay life indeed.

If Jack's mother had not objected to his attentions to me because I was a poor, working widow, a society editor instead of a socialite, it is doubtful that his courtship would have been so successful that we were married in March, 1920. My mother begged me not to marry him, for, said she, "he has no soul." His mother had met me only once before the morning of our quiet wedding in the chapel of St. James' Episcopal Church.

Chapter 4

I never saw much of Charlie MacArthur after he moved to New York and married Helen Hayes, although I went to several parties for both of them when she was playing in Chicago. My husband Jack met Charlie at one of these parties. Jack took our wraps upstairs while I spoke to various people in the entrance hall. When I entered the living room and Charlie saw me, he lunged at me, throwing his arms around me, I fell, and he landed on top of me. At that moment Jack walked into the room and said, "Well, I never expected to see my wife in that position even with an old friend." Anyone who knew Jack realized he was joking but Charlie must have thought he was serious, for his apologies and explanation were profuse as he scrambled to his feet and helped me up. His nimble wit deserted him entirely that time.

The last time I saw Ring Lardner was in the spring of 1931 when he visited me in a house on the desert at the foot of Camelback Mountain outside Phoenix. I had gone West with my children to try to get rid of the attack of asthma that had been bothering me since the hay fever season ended in 1930. The children and I were living in a thick-walled adobe house which kept us comfortable even when the temperature rose to well over one hundred degrees.

Ring wrote me from the Desert Sanitorium in Tucson early in March:

"On my way out to this garden spot, I stopped off in Chicago and saw Lady Massee for ten minutes and she gave me your address and if you are receiving and I am permitted to wander and if you'd like to see an old man like me, I'll come up some time in the next week or so. I don't know the rules here, but I have never seen any that couldn't be broken, and if I were punished by banishment, I'd try to survive. Write to me if you feel like it, and don't be afraid of turning me down cold. I am not used to anything else."

A few days later he wrote a brief note as follows: "My sheriff has put his ft. down on my projected trip to Phoenix this week. I'll just have to make it later and will let you know when just as soon as I know myself. I hope you're as disappointed as I am, but I don't believe it." On March 7 he wrote: "I'll come to Phoenix on a respectable train that arrives there about noon next Friday. Your sole duty is to write me directions how to reach your house by taxi from the station. This date depends, of course, on my warden's consent. If he says no, I'll telephone you and make it later. But I don't believe he'll say no." I wrote that I would drive down and get him and enclosed a photo from the paper showing his house on Long Island. He wrote back: "You know very well that a motor trip down here would be bad for you and you have no business trying it. As soon as I am a little more 'rested' (or can convince the doctors that I am) I'll come and partake of your hospitality. Thanks for the clippings from the *Tribune*. The house pictured is Grantland Rice's, not ours, but he lives next door and it's the same ocean."

On March 27 he wrote: "I would have defied the sheriff and come to Phoenix before this if my ordinarily shapely ankles hadn't decided suddenly to swell to such a state that I can't wear shoes. Maybe I have contracted elephantiasis. Anyway, you wouldn't want me to visit you bare-footed. I *am* anxious to see you—a great deal more so than you are to see me—and I'll make it before I go back east, ankles or no ankles." On April 1 he wrote: "If you have no objection and if my ankles don't start acting silly again, I will be there day after tomorrow (Friday) noon. I haven't got permission, but I'll sneak out anyway. Please disabuse the kids' minds of the idea that I can tell stories. I am probably the world's worst raconteur, particularly for an audience of children."

Ring had tuberculosis and indulged too much in alcohol most of the time, so I hoped he would be "on the wagon," but the first thing he said when I met him at the train was where could he get some whiskey. I knew no bootlegger in Phoenix and I tried to persuade him to give up drinking while at my house. I was sure he could not drink in the sanitorium but he insisted upon having the liquor. I called a Chicago friend who was staying at the Arizona Biltmore Hotel and he procured some for us. Ring looked like walking death and his ankles still were terribly swollen. He admitted not only had he left without permission but had also bribed a male nurse to get his clothes for him.

He drank steadily and would not let me drive him around the desert, as I kept trying to do. In the evenings it was cool enough to have a fire in the big fireplace which he loved. He enchanted the children with the lifted eyebrows that gave him the appearance of always being surprised. He ate practically nothing and I truly was afraid he was going to die right there in my house. I wanted to call a doctor to see him but he would not let me.

He stayed for about four days, seemingly enjoying talking about the old days on the *Trib* and, in a manner completely different from the way he had been in the old days in Chicago, talked a lot about his four sons. As always, he deprecated his own writing but said he expected great writing from one of the sons. I cannot remember which one he thought the most talented: John, James, Ring, Jr. (called Bill) or David. All four became writers and achieved considerable success but none outshone their father in the field of writing.

When he got back to the sanitorium he wrote a short article for some magazine describing his visit. From the way he wrote about my driving him the ten or twelve miles from the railroad station to my house at the foot of Camelback Mountain, I could understand why he did not wish to have me as chauffeur for any sightseeing.

I always have been a law-abiding, careful driver, so I think he made it out that I was a wild, fast driver in order to put a little zip into the story, which fell far short of Ring's usual writing. Poor Ring. He was the wittiest and most entertaining person I ever have known.

In October of 1952 I was reminded of Ring and my early days on the *Trib*. I received a typed copy of a column written by John Wheeler, president of the Bell Syndicate, Inc. He started out with reporting that he was on the road to find out if he still could sell and then he wrote, "The first town I hit was Washington. Drew Pearson had lunch with me at the Mayflower Hotel and told me a lot of interesting inside stuff which I will leave for him to write in his column. A lady came over to the table and spoke to me cordially, even though I was wearing an Ike button. To make me comfortable, she began, 'I guess you don't know who I am.' 'I certainly do. You are India Edwards, and you are the chairman or chairwoman of the ladies' department of the Democratic National Committee. You also appeared on television at the convention. I can remind you of the first time I met you, which was a lot of years ago, if you want me to.'

"She nodded her head, so it is her own fault. 'It was in 1919 in Chicago when you worked on the *Tribune*. I was going to take Sidney Smith, who drew the Gumps, for dinner to try to hire him, but I ran into Ring Lardner. "What are you doing tonight?" he asked me. I told him. "There you are—always thinking of money, and besides that Smith guy is an awful bore. I have invited two beautiful young ladies to dinner, so forget him and come along," he said. I did, and you were one of them. Incidentally, we never signed up Smith.'

" 'That's a long time ago,' she agreed.

" 'What do you think of the election?' I asked her.

" 'Stevenson looks better every day,' she answered. 'He'll win. Do you want to bet?'

" 'Which one do you take?' I said.

" 'Not R. H. Macy or Senator Taft or President Truman, but Stevenson,' she answered.

" 'To show there is no hard feeling, I'll make it ten dollars and back Ike,' I said.

"I got out my notebook and wrote it down. She looked at my Eisenhower badge. 'I hear the Republicans are long on those—overstocked—and having trouble giving them away,' she remarked as she shook hands and departed. 'A smart woman,' commented Mr. Pearson. I think he meant her general conduct and not the wager."

I sent Jack Wheeler a check for ten dollars after the election and he replied, suggesting I write some columns for his syndicate but I never did it. He had a special project in mind but I cannot remember what it was. I do remember, though, what an interesting companion he was during the several times I saw him when he was in Chicago after that initial meeting with Ring. I also remember that once when

I was waiting for him on the mezzanine of the Sherman House, the hotel detective warned me that I was showing too much of one leg with my knees-crossed position. Women then were wearing skirts down to the ankle and I must have caught my skirt under a knee as I crossed them, with the result that most of one leg up to the knee was in evidence. I was so horrified at the idea of being reprimanded by an officer of the law that I would not have dinner in the College Inn in the basement of the hotel as we had planned. The Inn always had a good band and entertainment and everyone I knew frequented it. I never knew until Jack explained to me that the hotel itself was not first class and that the house detective thought I was a loose woman trying to pick up a man, not just a respectable young widow waiting for a friend to take her to dinner.

Chapter 5

In my years of opera-going I had many amusing experiences, but one that I particularly remember occurred when I had seats in the same box as Lina Cavalieri, the beautiful prima donna, who at that time was married to Lucien Muratore, the leading tenor with the Chicago Opera Company. No longer singing herself, Cavalieri did not spend the entire season in Chicago, but she came to hear her husband singing in *Monna Vanna* with Mary Garden. Cavalieri's pearls were famous, and she seemed to be wearing them all that night.

Monna Vanna, wrapped only in a cloak, has to come at midnight to the tent of a warring lord who had demanded this as the price for leaving her husband's city unharmed. During that act Cavalieri leaned so far forward I was afraid she would fall out of the box. She kept her opera glasses to her eyes every minute. She acted as if she thought Garden might drop her cloak and—well, do anything. Garden was noted for the verisimilitude of her acting, so when the curtain fell, Cavalieri rushed backstage, no doubt to make sure Garden and Muratore were not playing to the finish.

Garden was one of the greatest singing actresses I ever saw—and I've seen them all since about 1915. It was remarkable to see a wom-

an play and sing so many parts that demanded such different charac-
terizations. One night she would be the courtesan Thais, letting her
full-blown bosom fall out of her gown and calmly putting it back
where it belonged; two nights later she might be the sexless boy in
Le Jongleur de Notre Dame; another time she would be the young
Parisian seamstress Louise; and another the fiery Spanish gypsy
Carmen. Garden did not have the greatest voice I ever heard but she
used it with perfect technique and taste; her training must have been
done under the best teachers and coaches available, both here and in
Paris. She was not a tall woman but she carried herself so regally
that on stage she seemed to be above normal height. I was surprised
to find that she was not as tall as my five feet, four and one-half
inches. She and Muratore made a stunning pair.

Occasionally I treated myself to a masseuse who would come to
the house around 9 at night and give me an hour's massage, which
guaranteed a good night's sleep no matter how tired I was. When
Garden was in Chicago she had this masseuse every day. The woman never gossiped, but one evening as she massaged me, she chuck-
led now and then. Finally I asked her what had happened to make
her find life so amusing. She said she had just come from Garden's
apartment in the Lake Shore Drive Hotel, where she had left the prima donna striding back and forth across her bedroom in nothing but
a wisp of a chiffon bed jacket instead of relaxing in bed, as she
should have been doing after the massage. Garden had abruptly interrupted the massage when her maid had announced that a certain
man was on the telephone.

"No, no, no," Garden had said. "I want that house, not any more
stock. You promised me and I am going to hold you to it." Apparently becoming too angry to stay in bed, she threw off the sheet the
masseuse had covered her with and pulled on the bed jacket. Holding the telephone in her hands, she paraded as far as the wire would
permit—up and down—up and down—getting into more of a rage
every second. "I want that house, not any more stock," she repeated over and over. Finally the man on the other end of the telephone
wire must have agreed enough to placate his angry mistress, for she
said, "All right. Come in an hour." The masseuse said she was
shaking so with anger that it took some time to calm her down. Garden made no bones about whom she had been talking to. Although
the masseuse did not mention his name to me, I knew who it must

have been. It was fairly well known in newspaper circles that a very prominent packing company executive had been her "best friend" for years. He was married and, since his wife was one of those to whom the masseuse went every day, it well might have been he who recommended her to Garden in the first place.

Garden continued to come to Chicago for the opera season for many years after this incident in the early twenties. But I do not remember her ever living in a house. I think her portfolio of investments must have been enlarged and "her best friend" did not keep his promise to buy a house for her.

Anna Pavlova, the first Russian ballerina to enchant Americans; Nijinsky; the incomparable Sarah Bernhardt, who by the time I saw her, had lost a leg but still was a marvelous actress; Eleonora Duse, the Italian actress who inspired D'Annunzio for many years and then retired for twenty years after he had "kissed and told" in *The Flame;* Nellie Melba, the Australian songbird who sang Mimi in Puccini's *La Boheme* beautifully but was as fat as a butterball; Mme. Schumann-Heink, who gave many farewell performances but I heard her only in one—I saw and heard these and practically every other great artist performing from World War I through the thirties. I was present at the performance when Amelita Galli-Curci made her debut in this country in the old Auditorium to an ovation such as I never had heard before. The first time this coloratura sang in French was in a performance of *Romeo and Juliet.* I did not hear much of the performance, for I was in the second floor foyer holding the hand of her little husband, whom I discovered biting his fingernails.

It was rude and ugly of us in the Auditorium to laugh when Marguerite D'Alverez, the beautiful Peruvian contralto, fell flat when she was doing her most seductive scene in *Samson and Delilah.* It must have been very difficult to finish the seduction scene when she was helped to her feet, but she carried on valiantly. I recall another time in the Civic Opera House when the audience broke up. Maria Jeritza, the Austrian blonde beauty, was doing the Dance of the Seven Veils in *Salome.* Each time she undraped a veil it sounded as if she had dropped a piece of armor. I was sitting well down in front, so I got the full sound effect of the "veils" dropping. It was one of the funniest things I ever have experienced in an opera performance. Jeritza was beautiful and had a gorgeous voice but she was too large a woman to pretend to dance like Salome. Garden was a superb Salome but she did not attempt much of a dance. She did wear chiffons, though, not armor.

The Chicago Opera Company never was as good after it moved to the Civic Opera House as it had been in the old Auditorium, which had acoustics not surpassed by any other opera house in the world, so experts said. Nor did the new house have the warm elegance of the old theater. It seemed sad to many that Samuel Insull insisted upon building the Civic Opera House, in reality a skyscraper office building with the Opera House occupying the lower floors. I remember Insull calling a meeting of women's page and society editors of the Chicago papers a week or two before the opening night to give us orders as to how he wanted the gala premiere covered. We all listened, I for one becoming more angry every minute. When he finished, I said that his ideas were interesting but not practical and that the *Tribune* would continue to cover socially the opening night of opera in the way we thought best. He glared as if he could not believe that I was daring to question his authority. The other women immediately spoke up and said they agreed with me, whereupon we all rose and said good-bye. As we left, he called out that he would talk to the publishers about this, but if he got in touch with Colonel McCormick I never heard about it.

The worst performance I ever attended was given in the Civic Opera House when Samuel Insull was running the show, something for which he was about as well suited as I am for space travel. He would do anything to fill the house. Once he let the young wife of a very wealthy man sing Micaela in a performance of *Carmen*. In return, her husband had to buy out the house. In the third act, Micaela appears in a wild, rocky mountain pass where the smugglers stop to rest, to beg Don José to return to his dying mother. The aria is Micaela's big moment in the opera, but the poor woman had such a pitiful off-key little voice that the audience tittered. When there was a shot in the wings someone in the balcony shouted, "They've shot the wrong one. It should be Micaela."

Chicago is a city of balletomanes and whenever the Ballets Russe de Monte Carlo came to the Auditorium the theater was filled. Complete egotism must be a necessary part of success in any one of the arts, for it is seldom that I ever have met a singer, dancer, stage star, painter or great writer who had any real interest in any artists other than him or herself. This was brought home to me forcibly when I asked sixteen-year-old Tamara Tamanouva of the Ballets Russe which ballets she liked best and she replied, "The ones in which I am the premiere ballerina, of course."

Once when I went to interview a very young Russian musician who had just made a sensational debut in New York City, he was totally uninterested in talking about anything but "bass-ball," as he called it. All the time I was with him and his parents in their Michigan Avenue hotel suite overlooking Grant Park, he watched a baseball game being played there. When I left, the boy barely said goodbye, but his parents followed me into the corridor and in halting English told me they knew their son was a genius but that he needed to have some sentimental experience, something to make him a warmer person. They wondered if I would not like to help him acquire a warm, sentimental experience. I could think of nothing I would like less. From what I have heard and read about him over the years, he developed into a great ladies' man.

During the years I was on the *Tribune* I met practically everyone of newsworthy interest who came to the city. Sometimes I interviewed the notable but often the encounter was social. It was at a dinner dance that I met Rudolph Valentino and had the thrill of dancing with him. I had seen him in every picture he had made until then and was enough of a fan of his so that I had gone to *Monsieur Beaucaire* four times! Our dance was not as thrilling as I had expected. I knew several men in Chicago who were better ballroom dancers than the adored Rudy. I found his sleek, Latin appearance much less attractive off the screen than on it. I often found a great discrepancy between the charm of a person on the stage or screen and that same person in real life.

One of the first things I was told when I became society editor of the *Tribune* was that I could accept nothing of great value from an individual, organization, company or corporation, etc. Well, I was offered everything from a thin dime to a five-thousand-dollar-check to get certain brides' pictures in the paper.

One of Chicago's most energetic social climbers once sent me a large box of her clothing, all of it expensive and beautifully made but all in need of dry-cleaning. I returned it with a note in which I wrote, "The *Tribune* pays me enough to dress myself decently, if not extravagantly. I also can afford to keep my clothes cleaned. I am returning your dirty ones." She never mentioned the incident and neither did I, but when she gave me a lovely "teddy bear" from Paris the next Christmas, with my initials on it, I kept it. Any reader who is not old enough to know that a teddy bear is not just a stuffed animal will have to remain in doubt as to what the gauche climber gave me.

During the thirties both Japan and Germany invited me and my guest to visit with all expenses paid. The Japanese representative also said his government would like to give me two hundred dollars in cash to buy souvenirs. I was horrified by the invitations, which I suppose was a naive way of considering them. The Japanese and the German said nothing would be expected from me in return: it was just that they wanted me to know their countries. Our government has been bringing journalists and other opinion-makers from other countries in large and small groups for years.

The only other time my services were solicited by a foreign government was in 1960 when a prominent Chinese man who had come here before the communist takeover of his native country wrote to ask if I would be willing to "help in the furtherance of good relations between Free China and the United States . . . either confidentially or openly." I had no desire to become involved in the work of the powerful China Lobby, which operated in Washington on behalf of Nationalist China in Formosa. It was very effective in years past but has not been very successful in recent years.

Somewhere in my mementos is a picture of all the stars of the Chicago Opera Company arranged on a fan and autographed by Cleofonte Campanini "to the greatest fan of them all, India Gillespie." I did not miss a single performance of the ten-week season.

After I became society editor my opera seats for every performance were on the side in a row that included only those two seats. They were excellent seats and afforded me not only a magnificent view of the stage but of all the boxes, where the people in whom I had to be interested usually were seated. One night during the second intermission (I had done my work during the first), I did not leave my seat, but sat there chatting with my guest. I did not suspect that I was about to get a scoop important enough for front page news. Harold McCormick came through the door nearest us and sat on the aisle step to talk with the women seated in back of us. "Mathilde is here," he said, "but no one knows it, and we want to keep the press from finding out, so she is not sitting with me in my box, nor with her mother in hers, but in the gallery up there [pointing to the left], with her Fräulein. You will see her tomorrow.'' (Mathilde McCormick, the younger daughter of Edith Rockefeller and Harold F. McCormick, had returned to Chicago from Switzerland, where she and her sister Muriel and Mrs. McCormick had been living since the parents' divorce. Mrs. McCormick had returned some time before to open her stately mansion on Lake Shore Drive, and Muriel followed later. Everyone was wondering when Mathilde would arrive, but this was a well-kept secret.) I had not noticed who the women were to whom he was talking, and of course I could not turn around then and look. In fact, I was petrified for fear he would recognize me. If he had paid any attention to who was sitting in front of his friends, he would have seen that a member of the press was there. But he was so full of pride at the way the press was being kept in the dark that he never looked ahead or behind, to the right or the left, just up toward where the plain little dark-haired girl was sitting.

He left just as the lights were being dimmed, and so did I. He went back to his box, and I rushed to the telephone in the press room, where I told the city editor to kill the story I had sent over previously and to send a photographer to meet me at the front door. When he came, we waited for the next intermission (luckily, there was another in that opera), and then I took him to the gallery, where he managed to get a fairly good picture of Mathilde. Her father had pointed her out so carefully to his friends that there was no trouble identifying her. I suppose the McCormicks were mystified how the *Tribune* discovered the girl and never dreamed that it was Mr. McCormick's own carelessness and garrulousness that had betrayed her whereabouts. Colonel McCormick and Harold McCormick were distant cousins.

Another front page story also came to me through luck. One Sunday afternoon, I went to the Henrotin Memorial Hospital to call on a friend. I found a crowd of about 150 people assembled on the sidewalk, on both sides of the front entrance to the hospital. An enclosed canopy was stretched from the top of the stairs to the street. No one could go into the hospital nor pass it without going out into the street and walking around an ambulance. Smelling a story of some sort, I went into the street so I could see who or what went into the rear of the vehicle. Some of the waiting crowd had been

muttering that they had been there for a long time and that they were
going to call the police if they did not gain entrance to the hospital
soon. I had only a short time to wait until my story began to unfold.
An incubator, or at least what looked to be one, was in the vehicle,
and a man and a couple of nurses got in with it. I could not see the
baby, but I was sure there must be a baby. When a limousine drew
up as the other large vehicle drew away, several more adults, including Mrs. Emmons Blaine, Sr., one of the McCormick clan, and a
younger, rather delicate-looking woman got into it. I knew immediately that the baby must be the surviving twin of the babies that had
been born about four weeks before to Mrs. Emmons Blaine, Jr. Her
husband, the senior Mrs. Blaine's only child, had died from influen-
za not long before his young wife became a mother, so naturally the
grandmother was doing everything humanly possible to protect the
life of the girl baby whose brother had died shortly after birth. When
the crowd was admitted to the hospital, I had no trouble in getting
the information I needed for a story from hospital employees. I telephoned it to a rewrite man. Through some fluke this is one of the few
clippings from the *Trib* that I still have. His style and mine were not
alike and if I had written the story it would not have been quite so
flowery. Here are the salient parts: "Never in the history of Chicago
were more elaborate precautions taken to shelter and protect an infant. For this is an incubator baby, a baby that must live in a regulat-
ed temperature, held under glass, watched day and night to guard
the sacred flame of life. Everything stopped at the hospital for three-
quarters of an hour until this precious charge was delivered safely to
the waiting ambulance. No one was allowed in or out of the place.
'A lot of fuss over a baby,' said one curious bystander. 'Not a bit,
lady,' said one of the guards. 'I'm for it. I'm getting $5 for this.'

   "All the floors and walls near the place where the baby was to be
carried had been scrubbed until they shone. Carpets and rugs covered steps and sidewalk. . . . The ambulance doors closed and the
machine started without the slightest jar. Not a breath of air except
that especially warmed and purified reached the infant's soft nest.

   "An entire floor in the hospital had been rented by the family for
the event four weeks ago. All the walls were repainted and the floors
prepared, special furniture installed, and the whole place trans-
formed into a home. There was danger at first that the baby's life

could not be saved, but the physicians expect now that she will grow into normal babyhood soon.''

That baby, Nancy Blaine, grew up to be one of the finest, most generous, most understanding, and most liberal women I know. She is Mrs. Gilbert A. Harrison of Washington, D.C., until recently co-owner with her husband of *The New Republic* and president of the board of the New World Foundation, the corpus of which is the Anita McCormick Blaine fortune.

I do not know about other people who worked for the *Trib*, but I always knew that my bosses would back me if I had a dispute with the business or advertising offices or someone about whom I had written. The surest way of not getting into the society columns of the *Trib* was to try to make it through pressure from an advertiser. During my early years at the paper, press agents also were persona non grata in the editorial departments but gradually over the years that feeling changed and legitimate press agents became more welcome.

On one occasion one of Colonel McCormick's relatives and another society leader called on the Colonel to complain about a story I had written on a benefit they had sponsored the night before. For weeks they had given out information about a recital by Ganna Walska for the benefit of one of the many charities with which these two busy ladies were concerned. The *Trib*, as well as the other papers, had given them columns of publicity enabling them to have a sold-out house for the affair. Ganna Walska was a Polish opera singer who was acclaimed as much, if not more, for her beauty than for her singing. Chicagoans were tremendously excited at the prospect of seeing and hearing her. She had been married for a short time to Chicago's own Harold Fowler McCormick after he was divorced from Edith Rockefeller McCormick. The stunning prima donna had never sung before in Chicago, so her promised appearance, sponsored by two leading socialites for a popular charity was an important occasion. The professional press agent for the concert hall, not the volunteer publicity chairman, told me that Walska was not going to be in Chicago at the time of the recital. When I asked the two leading sponsors about this, they both insisted that Walska would be there. The press agent was right: Walska was not there and the audience was not at all pleased with the substitute.

In the lead of my story I wrote that even to aid a worthy charity it was not cricket for the women to use the name of an artist who they knew would not be present. The press agent had assured me that there was no misunderstanding about this. The ladies were furious with me and told me so over the telephone in no uncertain terms. They called the Colonel's secretary to ask for an appointment that same morning. They were going to ask him to fire me. I doubted that he would if he knew the full story. I never had to tell him because he never asked me.

Once the Colonel did demand that a young reporter, who had written an item for a Sunday column during the World's Fair, be fired. The column consisted of items that did not fit into other stories about the fair. I edited the column and it also was read by the Sunday editor and the copyreader and goodness knows how many other people. The young girl who wrote the item in question heard the story from several young men she knew socially. They said they had met a handsome, white-haired gentleman one night in the fair's "Streets of Paris." They all had a gay time, and when they parted the unknown gentleman asked them to come and see him if ever they were in Indianapolis. "How do we find you?" they asked, and he said, "At the governor's mansion. I am the governor."

Democrat Paul McNutt, the governor of Indiana, was certain the Colonel, with whom he was having a political feud unbeknownst to me or the Sunday editor, was responsible for the item. McNutt sued the *Tribune*. The Colonel ordered Mr. Beck, the managing editor, to fire whomever had written the item. When the M.E. asked me who had written it, I said that it was my responsibility, so I should be the one to be fired, not a nineteen-year-old girl. Mr. Beck rejected that idea. When he could not get me to name the writer, he asked the city editor Bob Lee, to deal with me about it. I refused to tell him either who wrote the item, and for days we argued about it. Finally Bob said something would have to be done for the Colonel was asking each day if the reporter had been fired. "Fire her and then take her back in a couple of weeks after the colonel has cooled down," the two editors said. I agreed to this if they would assure me that she would be taken back. They did that willingly, so Eleanor Page was fired after I explained the situation to her.

After a couple of weeks I began asking if I could take Eleanor back and each time Bob or Mr. Beck would say to wait another week. This went on for so long that I suspected they would never give me the OK to take Eleanor back. I gave her some money and told her to take the train to Indianapolis and go to the State House and to stay there until she saw the Governor. I advised her to tell him the whole story and to assure him that the Colonel knew nothing about the episode she had reported. She went to Indianapolis. After waiting quite a few hours she saw McNutt in his office. She was a tall, pretty young woman with a great deal of charm. After she told the governor that she had lost her job, which she needed, he picked up the telephone and called the Colonel. He said he had decided to drop the suit and hoped any reporter who had suffered because of it would be put back in the paper's good graces.

I did not know the McNutts at that time but met them a year or two later when I spent the Derby weekend at the home of "young" Tommy Taggart, owner of the popular Indiana spa, French Lick Springs, which had been started by his father, "old" Tom Taggart. The McNutts were Tommy's guests the same weekend, and Paul was much amused when I told him I had sent Eleanor Page to see him.

The day after Eleanor visited Governor McNutt, Mr. Beck showed me a memorandum from the Colonel permitting the reporter to be rehired. Mr. Beck never dreamed I had anything to do with it, but Bob Lee, who knew me better, immediately asked what I had done to bring this about. "Wouldn't you love to know?" is all I ever said about the affair to him after that.

Ned Beck asked me once when I was with him and his second wife, Clare, at their retirement home in Palm Beach, "Why was it, India, that you were the only woman on the *Tribune* who never seemed afraid of me?"

"Because I soon found out that you were more afraid of me than I was of you. You were so shy you were afraid every woman who walked into your office was going to attack you, so you growled and acted real tough whereas you are really a sweetie-pie, tender and darling." Clare laughed until she almost cried, and Ned admitted he really was afraid of newspaperwomen until he got to know them very well.

Mr. Beck, as I always called him when I worked for him, was a stickler for the correct spelling of names and he insisted upon full names, not initials. A middle initial might get by, but if a society re-

porter wrote "H. F. McCormick" for instance instead of "Harold
F. McCormick," she would hear about it. She would hear about it
once; the second time she would be fired. "If a person is important
enough to be mentioned in the society column of the *Tribune,* he is
important enough to have his full name used, not just initials," he
would say. He was not the only one who had specific ideas about editing. Bob Lee used to say, "Never use a two-syllable word if a one-
syllable one will do; never use a three-syllable word if a two-syllable
one will do; and never under any circumstances use a four-syllable
one. Remember newspapers should be well-written but they must be
written simply."

There was one copyreader on the paper who would not allow anyone in Chicago to give a "ball" or at least to have it written about in
the *Tribune.* He always changed that word to "dance." Explain as I
would to him that there was a difference between a ball and a dance
and that Mrs. Astorbilt did not like having her ball described as a
dance, a dance it would be no matter if the reporter who covered it
wrote that it was the most elegant and largest debutante ball of the
season. The man just could not bring himself to let such a word go
into the columns of a family newspaper. Ye gods, what would the
poor man do if he were copyreading today!

This same copyreader opened a note to me from Lloyd Lewis.
Lloyd started out by writing that he was using purple ink for no other could express the mad passion in his heart for me. Lloyd, one of
the most brilliant writers and most attractive men I ever have
known, was not in the least in love with me. Until he fell in love with
young Kathryn Daugherty, this was his usual way of writing any one
of a dozen young women he knew. The copyreader was so embarrassed after he had opened this note (he opened all mail that came
after I had left for the day) that he gave it to Bob Lee with the request that he pass it on to me. Bob, who knew Lloyd, understood
the kidding manner in which Lloyd was writing, but I doubt very
much that the copyreader believed him when he said that he was
sure Lloyd and I were not having a wild, passionate love affair.

The simplified spelling that Colonel McCormick had decreed
should be used in the *Trib* never bothered me, for I paid no attention
to it, leaving it to the copyreaders to change my spelling. If I had a
young reporter who was not a good speller I had difficulties, though,
for often I could not be sure whether she was obeying the Colonel's

edict or just misspelling a word. There were eighty words that appeared in *Trib* print in the Colonel's shortened and simplified method. "Though" was "tho"; "through" was "thru"; "aisle" was "ile"; "island" was "iland"; and so it went. I was interested to read in the Los Angeles *Times* in 1975 that the editors of the *Tribune* had "thrown in the towel, admitting that it is almost as difficult to change the way people spell as it is to get a Republican elected mayor of Chicago." The article went on to report that two words would continue to be spelled in McCormick style: "dialogue" is "dialog" and "synagogue" is "synagog."

Chapter 6

I was a late bloomer. I thought of *a good time* as the ultimate. It may have been the depression that made me realize how much more there was to life than good times, although I always have had my share of them. I enjoyed working for the *Trib* and it was a good preparation for politics—but in many ways I wish I had gone into politics earlier in my life, for if I had I might have accomplished much more.

The first place Jack and I had was a one-room apartment with kitchenette, dressing room, bath and front and back doors. Usually we came home together, never before 6 or 7 in the evening. One afternoon I went home about 4 to change clothes for a wedding. As I unlocked the front door I heard someone running out the back. He left the door open, so I caught a glimpse of him as he neared the foot of the stairway and raced down the alley. I immediately called the police and they asked what he had stolen. I said I would call back as soon as I knew what was missing. When I called again they said they had picked up a man with pockets stuffed with jewelry and other things, and they asked me to come to the station to see if any of the things were mine.

The burglar had come through the back door transom and had

packed all our luggage with our clothes and then, no doubt thinking he had a couple of hours before we would come home, had opened a bottle of Scotch and a carton of cigarettes and sat down to enjoy himself. I must have disturbed him, for he left half a glass of Scotch and a half-smoked cigarette in an ashtray. Also the six suitcases which contained practically all the clothes we owned.

The contents of the desk and dressing room drawers were dumped on the floors, and I had no way of knowing what was missing until I reached the police station. There on a table, filled with the loot found in his pockets, were several pieces of jewelry, none of great value but cherished because they had been my grandmother's; a handsome watch that had been Jack's grandfather's; a dozen pairs of new silk stockings which I had bought at a sale just a few days before; and a pile of thousands of pennies which we had collected in a large Mexican jar on the bookcase. How many there were I did not know but I know the jar was so heavy I could not lift it.

After identifying my things I started to put the jewelry and stockings into my large handbag and I asked for a paper bag in which to carry the pennies. "You cannot take these things," the police officer said. "We have to keep them for evidence." That sounded reasonable to me.

Months passed and at least five or six times during that period a date was set for the man's trial. Jack appeared at the court each time and each time the defense attorney asked for a postponement. Finally the man jumped bail and disappeared, so the case was dropped. Jack asked for our possessions and the police asked for a receipt. Without one they said they could not give us anything—too bad, but that was the way it was. I had never thought to ask the police for a receipt.

I was so furious when he told me about this that I asked the managing editor of the *Trib* if there were not something to be done. He called Jake Lingle, a police reporter, to his office and told him to help me. Jake and I were good friends. In fact, about once a month he would take Katie Webber and me to luncheon, each time paying the check with a hundred-dollar bill which he peeled off a huge bankroll. Katie and I thought it strange that a reporter who probably did not make over $65 a week could have so much money, but we thought he probably was one of those we read about who were making killings on the stockmarket all the time. It was said that even some elevator operators and starters were millionaires on paper. We enjoyed his stories about the gangsters and other underworld figures who were so much in the news in Chicago during those prohibition years. Jake never could write a story, for he murdered the King's English, but he was a super investigative reporter and rewrite men wrote his stories.

Jake asked me for a list and minute description of what the police were holding, and about a week later he brought me all the jewelry. "Babe, the stockings and the pennies are gone," he said. Then he explained that the policemen in the Rogers Park station had divided up some of the evidence among their wives and girl friends. After severe prodding they had recovered the dozen or more pieces of jewelry, but the stockings were long since worn out and the pennies had been spent.

I have always thought of myself as a law-abiding citizen, but when I remember how we used to ignore the Prohibition Amendment to the Constitution which was on the statute books from 1920 until 1933, I must admit that I was a lawbreaker then, as was almost everyone I knew. Several summers we visited friends who had a summer place in northern Vermont. If we went by train we would go through Canada. Our trunk would be sealed in Chicago. If the seal was unbroken when we arrived at the Vermont town where our friends would meet us, the trunk could be picked up without any trouble. There was no inspection such as our hand luggage would have to undergo by the customs office to see if we were bringing contraband liquor into the "dry" United States.

Whenever we drove over the border to an inn for dinner and Canadian ale, we would buy several bottles of Scotch, and since our hosts were well known to the customs officers their car was never searched. By the time we were ready to return to Chicago we had accumulated about seven or eight bottles of Scotch, so we decided it would be safer to ship the trunk by express. It was sealed at the Newport express office and eventually was delivered to our apartment on the near north side of Chicago with the seal intact.

One summer when I began to pack I found that we had a dozen bottles of Scotch and several bottles of liqueurs. I told Jack I thought these would make our trunk so heavy that it would be suspect and that we would have to give our hosts some of the bottles. Jack said he was sure everything would be all right but he thought it would be better to check the trunk on our train tickets. Though this made no sense to me, he insisted that expressing it would be too expensive because of the weight, so he checked it at the railroad station.

When I gave the check to a man to pick up the trunk at the railroad station in Chicago, I expected it would be delivered no later than the next day. The trunk did not come. Instead the man called to say the trunk would have to be opened at the station before it could be released. The trunk could not be opened without exhibiting many of the bottles of liquor. It was a wardrobe trunk, and I had packed some of the bottles in clothes in the half of the trunk ordinarily used for hanging garments.

Jack and I worried for days but could see no way in which we could obtain our trunk without having the customs officer see the liquor. So, I asked one of the editors at the *Trib* if he could have someone look into the case and see what could be done, if anything. The report came back that the man in charge of the federal unit to enforce prohibition in the area was going to make a test case of ours; too many private citizens were breaking the law just as we were doing, and Jack would have to go to prison. Finally I was told to stay at home all the next day and to be ready to take the trunk key to the customs office at the railroad station the moment I received a telephone call. I sat near the telephone all day, afraid to leave it. I decided to whip up a sunshine cake for it was then 5 o'clock and I did not suppose I would get the call so late. Just as I was putting the cake into the oven the phone rang and a man's voice said, "Mrs. Moffett, come at once." I pulled the cake out of the oven, dashed to the garage and exceeded the speed limit getting to the Twelfth Street Station.

When I went into the storage room where an attendant told me my trunk was, I found a man standing there whom I recognized as the head of the federal enforcement agency in the Midwest. Without a word he took the key, opened the trunk, thus breaking the seal, and then handed the key back to me. The editor who had given me instructions about the part I was to play had told me to offer whoever opened the trunk some Scotch, so I asked the man to take what he would like. He took several bottles and then suggested there were men in the adjoining office who would enjoy some, so when I shut the trunk there was one bottle of Scotch and the three bottles of liqueurs left. The Scotch and one bottle of liqueur were taken to my friend, the editor, the next day, but he did not drink so he suggested I give them to the reporter who had arranged the deal. Yes, it was Jake, bless his heart.

During the years I was not working for the *Trib* I often dropped by the local room when I was in Chicago. Coincidentally, I was sitting chatting with Ralph Ellis, the day city editor, one afternoon when he received the news that Jake had been shot to death in the tunnel that led from Michigan Avenue to the Randolph Street Illinois Central station. We later learned that Jake was so involved with gangsters that he suffered the same fate as many of that group. The source of his mammoth rolls of large bills became known. While I was shocked, I was also saddened, for I was fond of Jake.

A "friend" who worked in the Sunday room had a tongue that wagged unmercifully after she had had a few drinks. Once when she and her husband were having Sunday luncheon at our house in Geneva, she confided to Jack that "everyone at the *Trib* thinks India and Bob Lee are lovers but I want to tell you I am sure they are not." Jack did not need her assurance that Bob and I were nothing more than good friends. Jack had laughed with me when I told him that Bob had told me that when I first came to work for the *Trib* Bob and Fred Pasley had thought I was about "as cute a dish as they had seen" and that they had matched coins to see which one "would make a play for me." He did not tell me who had won, or lost, but neither ever tried. Bob said they decided I was too nice a girl for any hanky-panky. This was approximately sixty years ago and nice girls didn't "do it." When I would go into the *Trib* local room to write one of my five-dollar assignment stories, Bob and Fred, rewrite men, sat with their backs to me at the desk I used. I usually had to ask one of them to help me with my lead. They gave me a crash course in journalism, teaching me to write the most important facts in the first paragraph and always to keep in mind that if a story had to be cut to fill the space, it was better to have the story written so that it could be chopped off at the bottom instead of in the middle.

Caroline Kirkland, who under the pseudonym of Madame X wrote a very interesting society column in the Sunday *Tribune,* and James O'Donnell Bennett, one of the best newspaper writers I ever have read, took me under their respective wings and taught me many niceties about the English language that I hadn't learned in high school. Miss Kirkland was descended from some noted New England authors and had a distinctive aristocratic writing style. Jamie Bennett and his wife Susan became close friends of mine even though they were much older, and to spend an evening in their home was a great treat. Jamie had been chief of the *Tribune* writers abroad from 1914 until 1918, and his style was philosophical but not pedantic. He never used a typewriter and, although copyreaders complained, the Colonel said he wished other writers would write in longhand if they could turn out stories like Jamie's. We had some great men on the paper in my early days there: Bert Leston Taylor, Richard Henry Little, John T. McCutcheon, Ring Lardner, among others. When we moved from the building at Madison and Wabash avenues to Tribune Tower on North Michigan Avenue, we had a splendid, high-ceilinged city room with good light and many other improvements. "But where is the women's rest room?" I asked the first day we were in our new quarters.

"There is one on the fifth floor," said Jimmy Durkin, our colorful copyboy, who was almost an old man then. The city or local room was on the fourth floor, so it was a definite inconvenience to have to take an elevator or walk up a long flight of stairs if one was rushing to make a deadline.

I inquired of Bob Lee what facilities there were for the men on the fourth floor, and he said they had a nice big room. "Well, the women must have the same," I said, and he agreed that it was a sad mistake to have put their rest room on the fifth floor and said he would see what could be done to rectify it. Weeks passed and nothing was done. So finally I went into his office one night when only one elevator was working and I was tired and did not feel like walking up the long flight to the floor above and I declared that if they did not start work the next week on turning some fourth floor space into a women's room I was going to use the men's room. "I'm married with two children so I've seen everything," I said, "and you'd better believe it won't embarrass me to use the same toilet as the men. They do it in France, you know." We soon had an adequate women's rest room on the fourth floor.

Occasionally Bill Bockelman, who was the Colonel's bodyguard and chauffeur, would come and sit beside my desk after he had delivered the Colonel to the 24th floor and tell me stories about the Colonel that were so amusing I had great trouble not to laugh aloud.

My response would have been most unsuitable, for Bill saw no humor in his tales. For instance, one morning he said, "I just want to tell you what my boss did last night. It was terrible. Somebody told him there was a good show at the Cort Theater, so he says to me, 'Bill, get two seats and we'll go.' So, I gets two seats in the second row but we were late, so we had to crawl over a lot of knees to get to our seats. I sorta liked the show but after we'd been there about ten minutes the Colonel said in his booming voice, 'C'mon, Bill, let's get out of here. I've seen this show.' Now, wasn't that a hell of a thing to do?" I agreed that it was. The show was Shakespeare's *Romeo and Juliet*.

There were many such stories, for the Colonel often took Bill to places of recreation with him. Bill was rough-talking but he was kind and tender-hearted, and in addition to amusing me he often made me feel great sympathy for the Colonel, who Bill said was terribly afraid of being assassinated by gangsters. This worried Bill considerably and he always was trying to think of some way in which he could make his boss feel secure and safe for he had a sincere and deep affection for the man he was engaged to protect.

Almost all who worked for the Colonel for any length of time felt the same affection for this man in spite of the fact that some of his closest associates thought he was arrogant and despotic. He may have been—I never saw any evidences of this in his behavior to me. I was glad that I was able to tell Pat Maloney and Don Maxwell when they were managing and city editors that his deafness accounted for what sometimes seemed very rude treatment of them and the others who attended the daily editorial conferences. It did not seem possible to me that these men did not know he was deaf. I mentioned it one night when they were questioning me about a visit I recently had paid to his house in Palm Beach.

"Deaf?" they both yelled. "What do you mean?"

"Just what I am saying," was my reply. "He is as deaf as a post. How could you possibly not be aware of it? You deal with him every day. I only see him once in a while and then we are talking directly to each other, so he hears me. But I wasn't in his house more than a few hours when I discovered how deaf he was; we were sitting on the veranda looking out at the ocean and I said something about how beautiful it was. He said nothing, so I repeated my comment in the form of a question and he still said nothing. Now the Colonel is a gentleman if he is anything, so I knew he did not hear me. I tested it several more times that evening and sure enough, he never paid any attention to anything I or anyone else said unless he was looking straight at the speaker. I asked Maryland about it the next day and she said I was right, that he was deaf but would not wear a hearing aid." Maryland Mathison Hooper had been the best friend of his first wife. After Amie's death, Maryland had continued to be the Colonel's best friend and became the second Mrs. McCormick. At the time of which I am writing, Pat and Don never had heard of her. They thought the Colonel was involved with a singer who sang every Saturday night in the WGN radio operettas, in which the Colonel took occasion to air his views on anything and everything during the intermission.

The singer in question, a pretty blonde, behaved in a manner suggesting she was mistress of all she surveyed, but I never believed that because I knew Maryland. Maryland had married Henry Hooper of Chicago. It was her prowess as a horsewoman that brought her and Amie McCormick together, although the latter was considerably older than Maryland. Amie McCormick was the master of the foxhounds of the Du Page Hunt in Wheaton, where the McCormick country home, Cantigny Farm, was located and where the Hoopers spent the summers. The first Mrs. McCormick was an artist, an art patron and a lovely person.

When Pat and Don found out that the Colonel had invited me to visit him in Palm Beach they were delighted and urged that I make an effort to displace the singer in his affection. They said they would much prefer to have a newspaperwoman as the second Mrs. McCormick than the singer. I could not seem to make them understand that the Colonel had not invited me to be his guest because of any personal interest in me but only because he knew I would be in the resort to write feature stories.

I think I finally convinced the two editors that the singer was not the queen bee on the opening night of opera the next season. I went to the *Trib* after the performance to help pick out the pictures to be used in a full-page display. The photographers had the lady in question in at least a dozen pictures and Pat and Don had picked one of her before I joined them.

"We won't use her," I said, "we have plenty of socially prominent women, and she was trying so hard to get into pictures that it will serve her right not to use her."

The men were shocked and asked what I thought the Colonel would do if she were not pictured in the next morning's paper.

"Has he told you he wants her picture used?" I asked. "He certainly has not told me and I think he would have if he desired it. If he complains, you can put the blame on me, but I can assure you he won't." And of course he did not.

It was sickening to see how most of the men always were trying to anticipate what the Colonel would want used. So many times they were completely wrong. Colonel McCormick was a superb newspaperman. Although he had some peculiarities (who doesn't?), he was made by some who worked for him to appear much more erratic and unreasonable than he was. Maryland was a wonderful wife for him, for she treated him in a perfectly natural normal way, something few men and women with whom he came in contact did.

I am the sort of person who always has treated everyone in the same way; rich and poor, powerful and weak. I respect achievement or high status, but I cannot behave as though I were an underling and anyone was my master. One day a young assistant at the *Trib* said, "Mrs. Moffett, you treat everyone alike, the rich society women, Colonel McCormick, Mr. Beck, Mr. Lee, me, the copyboy, everybody. I wish I could be like that."

Few of those who worked at the *Trib* would have believed that the Colonel had a sense of humor, but he did. One winter in Palm Beach he asked me what I was going to write about for the next Sunday, and I said, "All the titled people who are lapping up the Palm Beach colony's food and liquor this winter, while England and France are at war. I have counted the titles that appear regularly in the Palm Beach society columns, and half of them are not registered in the Almanach de Gotha."

"Well," the Colonel said, "if you list the phony titles be sure to include the Duke of Chicago." A two-piece saga about Colonel Robert Rutherford McCormick by Jack Alexander entitled "The Duke of Chicago" had appeared in the *Saturday Evening Post*.

Colonel McCormick once gave me an assignment that would have been a complete failure if I had not had my accustomed good luck. I was in a hotel in Palm Beach having a delightful working vacation, for there were beautiful parties every day and night and nowhere are there more elaborate parties than in Palm Beach during the season. Nothing would be more boring to me than a regular diet of such festivities but a week or two of it was fun. One night after returning to the hotel from a gorgeous party given by the Marquis de Cuevas and his Rockefeller heiress wife, I found a message to call the Colonel. I was dismayed to hear the Colonel say that John L. Lewis was in Miami Beach, giving no interviews and that no one could find out why he was there. I could see what was coming and sure enough, he went on to add: "I have made a reservation for you at the King Cole Hotel, where he is staying, and I think if you go down there for a few days you will be able to find out why he is in Miami Beach." The next morning I was in my rented car, driving south to join the other newshawks or hens who were after the story of why the president of the United Mine Workers Union was in Miami Beach. An Associated Press reporter and photographer already had been thrown out of the dining room when they approached Lewis and his party.

For three days I sat on the lawn in front of the hotel, which was located on a canal, where I could see the door to the cottage which Lewis and his daughter Katherine and a chauffeur-bodyguard were occupying. My room was in the hotel, but I spent every waking moment on the lawn, only going to the dining room when the Lewises went. It was terribly boring for I did not dare to become engrossed in a book for fear Lewis would leave the cottage and I would not be aware of it. At length, fairly late on the third afternoon he and his chauffeur left, rushing so fast to the sixteen-cylinder Cadillac parked at the curb that by the time I reached my little car and started it, the big car had disappeared. I had no idea whether it had gone towards Collins Avenue, the "main drag" on which were located the ocean-front hotels and apartments, or towards one of the causeways which connected the Beach with Miami. I was so discouraged that I decided I would avail myself of a standing invitation I had from a friend who handled public relations for the Pancoast Hotel, then the most exclusive hotel on the beach and one very popular with wealthy Britishers as well as Americans. She was one of the few people I had telephoned since arriving at the King Cole. When she had invited me to come for cocktails, I told her I was very busy and would see her when I could. "Come any day," she said, "I always am here at the cocktail hour."

At the Pancoast I asked for Agnes at the desk and was told she was in the cocktail lounge. When I found her, she said she wished that I had come a few minutes earlier, for John L. Lewis just had walked through the foyer, occasioning much excitement among the conservative guests. She used an expression I never had heard before but never have forgotten: "They all acted as if a skunk had appeared at a lawn party." I asked if she could find out where he was and she did so immediately.

"He is in the suite of Harry J. Kelly, vice president of the Dominion Steel and Coal Company of Sydney, Nova Scotia," she said. The *Tribune* used the story of Lewis' meeting with Mr. Kelley as a news story. It was picked up by the press services and used in many papers, both here and in Canada. Apparently the fact that the powerful head of the American United Mine Workers Union was calling on a prominent member of Canadian management in the coal industry was of more than passing interest to certain Americans and Canadians.

I was determined not to eat dinner that night in the King Cole dining room, so I called some friends who invited me to join a party at Jack Dempsey's newly opened restaurant. My friends were a conservative automobile company executive and his wife from Detroit, and I think they were more than a little shocked when the maitre d' at the restaurant greeted me with a loud, "Hi, India, I'm sure glad to see you. How many in your party?" He gave my Detroit hosts and their other guests and me a very good table in spite of the fact that we had no reservations and there was a good-sized crowd waiting. The maitre d' used to run a speakeasy on the lower level of Michigan Avenue near the Tribune Tower, and I had been there with some of the *Trib* gang many times.

I have attended more weddings than most women, for not only have I been a bride three times and celebrated the nuptials of many friends during my long life, but as society editor of the *Trib* I went to many ceremonies. Personal ones as well as those in which I had only a professional interest. The most spectacular of these was the wedding of Mary Landon Baker, eccentric but exquisite daughter of the Alfred Landon Bakers of Chicago and Lake Forest, and Allister H. McCormick, younger son of the Hamilton McCormicks of Chicago and London. Both families were well-known socially although the McCormicks were more "top drawer" than the Bakers. The wedding was planned for New Year's Day at 4 o'clock in the Fourth Presbyterian Church, Chicago's largest and most prestigious church of that denomination. I knew the McCormicks personally, so instead of sending an assistant I decided to go with my mother-in-law, also an acquaintance of both the McCormicks and the Bakers. When we arrived the church was over half-filled, and soon it was bulging with guests but no families of the bride or bridegroom appeared. Four o'clock came and went, and every few minutes we could see Allister or his brother Leander peep out of the room in which they and the minister, the Rev. John Timothy Stone, the apotheosis of religious dignity, were waiting. The organ droned on and on. At last Mary's sister, Mrs. Robert M. Curtis, her husband and their small children were escorted to the front, and then came Mr. and Mrs. Hamilton McCormick, looking the way I would imagine Queen Victoria and the Prince Consort might have, except that Mrs. McCormick would have made two of the Queen, for she was a tall, handsome woman with a regal bearing.

At 4:25 Dr. Stone came out and said in biting tones, "I am asked to say that there will be no ceremony here this afternoon owing to the in-dis-po-si-tion of the bride."

The gasp that emanated from the hundreds of guests was a mixture of horror and surprise, horror that Mr. and Mrs. McCormick should have been subjected to such unforgivable rudeness by a young woman noted for her eccentricities and constant desire to be "different," and surprise that the rumor that had been circulating for days that Mary was going to give society a real shock at her wedding was an actuality. I grabbed a pencil and notepad from my handbag and wrote down the word indisposition, then dashed for the door. The Bakers' apartment on Lake Shore Drive was only a few blocks away, so I ran to it and managed to get inside the apartment but not past the entrance hall. The only person with whom I spoke was a maid who said, "Yes, Miss Mary is here but no one can see her." The reception was to have been in the apartment, but there were no signs that any preparations for it had been made.

By the time I reached the *Tribune* the press services were sending in the story but they all used the word illness instead of indisposition. Apparently none of the society editors or reporters of the other papers was in the church, for the *Tribune* was the only paper that quoted Dr. Stone correctly. Helen Walker, a friend of mine who later became very close, was to have been Mary's only attendant, but because she was a friend I did not try to get a story from her. Bob Lee used to say that a newspaper writer should not have friends, and there were times when I agreed with him. If one had certain ethical standards it sometimes happened that one could not take advantage of friendship. To attempt to get Helen to give me the inside story of why there was no wedding that afternoon was unthinkable to me, and I am sure Helen would not have betrayed her long and warm relationship with Mary anyway. Years later, Helen told me that Mary had broken down at the rehearsal the night before and said she would not marry Allister but that the families and the bridegroom went ahead with plans, thinking they could persuade the bride to go through with the ceremony in spite of her protestations. Mary and her mother left shortly after for Italy and England, where they lived thereafter.

Quite a different sort of wedding was one at which I served as a witness in Woodstock, Illinois, some years after the Baker-McCormick fiasco. Orson Welles, who during his early teens had been a student at the Todd School for Boys in Woodstock, decided to return to that little town after he had become famous and stage a performance of *Svengali* in the old opera house for the benefit of the school. The opera house had been used as a moving picture theater for years and was in pretty rundown condition, but the school and townspeople renovated it and the performance took on the aspect of a glittering social event. Many Chicagoans and North Shore residents drove out to Woodstock for the performance.

I made arrangements with the local Western Union office to stay open so that I could file a story by 10:30 P.M. I had to leave the theater early, of course, in order to make my deadline, but fortunately the Western Union office was next door to the theater. When I walked in the telegrapher greeted me with the words, "Well, I'm glad to see you. I need a witness at this wedding." The bride was a shy-looking young country girl with a little tot hanging onto her skirt and another one well on the way. The bridegroom, sullen and greatly in need of a shave, was staring at the floor. The girl's parents might have posed for Grant Wood, and although there was no weapon in sight, the atmosphere definitely was that of a shotgun marriage. The telegrapher's wife and I signed as witnesses and then the tragic-looking wedding party left.

Never having worked for any newspaper except the Chicago *Tribune* I cannot compare conditions there with those in other offices, but I am sure there could have been no more stimulating and fun place to work than the *Trib* in my years there: 1918-1924 and 1931-1942. During the first six years it mattered not in the slightest that I was a Democrat and that the paper was Republican, and according to my memory it did not matter when I first returned. It was not until 1936 that Colonel McCormick became so rabidly anti-Roosevelt that he really thought Roosevelt's re-election would destroy our form of government.

Colonel McCormick always knew I was a Democrat. When someone asked the Colonel how he could stand having such a rabid Democrat on his staff, he said, "If she can stand me, I can stand her," and then he went on to say that since I came from Tennessee it was only natural that I was a Democrat. Actually, most of the *Tribune* editorial staff was Democratic, but there were few who openly professed their political allegiance. I sported a huge Roosevelt button about five inches in diameter during the '32, '36, and '40 campaigns.

If I had written political news I could not have stayed on the staff after about 1934, but since the Colonel's political bias did not extend to the women's pages I had no difficulty in doing my job and being loyal to my own convictions and also to my boss. Only twice did the Colonel ever question anything for which I was responsible, although the managing editor was sure several times that I would be fired when the Colonel saw the first edition. The M.E. called me one night and said he was removing an interview with Mrs. Roosevelt and a flattering picture of her from the first feature page. "Remove them," I said, "and start finding my replacement tomorrow, for I will not be working at the *Trib* any longer." I had not written the interview but I was responsible for it and I had ordered the photographer to take the pictures and then I had chosen the one to be used. The M.E. did not remove them and neither did the Colonel remove them—or me.

After the great naval battle off Midway Island early in June, 1942, A *Tribune* correspondent, just back from the Pacific, wrote a story which the government felt indicated to the Japanese that their codes and ciphers were broken. The Department of Justice brought suit against the *Tribune,* and Pat Maloney told me they expected me to be an important witness for the paper. This was because the women's pages always were harmonious with government policies, and the column I had started just after Pearl Harbor, "Women in War Work," had received favorable comments from numerous government agencies. The column, which was the first of the sort in the country, was about volunteer activities and the training that was being given to thousands of women so that they could engage in professional war work, thus relieving men for active duty. The suit against the *Tribune* was suddenly dropped, or perhaps it never really was brought, only threatened.

Twice when we had articles and pictures concerning British War Relief and Bundles for Britain in prominent places on the first feature page, I received pages torn out of the paper and written in the margins in the Colonel's handwriting were his comments that he wondered if the women's pages did not have the same editorial policy as the rest of the paper. Since an answer quite evidently was expected, I wrote one in each case right under his "R.R.Mc." "We have the policy of reporting the news as faithfully and fully as possible. If you want us to do otherwise, please notify me. India Moffett." That was the last I heard of either incident.

One time shortly after World War II had commenced the city editor told me the Colonel wanted me to write a story about the American Red Cross, pointing out its deficiencies and inefficiencies, in short, doing what we could to undermine the confidence of the paper's readers in the organization. I said I would not do so, feeling that it was unpatriotic at that particular time to have such a story appear. I knew that the Red Cross in peacetime deserved to be looked at critically, but it seemed to me that the start of a war was the wrong time to publicly criticize an organization that was going to be needed badly. I heard no more about that project, either. I must say that the Chicago *Tribune* was a marvelous place to work and that Colonel McCormick always was a considerate and fair boss to me. The kind of treatment I and the other women received at the *Trib* did not prepare me for the way in which women were discriminated against in politics.

Chapter 7

Today's young women are often satisfied with combining two vocations, that of wife and professional woman, not being forced to be mothers unless they want to be. But I always wanted a family and was very disappointed not to have my first baby nine months after I was married to Jack. I put my application in at the Cradle, an adoption agency in Evanston, Illinois, after the doctor told me he thought it would be wise to adopt a child if I really wanted one, for I had been married almost five years. Fortunately, the month after I decided to follow the doctor's advice, I became pregnant, due to the fact, the doctor said, that I had relaxed and ceased to worry about having a baby. At the Chicago *Tribune,* I am said to have told the elevator starter, the lobby guard (there was an armed guard on every floor of the Tribune Tower), the elevator operator and, of course, everyone in the local room when I returned to the office after seeing my doctor in midafternoon. I cannot believe this to be literally true, but it might well have been, for I was delirious with happiness.

I know I went to the managing editor's office late that afternoon and told him I would be leaving because I was going to have a baby. He looked at me closely and said, "When?" Upon hearing that the baby would be born in seven months, he laughed and said, "Well,

you do not need to leave immediately, do you?'' As it turned out I
did have to leave almost immediately. The doctor told me I would
not be able to carry the child full term unless I was very careful and
spent at least half of every day in bed. I was not to ride in an automobile or on a bus; only the streetcar was permitted. In spite of all
these restrictions, I never spent a more joyful period of time than
when I was awaiting the birth of my first child. He was born October
8, 1924. The doctor advised that if we wanted a second child, I
should use the Cradle. I ignored this advice. I was afraid I never
could feel the same about an adopted child as I did about my own (I
am sure I was wrong about that), so when Johnny was sixteen
months old he had a little sister. I would have welcomed a larger
family but that was not to be. Considering the life I lived, I suppose
it was just as well. I might not have been able to support more than
two children when the time came for me to do so.

In December, 1930, an asthmatic condition made it necessary for
me to go to a warm, dry climate for the rest of the winter. I knew I
never would stay more than a few weeks if I left the children at
home in Winnetka, so it was decided to close the house and take
them with me to Phoenix. Jack would stay with his mother in Chicago, which suited him, for it would give him a chance to live a care-
free life. In fairness I must admit when I look back that I was not the
best wife for a man who thought suburban living was great and
whose idea of a pleasant evening was to play bridge with another
couple, both men drinking so many highballs during the evening that
it is a wonder they could see the cards by 11 p.m.

Being a golf widow every Saturday afternoon and every Sunday
when the weather permitted the game to be played—it was an unex-
plained mystery that it never rained at the country club even if it
poured at home—and not enjoying vacations that consisted of
fishing from early morn until late evening, rain or shine, I really had
a low rating as the wife of a man who never read a book and cared
nothing for classical music. Walking into a friend's kitchen one evening to find the friend and my husband in a close embrace did not improve Jack's and my relationship, so it was not surprising either that
I was glad to go to Phoenix although I knew no one there and felt as
if it was practically at the end of the world and that he was happy to
see me go.

My state of mind may have been what triggered the asthma for I was rid of it just a few weeks after I arrived in the desert.

Phoenix was starting to boom and Scottsdale, near my desert home, where I went to buy alfalfa for John's white rabbits, consisted of a general store and post office and several shacks. I had met a number of people living in Phoenix or near me in the desert and I thought we could have a pleasant life there. At the time I was sorry Jack would not pull up stakes and move West.

Jack had sold our house in Winnetka when the children and I were in Arizona. Upon our return we were living in his mother's apartment at 999 Lake Shore Drive, one of the most fashionable neighborhoods in the city. We did not stay there longer than was necessary to rent the apartment for Jack's mother, who was in Europe, and then we moved to Geneva, a delightful little town forty miles west of Chicago on the Fox River.

I was persuaded by the managing editor of the *Tribune* to return to work in the autumn of 1931. Jack was opposed to my returning, but I told him I could not turn down the offer of a five-day-a-week job (everyone worked six or five and one-half days then) with a good salary at a time when investment banking houses were going broke at a fast rate. Jack was sure his firm was stable, but it was only a few months after I went back to the *Trib* that it failed, carrying with it not only his investments but all of his mother's as well. I surely would have had a hard time getting a job then, so I was thankful that the *Trib* had given me the chance to start earning money each week before I actually needed it. That salary was all we four adults (his mother and mine) and two children lived on for a couple of years.

As hard up as we were, we were affluent compared to the thousands who were dependent upon bread lines and were sleeping under newspapers on the lower level of Michigan Avenue near the Tribune Tower. I felt great sympathy for these unfortunates and gave orders that no one who asked for food was to be turned away from our house. If he were ablebodied, he was to rake leaves or sweep the sidewalk or do something to pay for the food, but if he were old he was to be fed without having to work. Reuben, our Geneva man of law, told me the X on our gate was marked by a needy person and meant that food could be obtained there.

In 1933 I decided that FDR's New Deal was not enough for me; I needed a personal as well as a national New Deal. I had become so disgusted with Jack's behavior, especially his willingness to do nothing and to let me support the family, that I took an apartment on the north side of Chicago and planned to move September 1. I told Jack that there would be no room for him or his mother in the apartment, so that he had better find a job of some sort. I was sure he could make enough to support himself. Although I did not tell him so, I was willing to help with his mother's support or even to assume full responsibility for her if necessary, but I was not going to continue to live with him and her. He begged me not to tell anyone of my decision, so that we could have the summer in Geneva just as if there would be no change in our family in the autumn. I agreed to this. No one but Jack and I, the Chicago real estate agent who had found the apartment for me and the head of the private school to which I intended sending the children knew that on September 1 my New Deal would start.

Early in August Jack and I went to a party given by a North Shore couple who were acquaintances, not close friends. There was no one among the guests who was more than just an acquaintance either. After dinner, the hostess announced that among us was a well-known numerologist from New York, Evangeline Adams, I think, who could be consulted by any of us. The hostess suggested I be the first to go into a private room with the noted guest, which I was delighted to do. I did not know the time of my birth but I gave her the date and the year. She did a lot of figuring on a pad of paper and then said, "You are about to take a momentous step which you should have done long ago. Much pressure will be brought to keep you from doing it, but do not let anything dissuade you. You have made the right decision for yourself and your children. You have fine children, a son and a daughter. You will stand beside one of them when the entire nation honors him. I do not know which child it will be. You are worried about the future but you do not need to do so. You are going to have a busy and interesting life and you will marry again, very happily. It will be a man in the diplomatic service whom you will marry and then you no longer will live in Chicago. You never will be rich but neither will you be poor."

I was a bit shaken by her first statement, for no one at the party except Jack knew we were separating.

Later I told the children what she had said about my standing beside one of them when the nation honored him and often we used to joke about which one was going to be famous. I had not thought of this for years until I stood beside John's grave in Arlington National Cemetery on January 12, 1944. After the flag-covered casket on a horse-drawn caisson had been brought to the grave from the chapel at Fort Myer, something the chaplain said as he handed me the flag made me think to myself—and I almost said the words aloud—"this is what the numerologist predicted"—for the entire nation honors every soldier who dies for his country and the funeral service for a young second lieutenant is nearly the same as for a general. How John would have laughed at this.

Although Herbert Edwards, my third husband, was not in the diplomatic corps, he was with the Department of State when we were married. And I never have lived in Chicago since then, either. And I have had a busy and interesting life, an unusually happy marriage, and I am not rich but neither am I poor.

My Cissy was born wise. An East Indian who cast her horoscope when she was only a few days old wrote that she was an old soul and I always have found this to be true. He also wrote that she would have many illnesses when she was young, that we would despair of her living to adulthood, but that she would be a healthy woman and live many years. She was knocked off her bicycle by an automobile when she was five and had to have dozens of stitches taken in her face but she bears no scar. She almost died, though, because she was allergic to the horse serum in which a tetanus shot was given. A few years later she again was knocked off her bike and this time she suffered a bad concussion. She had pneumonia three times while she was a child and we almost lost her each time. Sulfa drugs had not been discovered until her last bout with pneumonia, and then it was discovered she was allergic to the drug. In early 1945, she was paralysed for two months (more about that later). Even though she has negative Rh blood and her husband is a positive Rh, she gave birth to five normal daughters with no trouble of any sort to mother or babies.

I took the children to the World's Fair in Chicago a number of times during the first year it was held, in 1933, and made sure they saw all the exhibits I thought suitable and interesting for children their ages. The second year I asked if they could think of anything they had heard of at the fair that they had not yet seen, for otherwise

I did not intend to take them at all that summer. Bringing a nine-year-old boy and a seven-year-old girl from Geneva, forty miles from Chicago, to the fair involved making arrangements that were not easy for me since my job at the *Trib* kept me very busy. Cissy said she had seen everything she wanted to, but John said there was one thing he had not seen that he wanted very much to see: Sally Rand's fan dance. I explained that he was too young to be admitted and anyhow, I said, "There is nothing so interesting about it. Just a woman who dances holding several large ostrich feather fans and swirling them around so that they hide almost all of her body." His answer was "Yes, I know, but I want to see her because she might drop a fan and show her penis."

I remember overhearing Cissy when she was about eight reply to a question as to what her mother did at the *Tribune* by saying, "Well, she writes all that goes into the paper, takes all the pictures and draws all the funnies. At least I think that's what she does."

Cissy always was my champion. One evening when I was putting the finishing touches to my appearance in preparation for being taken to dinner and the theater by a male friend, John, aged about fifteen, said, "Mom, these men who take you out to places spend a lot, don't they?" When I agreed with him, he continued, "I can't understand it when there are so many pretty, young ladies around why they take you." Cissy bristled and quickly said, "John, how can you talk like that? Mother is charming and attractive and glamorous." John retorted, "Humph, as a glamour girl she's worn out."

When my escort came I could have walked under a snake and I wondered, too, why any man would take a woman verging on middle age anywhere. But thank goodness there were enough who did to give my life as a woman without a husband zip and pleasure. One of the most attractive, and certainly the finest man I ever knew, Herbert Edwards, even went so far as to be married to me when he was forty-two and I was forty-seven.

Cissy showed her wisdom when after her sophomore year in the Parker School she asked me if I wanted her to continue to do well in school and to go to college. When I answered that of course I did, she said, "Well, then you'd better send me away to school next year. I find studies and boys do not mix. Boys are fine during vacations and holidays, but when they are around all the time I just do not do good work in school." So, she spent her junior year at the

Sandia School in Albuquerque, New Mexico, and her senior year at the Warrenton Country Day School in Virginia. She had chosen Bennington for college when I had taken her on a tour of eastern colleges several years before we had moved east.

One reason Herbert and I were not married until six years after we met was because my John loved his Chicago school and never wanted to go to boarding school. A friend arranged for him to have a scholarship at the Phillips Academy at Andover, Massachusetts, but he would not accept it. I never gave him this reason for Herbert and I delaying our marriage but later I was thankful that John and I had spent the year Cissy was at Sandia together. It was a happy year for both of us.

Before I was married to Herbert, I went to New York City for the opening of *Kukan,* a documentary film he had produced. It was a spectacular account of China at war, photographed by Rey Scott. It included the building of the Burma Road and the aerial bombing of Chungking. After the showing, Robert Ripley of "Believe It or Not" fame, took a group to his apartment for a nightcap. Most of us were in a large pantry while he mixed the drinks. "Here's to the death of that s— of a b— in the White House," said the host. "I won't drink to that or touch a drop of your liquor," I said, "and how dare you, who make your living out of showing two-headed monsters and such, say a thing like that about our President? I'm leaving your home at this moment." And out I stalked, hoping Herbert would follow me, which he did. It was a moment of strain for us both, for I knew Herbert had been hoping Ripley would publicize the documentary. He did but not as enthusiastically as Herbert would have liked. *Kukan* later was awarded the first Oscar for a feature-length documentary film by the Academy of Motion Picture Arts and Sciences.

Chapter 8

Herbert T. Edwards, the man to whom I was married in 1942, was in charge of the distribution of campaign moving pictures for the Republican National Committee in 1936. We met soon after he came to Chicago from New York City around Labor Day. We saw each other very often during the campaign and he always urged me to vote for his man. He was not a very persuasive vote-switcher since he was but a nominal Republican who had inherited his political affiliation from his father.

I decided Governor "Alf" Landon of Kansas was not going to win when a mink-coated woman party leader from the East Coast addressed a huge Republican women's rally: "I gave up a trip to Europe to work for Governor Landon, and I want to tell you women no sacrifice is too great to make to defeat Roosevelt." Mink coats were not common in 1936, and any political party that allowed a woman in a mink coat to say she had sacrificed for her candidate by giving up a trip to Europe was doomed to defeat.

I would have liked to please Herbert, just as I wanted to please Colonel McCormick, so on election day when I went into the seclusion of the polling booth in the public garage where I kept my car, I cried and cried and cried. My belief in the principles of the Democratic Party and Roosevelt's New Deal were so strong that even to please my lover and my boss I could not vote Republican. I stayed in the cubicle so long one of the poll watchers called to ask if I were ill. They must have wondered why I had such red eyes and was sniffling when I came out after marking my ballot.

That election day was a sad one for me in spite of the fact that President Roosevelt was reelected. When I got to my office at the *Trib,* I found a message to call Weymouth Kirkland, the senior member of the law firm that handled the paper's business, and an old friend of mine. I was separated from Jack Moffett, but I had done nothing about a divorce. Each time I saw Weymie he would advise me to take steps to legalize the separation. Wisely he said if there were a chance that Jack and I would live together again not to bother with a divorce, but if I were sure that would not happen, it would be well to be divorced.

Since meeting Herbert Edwards, I was sure I would marry again, so I had told Weymie to give me a call some day when he was not busy and I would come to his office to start proceedings. That election day was the day he was not too busy to confer with me, so down I went to his office. Even if you know you have reached the end of the line and you have sufficiently good reasons for dissolving a marriage, it is not a pleasant experience to go through, especially when children are involved.

I left Weymie's office feeling anything but cheerful. I became more woeful when I met Herbert for luncheon and he greeted me with the question, "You DID vote for Landon, didn't you?" I admitted I had not. It was not the gayest meal we ever shared. Dinner at the Tavern Club that night was not much better, and the two "victory" parties to which we went later, one for Governor Landon given by John Hamilton, chairman of the Republican National Committee, and the other by Colonel McCormick, were worse than wakes. I was the only one at both who was elated.

Six years elapsed between our meeting and our wedding. I always said it took me that long to get such an attractive bachelor to say yes and he said it took him that long to get me away from the several serious beaux I had in Chicago who formed what they called "the anti-Edwards Club." One who asked many questions about my New York beau and found out that I did not know all the details of his personal and business life put a detective on Herbert's trail and then disclosed with disappointment that there was nothing in the report to indicate that Herbert was not a decent man and unfit for me to marry, "if you want to be a poor man's wife and not give your children the kind of life I could give them."

Herbert Threlkeld-Edwards, Jr., was born in Bethlehem, Pennsylvania, August 19, 1900, the only son of Dr. and Mrs. Threlkeld-Edwards. After graduating from the University of Pennsylvania, he served for several years as a volunteer assistant to Sir Wilfred T. Grenfell, who headed the International Grenfell Association in its great medical and social work in Labrador and north Newfoundland. It was while there that Herbert became interested in documentary motion pictures, a field in which he became a professional. He joined the newly created Division of Cultural Affairs in the United States Department of State in 1942, shortly before we were married. At the end of World War II, the Office of War Information, which was headed by our good friend Elmer Davis, and the coordinator of Inter-American Affairs, the director of which was Nelson Rockefeller, were transferred to the State Department and these two agencies were abolished.

President Truman realized there would be a continuing need for programs to explain American postwar policies to peoples overseas and to counter anti-American propaganda, so the United States Information Agency was established in the Department of State. Herbert became assistant administrator with responsibility for the international motion picture program, which produced and distributed documentary films, newsreels and animated films recorded in fifty-three languages. His was not a political appointment, since he was already with the Department of State when we were married.

Since I did not belong to any church, I was agreeable to being married by a minister of Herbert's church. Bishop George Craig Stewart of the Episcopalian diocese in which I lived would not give dispensation for one of his clergy to marry a divorced woman. I asked Dr. John Anderson, pastor of the Fourth Presbyterian Church—I had been brought up a Presbyterian in Nashville—if he would officiate at the quiet ceremony in my apartment. It struck me as being the height of absurdity to hear Dr. Anderson say that he could not marry a divorcee unless she had obtained the divorce on the grounds of her husband's adultery. I said that I had not used such grounds but that I could have, so that made it all right for me to become Mrs. Herbert Threlkeld-Edwards.

I never tried to get Herbert to become a Democrat. I felt sure he was too intelligent not to see the error of his political ways. When he went to work for the Department of State in 1942, I knew he believed in FDR's foreign policy. I've never asked him how he is registered and I never shall.

Our wedding took place on June 19, 1942. Herbert could not reach Chicago until the morning of the 19th, so I had to get the *Trib* to arrange for him to have a blood test and the result that same day, thereby avoiding the usual three-day period before obtaining a license.

Only a few of my friends were invited to the wedding, which had to be at 3 p.m. so that we could take a train for the East later that afternoon. Herbert had spent many vacations at Atlantic City when he was a boy living in Bethlehem, Pennsylvania. Since I never had visited that seashore resort, he wanted to take me there on our wedding trip.

When I told the *Trib* managing editor Pat Maloney in the early summer of 1942 that I was going to be married and move to Washington, he urged that I take a leave of absence in order to retain my pension rights and other benefits a long-time *Trib* employee had. I took this advice until I started accepting a salary from the Democratic National Committee in April of 1945. During my first few months in Washington I did a few Sunday feature stories for the *Trib*, but I soon realized this could not continue due to our differing philosophies.

Chapter 9

This is a book of memories, joyous ones and sad ones. The last time I saw my nineteen-year-old son was on a night in September of 1943 when John was leaving on a bus to catch a plane to return to Wendover Field in Utah where he was teaching men older than he how to be bombardiers in the U.S. Air Force. John had enlisted on his eighteenth birthday, October 8, 1942, and very soon had been shipped to Texas to be trained, so he thought, as a fighter pilot. Since he was a mite too tall for that, he decided to become a bombardier rather than "the motorman of a bomber," as he told me on the telephone. He was the youngest lad ever to receive his wings at the time he was given them by Governor Coke Stevenson of Texas in July. The presentation amused John very much: all the other new airmen had their wings pinned on them by the commander of the field but the governor elected to honor John because the *Tribune* had ordered a photographer to get a picture of "India's Johnny" receiving his wings. John had won the 1942 competitive college scholarship awarded to the child of an employee every year by the paper, but he had elected to go into the service rather than to college. He came to us in Washington for a brief leave after Texas and then went to Utah. He hoped to be sent overseas soon. I was happy when he was assigned to teach, for I thought he would be safer in this country than in Europe or the Far East.

John had no friends in Washington, nor did Cissy, who had gone to preparatory school in Virginia the preceding winter. Although they enjoyed his stay with us in our little house in Kensington, a Maryland suburb of D.C., they missed not having any young people with whom to have fun. When John called me just before Labor Day and said he had a week's leave, I suggested that he meet me in Chicago rather than coming to Washington. Cissy was off visiting a friend somewhere before going to college, and Herbert was going to go to New York on Labor Day, so I thought John would enjoy being in Chicago more than in Washington. I called the Drake Hotel and engaged a two-bedroom suite.

By the time I reached Chicago, John had met a beautiful eighteen-year-old girl with whom he had fallen madly in love. He brought her to meet me the first night I was there, but I saw little of him during the next five days because he was with her every afternoon and evening. He and I had breakfast together each day and I had my other meals with friends of mine. The night John was to leave he said Patty and I could ride with him to the airport on the Air Force bus scheduled to pick him up at the hotel at 1 a.m. At 9 that evening, John called to ask if I would join him and Patty in the Drake's Camellia Room. When the champagne he had ordered came, John announced that he and Patty had just become engaged to be married. I suggested that her mother and stepfather be told, so the young lovers telephoned them.

When it came time for John to take the bus, I walked out onto Walton Place with him and Patty and then I said, "Would you forgive me if I did not go with you? I seem to be very tired." The look on those two beautiful young faces will remain with me always. As much as John loved me, I knew they welcomed that last hour together. I am sure no mother and son ever had a closer and more satisfying relationship than we did. We had the same tastes, both enjoying the same things and having the same sense of humor. We both had a quick temper and fought often, but it never took either of us long to get back into a good humor and then we hardly remembered what we had fought about.

The only period of his life we did not enjoy each other was when he was about fifteen and began telling me he did not have to pay any attention to anything I said because I was just a woman. He was insolent and rude, which he never had been before. Everything I did and said was wrong, so finally I called Dr. Adler (nephew of the famous Dr. Alfred Adler, the Austrian psychologist and psychiatrist), who was John's counselor at the Francis Parker School and whom I knew John admired. I asked him if he would come and see me at the *Trib* some Saturday morning, for I did not want John to know I was consulting him. Dr. Adler very kindly consented to see me the next Saturday and he said I was not imposing on him for part of his duties was to counsel parents as well as students. He was greatly surprised to find out John's father and I were separated, but he said that explained many things to him. He had thought it strange that John talked and even bragged about his mother and never mentioned his father. I gave him my analysis of the problem—I always am inclined to diagnose my own ailment instead of waiting to have the doctor's opinion—saying that I thought John was beginning to feel his masculinity and that he resented being supported entirely by a female. He often had complained that his father did not contribute anything to his and Cissy's support. I always said it did not matter in the least as long as I was able to manage. Dr. Adler agreed with me and said he would have some talks with John that he thought would change his attitude. "Do not let him know I have seen you, please," I said. He said I would have to leave that to his judgment, but that it would be better if I said nothing about our meeting.

I do not know what Dr. Adler said to John, but several weeks later John told me in a rather casual way that he was glad I had consulted Dr. Adler because he thought it had done me a great deal of good. Me, mind you! Well, it did both of us good. His disdain of me disappeared and his rudeness and insolence were things of the past.

In the summer of 1941 John worked in the office of a yacht broker who was my friend. Since it was his first job, I suppose it made him feel very much like a man. One Sunday morning at breakfast I looked at him and realized he was different from the boy he had been the day before. A mother's loving intuition is keen, but I hardly could believe what mine was telling me. That afternoon I called his father, who was then living in Chicago with his second wife, and said I thought John had had a sexual experience Saturday night. I asked Jack to take John to luncheon the next day and talk to him about it. "Make sure he knows all that he should," I said, for I never had discussed this with John. I had taken it for granted that he was too young—he was almost seventeen—for sex.

Jack took John to luncheon and that night John said to me, "Mom, why didn't you ask me if I had had a sex experience Saturday night? Why ask Dad to take me to lunch and find out? I am much closer to you than to Dad and I would have told you more readily than I did Dad. He had quite a time getting it out of me. I knew when he called and invited me to lunch that something was up because he never had taken me to lunch before. Anyway, [naming his best friend] and I decided to try it Saturday night, so we got into a cab in front of a restaurant and asked the driver to take us where we could find some call girls. He drove us to a nice apartment building on North Dearborn, the same building in which some friends of yours live, by the way, and told us the girls' names. We rang their bell and they invited us upstairs. We had some beers, played the victrola and danced and then went to bed with the girls. It cost us each ten dollars and we thought they overcharged us. We were sorry we hadn't tried to get it for free from some of the girls we date, but we thought it best to start with pros. One of the girls is a telephone operator and the other a clerk in a shop. They probably couldn't afford to live in that building if they didn't make extra money at nights. They really are nice girls but we don't plan to see them again, so don't worry."

I did not worry, but I was sorry there was no affection nor tenderness involved in his first encounter with something that should be more than buying a moment of ecstasy. Perhaps I was wrong. I do not think a female who at that time believed in premarital chastity could judge the relative merits of finding out about sex with a professional or an amateur.

If I had known on that September night in 1943 when I said au revoir to him outside the Drake Hotel that I never would see him alive again, I might not have been able to send him off with a smile. He died December 29 in a night flight in which two of the huge bombers "touched wings" and all twenty-five men aboard were killed. The wreckage was not found for three days. Patty was on the train, having spent Christmas with us, on her way to New Year's with John. It was good for me that I had her to worry about. The thought of that young girl arriving in Salt Lake City, expecting to be met by her fiancé, kept me from the self-pity I might naturally have felt. I could not think of anyone I knew there, so finally I called the Red Cross and asked if it could have someone meet the train and tell Patty what had happened to John. Before the time of her arrival I remembered a young woman I had known in Chicago who had married a Salt Lake City man. She agreed to take over the sad task of meeting Patty. I suppose I could have asked the commander at Wendover Field to arrange for this, but I never thought of that. I found the Air Force under General "Hap" Arnold so solicitous and anxious to be helpful to bereaved families that I am sure I needed only to tell someone at the field of the situation and it would have been taken care of properly.

Since John loved the Parker School, after his burial in Arlington National Cemetery I sent the flag from his coffin to wave over the school. It did so until it was almost in shreds from the winds for which Chicago is famous.

"How long did it take you to get over John's death?" a man I had known for years asked when I saw him in New York some years later. "How long?" I repeated. "I never expect to get over it but I have learned to live with it, which is all I could do. One gets over the sorrow of losing a mate, but I am sure a mother never really gets over the loss of a child."

I did grieve terribly for John and it seemed especially cruel to me that he had been killed in this country before he had had a chance to go overseas to do what he had been trained for. That this was wrong on my part was brought home to me forcibly one night. We returned home from dinner to find a message to call Adela Rogers St. John in Connecticut no matter how late I came in. Adela and I were acquaintances of long standing, but I knew nothing of her family and she knew nothing of mine. We often had seen each other in Chicago because we both were in the newspaper business. Since moving to Washington I had seen her several times at the home of Mary Holmes, Steve Early's sister.

I called Adela, who said that she was at her daughter's Connecticut home (Adela herself lived in or near Los Angeles) and that I might think she was crazy but she just had to call me. Her daughter, who was psychic, had been receiving messages all day from someone named John who wanted her to call his mother India to tell her that it made no difference whether he was killed in this country or in battle and that his mother's constant grieving for him was holding him close to earth; that he could not progress and start the work there was for him to do, which was to help others who passed from mortal life in sudden violence.

Adela said her daughter disliked receiving messages and seldom did anything about them, but this impressed her so much because of its frequency and intensity and the fact that the name India was used. She finally asked her mother if she knew anyone named India. Adela did not know I had a son, but she said she felt she had to call me. It comforted me greatly to have this message, for I could not doubt its veracity.

I received one other message through a close friend in Washington. This message told me where to find the key to a little jewel case that had come back with John's things from Utah. The case was locked, and there seemed to be no key to it. Thinking it did not matter what was in the case, I just put it away. The message told me to find the key in the large case where John's dark glasses were. I never had opened that case, but when I did, there was the tiny key in one corner. My friend wanted to continue to try and make contact with John, but I felt that no good could come of that for either John or me, so I asked her to desist from seeking to communicate with him. This does not mean that I do not believe it possible for there to be communication between the living and dead for I know that in these two instances it was possible—it happened. Someday it may be a usual thing, but at this time I do not think it wise for the average person to attempt to live in two worlds. That there is another world than ours I firmly believe, but I do not know what it is like, of course. It will not be many years, though, before that mystery will be solved for me, for I already have lived more years than anyone has a right to expect. I do hope to live quite a few more, though, since I come from some long-lived female forebears.

Chapter 10

The first time I saw Harry S. Truman—the S stands for nothing; he told me it was just a middle initial he chose when he had to have one in the Army—was in Chicago in 1944 when he was nominated for the Vice Presidency at the Democratic National Convention. I cannot remember whether he spoke—he must have, for Vice Presidential nominees always do—but if I heard him he made little or no impression on me. The Democratic National Committee, for which I was working as a volunteer at the convention, gave me not a single ticket of admission. I only attended the sessions when my former boss, Colonel Robert R. McCormick, had me as a guest in his box. Maryland Hooper, our mutual friend, later his wife, was extremely gracious about inviting me to use the box, so whenever I could get away from my duties in the Public Relations Division of the Women's Division of the committee as escort to the feminine VIPs who were busy going to radio stations for appearances, I enjoyed the convention as Colonel McCormick's guest.

I next saw Senator Truman a day or two after his nomination, when the Women's Division gave a reception for him and Mrs. Truman at the Blackstone Hotel. It was a hastily arranged party because it was not known who Roosevelt wanted as his Vice-Presidential candidate until shortly before the actual nomination. Mrs. Charles W. Tillett, vice chairman of the committee and director of the Women's Division, and Mrs. Robert E. Hannegan, wife of the committee chairman, received with Senator and Mrs. Truman. Margaret probably was there, too.

Near the end of the campaign I saw Senator Truman in an elevator in the Biltmore Hotel in New York City. Someone introduced me to him as: "The speechwriter who always includes your name in every speech she writes." Whether Harry S. Truman remembered that comment after he became President I do not know, but in my heart I feel it helped my constant and often successful campaign to persuade him to consider and appoint women to important government posts. The fact that I was virtually the only person associated with the National Committee who felt he would be elected in 1948 was of enormous value to me. Loyalty is a virtue he admired, one that was a fundamental part of his own character, and one that very occasionally served him ill.

The fact that I became a speechwriter never ceased to astonish me. Until that campaign I never had written a political speech. In fact, it seemed unreal that I was in New York at all during the 1944 campaign. I had volunteered to go to Chicago for the convention. Since I had worked for a Chicago newspaper for many years, I knew I could be of value to the Democrats. It was Clare Boothe Luce who impelled me to work for my party. When I heard her say on the radio from the Republican convention in Chicago that GI Jim would blame Franklin D. Roosevelt for his death, I determined to do what little I could to keep the Democrats in office. John, my only son, had been killed, and certainly no Republican could speak for Second Lieutenant John Holbrook Moffett, USAF. My friend Lillian Dudley Owen suggested that I volunteer at Democratic headquarters, but I didn't do it until I heard Mrs. Luce's speech.

Having been turned down ignominiously when I volunteered to help the American Red Cross in any way possible, I was thinking of accepting a professional job with the United Nations Relief and Rehabilitation Administration. "I think if you take our staff assistants' course we might find something for you to do," said the Red Cross public relations director after I had told him of my many years of ex-

perience with the Chicago *Tribune*. "Who was that idiot?" Ells-
worth Bunker, at one-time president of the American Red Cross,
asked when I told him about this some years later.

I was received with open arms at Democratic headquarters, for although both national political headquarters are wary of volunteers
and try to be certain none is a spy for the other party, Louisa Wilson
Hager, capable director of public relations for the Women's Division of the DNC, had heard of me and could hardly believe that I
was volunteering to work full time without any pay. I cut my teeth
politically by writing biographies of the women who might be prominent in Chicago—I am sure I did none of Mrs. Truman or Margaret.

In those days, the Democratic Committee always moved its headquarters from the Mayflower Hotel in Washington to the Biltmore
Hotel in New York City for the campaign, so when practically everyone moved in 1944 I thought my campaign activity was over.
When Louisa called one night to ask if I would come up, I said I
could not possibly afford to do so. The next night she called and said
the committee would provide me with a bedroom at the Biltmore.
Since Herbert spent part of each week in New York I decided I'd
go, figuring I'd not spend much on food, for I needed to diet, as always. (As always, of course, I didn't diet.)

After I had been in New York only a few days, Mrs. Tillett, the
vice chairman and woman's director, invited me to dinner with the
national committeewomen from two New England states. Both of
these hearty, witty Irish women had been in politics for many years.
After listening to them talk for several hours about stealing elections, putting or keeping dead people on the voting lists and various
other practices in which old-style politicians indulged, I was so appalled that I did not see how I could continue to work for the committee. The next morning I expressed my doubts to Mrs. Tillett—
every inch a Southern lady and a League of Women Voters alumna
and one I was sure would not approve of what we had heard the
night before. Very wisely she said she did not think I needed to worry, that the national committeewomen just got wound up and after a
certain amount of Old Taylor, each tried to outdo the other. I am
sure this was true, for I soon discovered no women in any State had
enough power or authority to manage any of the actions about which
the committeewomen had bragged. Actually, I came to know that

they were decent, good women, just as most Democratic women leaders are. Republicans, too.

I've always worked hard, but I've never worked harder than I did during those seven or eight weeks of the '44 campaign. Since I slept as well as worked in the Biltmore, I often would go for four or five days without stepping outside. There was no deadline except that one big one, election day on November 7, so it was difficult to stop. It wasn't like working on a newspaper: there, when the paper finally was put to bed, there was nothing to do until it was time to start on the next day's edition. In politics if one is dedicated it is easy to work for eighteen or twenty hours, especially when one just takes an elevator to a hotel bedroom.

My speechwriting in 1944 was for women—perhaps some men— in all parts of the country. Due to travel restrictions we were sending out canned speeches by the hundreds. I was ghosting mainly, however, for Belle Willard Roosevelt, the widow of Teddy Roosevelt's son Kermit, who spoke frequently for FDR. Since I always ended every speech with the words "reelect Franklin Roosevelt as President and elect Harry Truman as Vice President," I suppose she spoke for HST, also. It was my naivete in doing this that occasioned a more seasoned politician to tell me that was not necessary to mention the Vice President. "Not necessary?" I remonstrated in a shocked tone of voice. "Of course, it's necessary. Harry Truman may be President. FDR isn't looking very well these days."

Since few speakers could travel in 1944, there was great dependence on live radio and recordings to carry the message of the Democrats to the voters. Adele Rosenwald Levy and Frieda Hennock, both now deceased, had planned a brilliant program for New York State that involved sending out recordings of speeches by numerous stars of stage, screen and other fields. Adele provided the money and organizing ability, and Frieda, then the only woman attorney in a prominent Wall Street firm and later the first woman member of the Federal Communications Commission, provided the aggressive imagination and business acumen that made the program possible. After hearing some of the recordings, I appointed myself head of an unofficial department in the National Committee to distribute them to all parts of the country. I first had to obtain permission to make pressings from the New York State chairman and vice chairman, and to get budget approval from Mrs. Tillett. These programs were made by such artists as Annabella, Joan Bennett, Franchot Tone, Orson Welles, Clifton Fadiman, Frank Sinatra, Martin Gable, Benay Venuta, Jerry Wayne, Ethel Merman, Ethel Barrymore, Fannie Hurst and others.

The National Committee *was* sending out recordings for use at rallies and on radio, but it was not using the brilliantly planned and directed shows that New York State was enjoying until I took on the task of making these platters available to Democratic leaders in various parts of the country. The most popular speech that the committee sent from New York was one made by the noted columnist and foreign affairs analyst, Dorothy Thompson, who spoke at her own request, "not as a Democrat, but as an American and as a close student of American foreign affairs." Miss Thompson's speech followed one in which Governor Dewey seemed to brag about his active, youthful legs. "When it comes to sitting tight with the United Nations in the Peace, I will bet a hundred to one on Roosevelt's *seat* against Dewey's *legs*," thundered Miss Thompson, who never had hesitated to voice her opinion—a woman after my own heart.

It was a tremendous job to push into quick action the men who made the six hundred pressings we distributed, packed the platters and delivered them to the Railway Express office so they could go out as quickly as possible. Many a night at 11 or 12 my secretary and I would trudge from the Biltmore to the Railway Express office, luckily not far off, so that the platters would be on their way long before the committee mail shop had opened the next morning. Sometimes we had to make more than one trip, especially if we could not find a cab. But we slept better, I'm sure, than if we had left the packages for someone else to look after the next day. (Imagine my dismay when I asked someone at the committee in mid-October during the 1968 campaign how material for the Far West was being sent. "By regular mail, of course," she said. I told the young lady I thought it would be cheaper to have the printers' trucks unload right into the Potomac or the city dump.)

Working with Belle Roosevelt was a joy, for she had a delicious sense of humor and always was willing to do whatever was required. She had volunteered to be a receptionist but was drafted as a speaker at once. In the mornings I would go to her charming house on Sutton Place overlooking the East River and find her in bed with papers spread out all over. We would start to assemble a speech. Scissors and paste pot were our faithful tools, since we'd salvage wherever possible paragraphs from preceding speeches.

I quickly learned to do this when writing for Mrs. Tillett also. I remember a five-minute speech I assembled for her when she was asked to go down to the White House on very short notice to appear on a nationwide radio program with President Roosevelt and Democratic Chairman Hannegan. There was no time for creative thinking, just time to grab ideas from other speeches she had made (written by others, for I had done little writing for her until that time).

The next night I listened to the program but heard only the men. What had happened to the vice chairman? I found out when she returned to New York and told us that the president and the national chairman had used all the time. "Why didn't the chairman cut his remarks if the President talked longer than scheduled?" I asked, not realizing that this wasn't the way things were done in politics. In spite of the fact that women voters were considered important then and have become increasingly so every year since, women are always edged out of a program if time runs out.

That episode was one of two that occurred during the '44 campaign that *should* have prepared me for the fact that women were second-class citizens in the opinion of the majority of male politicians. The other episode happened when Belle Roosevelt was to accompany the President to Chicago. Mrs. Tillett had asked if I thought it would be a good idea to have Belle go with him. I had responded that Teddy Roosevelt was popular in the Middle West and that it would mean a lot to have a member of his family in Chicago with FDR. As the time drew near for the Chicago trip, I asked Belle if she had been given any schedule or if she was sure she would be with FDR in the entourage and on the platform at Soldier Field. She had been told nothing, so I decided to ask Paul Porter, the committee p.r. man, what the plans were. I was beginning to learn that unless one made sure about planning such details, they often were aborted. There was no need for Belle to go to Chicago if a Chicago politician decided to squeeze himself into the picture with the President; thus Mrs. Kermit Roosevelt, a mere woman after all, would be pushed into the dim wings of the production.

I tried for several days to get Paul Porter on the telephone and I also dropped by his office a couple of times. He always was too busy to talk to me, according to his secretary, and he never returned my calls. Finally, two days before the Chicago meeting, I called and said to the secretary when told Mr. Porter was too busy to be disturbed: "OK, I'll call Steve Early [FDR's press secretary] at the White House if I do not hear from Mr. Porter in five minutes." In about three, Mr. Porter called from the Turkish bath establishment where he spent part of many afternoons, I was told later. I am sure he needed the relaxation of a Turkish bath (so did I and everyone else working in the headquarters), but, as I told him when I finally had the privilege to talk with him, I never had to wait more than a few hours to talk to the publisher, managing editor or city editor of the *Trib*. They knew I did not ask to talk to them unless what I had to say or request was important. He agreed that it was important for Belle Roosevelt to be right with FDR in Chicago and he said he would call Steve Early immediately. I could have called Early, but I always have followed the chain of command, if possible. Sometimes, however, in politics especially, one has to go to the top in order to accomplish certain goals.

I had met Mrs. FDR several times in Chicago and saw her several more times during the '44 campaign. I was always impressed with her—so soft-spoken but so decisive and sagacious politically. Mrs. Tillett, one of the most generous women politicians I've ever known, was exceedingly kind to me and included me in many things that inexperienced volunteers did not usually enjoy. An illustration of her generosity occurred the only time I ever met President Roosevelt. It was on January 19, the day before the 1945 inauguration, when he and Mrs. R. gave a luncheon for those who had worked in the campaign. It was the first time I had been to the White House, so it was quite an event in my life. My seventeen-year old daughter was ill, so ill that I was in doubt until the last moment whether I would attend the party. "Go, Mother," Cissy said, "And ask Mrs. R. to send me a kiss."

Mrs. R. received the guests before luncheon. We were told the President would receive us after the luncheon, but that due to his ill health we were not to shake hands with him. Mrs. Tillett preceded me to him. After he had spoken to her and the aide had said my name, Mrs. Tillett turned back and said, "Mr. President, I think you would want to know that Mrs. Edwards is India Edwards, who did such splendid work as a volunteer for us in the campaign." "Our India," said the president, taking both my hands in his, "Our India, who used to be Bertie's India, but now is all ours." Franklin Roosevelt and Bertie McCormick had been classmates at Groton and later at Yale.

When I told Mrs. R. what Cissy had said, she gathered up the roses from all the tables, put them in my arms, and gently kissed my cheek.

Cissy was spending her second work period from Bennington College as a nurse's aide. Before she had completed the one-week course at the Red Cross that preceded the hospital course, she became paralyzed. Luckily, her doctor was able to get her into a hospital room, but there were no private nurses, so I spent every day and many nights with her. The doctor and the four or five specialists whom he called into consultation were never able to diagnose the cause of the total paralysis, which began to disappear after about two months. It took another four months for her to learn to walk again, but by the time she returned to college the next fall she was completely recovered. She was able to dance, ski, play tennis, in fact do all the things she always had done.

I think I found out what caused the paralysis in 1951 when I was a member of the United States delegation to the World Health Organization meeting in Geneva, Switzerland. I had been appointed as the public member by President Truman. One day I was listening to what seemed to be an interminable speech when I heard the speaker, a delegate from Ceylon, say that his country never would go along with the U.S. policy of insisting that all citizens be vaccinated for smallpox . "Too many cases of paralysis result," he said.

I sat up with a start, suddenly remembering that Cissy had been vaccinated ten days before she started the nurse's aide training. None of the doctors who attended her ever inquired about recent vaccinations, so neither she nor I had ever mentioned it. I questioned doctors in our delegation as to whether Cissy's paralysis could have been caused by vaccination, and they admitted that there were cases of this sort occasionally.

At long last the campaign in 1944 ended and all of us who lived in Washington came home. From then until February, 1945, I did a bit of volunteer work for the Women's Division since Louisa Hager had left and there was no p.r. woman in the division. Mrs. Tillett was putting on a tremendous national campaign to support the Dumbar-

ton Oaks plan for a world security organization, the forerunner of
the United Nations Conference which opened in San Francisco that
spring. I helped prepare kits of material for meetings on Democratic
Dumbarton Oaks Day, April 4. Virginia Rishel, an excellent writer
and smart politician, editor of *The Democratic Digest* that the Wom-
en's Division published, was planning to resign. I had a strong hunch
I would be asked to take her place. I was totally unprepared, however, for the offer that Gladys Tillett, approved by Chairman Bob
Hannegan, of course, made to me in March: to become executive
secretary of the division when Lorena Hickok left because of ill
health. Lorena, or Hick as everyone called her, had been a star
Washington reporter for the Associated Press before she joined the
staff of the DNC. Mrs. Roosevelt was her beat, and she covered her
so well and enthusiastically that it seemed wise to both her and the
AP to sever their association.

I had worked with Hick during the '44 campaign, although not as
closely as with Mrs. Tillett and Louisa. My only hesitancy in accepting the unexpected offer was that my husband was a civil servant
with the Department of State and I was not sure that his wife should
be employed professionally by the DNC. He checked with his office
and was told the Hatch Act, which forbids civil servants from actively participating in politics, did not apply to the families of civil
servants. Of course, neither of us at that time anticipated that my
name would become fairly well known in Democratic circles, for, as
the executive secretary, Hick had worked behind the scenes.

Shortly after I joined the staff of the DNC, I discovered how
women were treated by Chairman Hannegan. When Mrs. Tillett
planned to come up from her home in Charlotte, North Carolina, to
spend some time at headquarters, she would ask me to arrange an
appointment with the chairman. I would have great difficulty getting
past his secretary and often would find it impossible to secure her an
appointment. The last straw came when the president of the Business and Professional Women's Clubs, Margaret Hickey, later public affairs editor of *The Ladies' Home Journal,* asked me for an
appointment with the chairman. His secretary made it clear that Mr.
Hannegan could not be bothered. I blew up, for this woman represented several hundred thousand women voters. It seemed to me
that a wise politician should see her.

That night I sent to the chairman's home, a special delivery letter in which I resigned and stated the reasons why I did not care to work for the DNC. My resignation really should have gone to the vice chairman, but I wanted the chairman to know why I was leaving. It did not take him long to get the message. He called me that night at home and said I need not worry, that from then on he would see anyone I thought he should and that he had no intention of treating me as a second-class citizen.

"Tell your secretary," I replied. From that time on I never had any trouble, and eventually his secretary, Loretta Larkin, became my friend. This was a valuable alliance, for she stayed with the committee through several chairmen after Bob Hannegan resigned. Irma, Bob's lovely wife, told me shortly after his death that I was the woman politician for whom he had the most respect, undoubtedly because I was so tough.

I was not much of a politician in those early days. It is a miracle that I did not get the Women's Division into really hot water, for I often had to make decisions that required more experience than I had. Mrs. Tillett spent more and more time in Charlotte. Although we talked every day—sometimes three and four times a day—it was not the same as if she had been sitting in the next office. Sometimes I feared she might resent my going ahead and doing things without waiting for her considered judgment, but she was pleasant to work for and with and did not object to the way in which I was running the Division.

There was no person in the country who had done more to build support for the idea of a world security organization than Gladys Avery Tillett. It seemed terribly unfair when the Department of State decided that she was "too political" to be given credentials to attend the San Francisco United Nations Conference. We got around that by having her share my bedroom on the special train that carried the press, both domestic and foreign, from Washington to San Francisco. I was representing *The Democratic Digest,* and who cared whether I had a traveling companion so long as she paid her fare? She was named a nongovernmental observer at the conference, joining a fairly large group of men and women in this category.

Our delegation in San Francisco was headed by the Secretary of State, Edward R. Stettinius, Jr., with former Secretary of State Cordell Hull acting as senior adviser. The other delegates in addition to Secretary Stettinius and Dean Virginia Gildersleeve of Barnard Col-

lege were Senator Tom Connolly, Democrat of Texas and chairman
of the Foreign Relations Committee; Senator Arthur H. Vandenberg, Republican of Michigan; Representative Sol Bloom of New
York, democratic chairman of the House Foreign Affairs Committee; Representative Charles A. Eaton, ranking Republican member
of the committee; and Commander Harold Stassen, former Republican governor of Minnesota.

I first met young John F. Kennedy at the San Francisco Conference. He was covering it for the Hearst newspaper chain and was
one of the young men I constantly saw at parties for the delegates
and press. He was charming, friendly, and among the most sought-
after young men out there. Another one, easily the "lion," except
for such delegates as Senator Vandenberg, Commander Stassen,
and Vyacheslav Molotov of the USSR, was Alger Hiss, secretary-
general of the conference. Many Democrats at that time were sor-
rowful that the young former governor of Minnesota was a Republican, for we expected great things of him. Whatever happened to him
that kept him from fulfilling the stellar role he seemed destined to
play in the political life of the country? In San Francisco he seemed
to have everything that would make him a success at whatever he
undertook.

Molotov was the star of the San Francisco show during the two
weeks he was there, although there was neither charm nor friendliness in his manner. Stassen was the star of our delegation as far as
the press was concerned, although Senators Connolly and Vandenberg and Representatives Bloom and Eaton were more knowledgeable about the organization that was being created at the conference. These four certainly had more to do with getting our Congress
to accept the organization than did any others of our delegation.

Alger Hiss was a personable young man, seemingly well liked by
all who dealt with him. It was hard to believe that he had been a trai-
tor to his country when the young and new Congressman Richard
M. Nixon persevered in having Hiss brought to trial for perjury in
connection with his denials concerning spying. Hiss was convicted
and served time in prison, but I always have believed there was
more to the story than came to light. Through one of Herbert's closest friends, a Baltimorean, I was asked if I would be willing to meet
Alger's brother Donald and advise him as to how Alger could get a
more favorable press. This was before the verdict, of course. Our

friend brought Donald Hiss to the house we were occupying in Georgetown that winter. The meeting was short but not sweet. Donald was even more arrogant than his brother was being in the ordeal which he was undergoing. When I suggested that Alger try to be more polite and agreeable to the press, Donald told me that he and his brother loathed and had contempt for the press and would rather be garbage collectors than journalists. He knew that I had been a newspaperwoman—the reason he had asked to meet me, I supposed. I felt that Donald was being unnecessarily rude so I terminated the interview at once.

I never knew any of our delegation well, although I met them at official parties in San Francisco. I knew Senator Vandenberg's wife Hazel, who had left the *Tribune* shortly after I started work there. One evening late in 1946 I saw Hazel and the Senator at a reception where she said to me archly, "What do you think of the appointment that will be announced tomorrow?" Not having the faintest idea of what she was talking about but anxious to know, I mumbled that I thought it was fine. Whereupon she said, "President Truman told Arthur that he would give Marian Martin a good appointment, and we all think she will be just right as a Federal Communications Commissioner."

I made my departure hurriedly, whispering to my husband that he could meet me later at my office in the Mayflower. I called Mrs. Tillett in Charlotte and George Killion, the treasurer of the committee, in San Francisco (the chairman was in the hospital in Boston), and asked them what they could do to prevent having Truman's first woman appointee be a Republican. Each seemed to think it was too late to do anything, but I, in my ignorance, did not accept that. I sat myself down at the typewriter and wrote the President a letter telling him how upset Democratic women would be if his first appointment of a woman was a Republican, especially the one who had been at the head of Republican women as assistant chairman of the Republican National Committee until very recently.

At that time, the Republican national chairman appointed the top woman as assistant chairman. The DNC elects the committee female vice chairman. Miss Martin had been eased out just after the 1946 Congressional victories of the Republicans because Senator Robert Taft did not appear to like her brand of politics. She was an extremely able woman from Maine, tough but feminine, as women in politics should be. I would have been happy to see her receive a Republican appointment to the FCC or any federal commission eventually, but the only Democratic woman President Truman had appointed up to that time was Eleanor Roosevelt, as delegate to the General Assembly of the United Nations.

At about 10 o'clock, my husband having joined me, I went to the White House, clutching my letter in my hot hand. The guard explained that he could not accept mail for the President. I suddenly had an idea: why not get the guard to give it to Rose Conway, the President's secretary, and ask her to put it on his desk? I went back to the office, wrote Rose a note and addressed an envelope to her in which to enclose the one for the President. It was about 11 by the time Herbert and I sat down to dinner.

I scanned the papers the next day for news of appointments that had gone to the Senate from the White House, and great was my joy not to find Marian Martin's name among them. I always felt a little mean about "doing" Marian Martin out of that appointment, but I am sure she would have done the same to a Democratic woman if a Republican President had been planning to name a woman of the opposition party as his first appointment on the distaff side.

Marian Martin was a tough debater and I was warned by some of the staff of the Women's Division that I should be wary about taking her on. She had reduced one director of the division to tears in a radio debate. But we had radio debates in 1946 sans tears! Later, she was appointed commissioner of labor in Maine. We met in Boston in 1952 as speakers at the national convention of some nonpartisan group. I told her the story of why she was not on the FCC. That Christmas she sent me a card with a handwritten greeting as follows: "I hope our paths will cross in 1953. I enjoyed seeing you in Boston last summer. Whenever you are in Maine, do stop off in Augusta and have lunch with me. We certainly have a lot of comparable experiences to talk over. Even though you've not been successful in changing my vote, I want you to know that I am one of your staunchest admirers and personal supporters. Good luck and all happiness to you."

On my way back to Washington from San Francisco in 1945 at the conclusion of the U.N. founding conference, I stopped in Chicago for a day or two. In order to see as many friends as possible, I gave a party at the Tavern Club. Since practically every one of my friends was a Republican, I expected no orchids to be thrown to me or to

HST. I was distressed when every one of my guests told me what a great guy HST was, but I should have realized that it was only in comparison with "that man" whom they feared and hated that they were willing to admit Truman was a good guy.

The Republicans I knew in Chicago were so violent in their hatred of FDR that during the '36 and '40 campaigns I never made a social engagement after a couple of harrowing experiences. One was at a formal dinner party at the home of dear friends when the host insisted that I drink a toast to Landon's victory. When I refused, saying I would prefer to raise my glass to the success of Roosevelt, he became so apoplectic I feared he would have a stroke. Another time when I was introduced to one of the *grandes dames* of Chicago society at an afternoon reception, she held up a lorgnette, inspected me carefully and said, "I am told you are a Democrat. You are the first one I ever met other than a servant."

Ever since the Tavern Club had been organized, one of the big events of each Presidential campaign year was the election night party. I had no idea how many Democrats were present in the early years, but in 1936 I realized there were only a few and in 1940 there were only two of us, Mrs. J. Hamilton Lewis, widow of the red-whiskered Senator from Illinois, and myself. When it was definite that FDR had been elected to a third term (fairly early in the evening, as I remember), there were groans and sighs from everyone but me. I stood, raised my glass of champagne and said, "To our President." Before I could be seated I felt a sharp slap on one cheek. A young Lake Forest matron, Mrs. William V. Kelly, Jr., who was sitting at an adjoining table, was the slapper. I was so astounded that I did nothing. Her husband grabbed her, sat her down, and made a sort of halfhearted apology to me. When I went to the powder room a minute later, I found dear old Mrs. J. Ham sitting on a stool in front of the dressing table, sobbing, "I'm so glad to see you, everyone else here is a Republican and just too rude for words. I can't stand it."

I often have wondered why so many Republicans can be so bitter against Democrats and try to make their Democratic friends change their policies. I admit I am not objective but I don't think Democrats are that way. We try to change votes on a wholesale scale but do not insult our friends and treat them as though they were halfwits because they do not see eye to eye with us politically.

When I arrived home in Washington from San Francisco via Chi-

cago, I feared there were things in HST that I did not see, for otherwise my Republican friends in Chicago would not have been so enthusiastic about him. I need not have worried, for they soon lost
their enthusiasm. By 1948 they were completely "off" him, not because he had aroused in them the fear that FDR had, but because
they considered him a little haberdasher from Missouri who was a
joke as President. Today even some of the most rabid Republicans
admit that Harry Truman will go down in history as one of our great
Presidents.

Congressman Chase Going Woodhouse of Connecticut was defeated in 1946 and early in 1947 was named executive director of the
Women's Division. Bob Hannegan had talked to me about this position and said he and President Truman would like to choose someone with whom I could work as harmoniously as I had with Gladys
Tillett, who was continuing as vice chairman but resigning as director of the Women's Division. Bob suggested Mrs. Woodhouse,
since he thought her prestige as a former Congresswoman would be
advantageous. When Bob called me at home one night to ask if I
were sure I could work with Mrs. Woodhouse, I said, "Of course, I
can work with anyone."

I soon found out I was wrong. It was possible for me to stay on
only because she and her secretary-daughter started off on a motor
trip that took them across the continent not long after her appointment. We got nothing from her except expense accounts for several
months, which did not at all please the new chairman, Senator J.
Howard McGrath. Her ambition to be reelected as a representative
from Connecticut seemed to outweigh all other considerations, and
she definitely was not in favor of nominating Truman in Philadelphia
in 1948.

When she returned to Washington, Senator McGrath told her he
felt it would be better if she resigned from the committee, which she
said she would when she was given another good position. He threw
that one at me, and what a time I had! I finally convinced Frank
Pace, Jr., Secretary of the Army, to send her to Germany to help
German women participate in politics. I have no doubt she did that
very well.

Chapter 11

Autumn was the time when the Women's Division of the DNC celebrated Democratic Women's Day, a fund-raising operation originated by Mrs. Roosevelt in 1939. Women's groups all over the country were urged to hold meetings and raise as much money as possible. Each group kept one third, gave one third to the State Committee, and contributed the other third to the National Committee. Much effort and time went into this project, but it never was enough of a fund-raiser to be considered a success, so eventually it lapsed. During the Roosevelt Administration, Mrs. Roosevelt always sent a message from the President to women.

In 1945 it was impossible to obtain free radio time from any of the networks, so I decided that we should buy a fifteen-minute period and have our four Democratic Congresswomen participate in it. When I approached the treasurer, George R. Killion, for an OK, he said that not one penny could be spent for such a broadcast.

"All right," I said, "I'll have to think up something different in order to get free time, for no network will donate it for a Presidential message to Democratic women." A little later I went to his office and said, "I have it. I am going to ask President Truman to play the piano as an accompaniment for Margaret to sing, and then we'll slip in a brief message to the Democratic women. I am sure a network will buy that idea."

"I honestly believe you would ask him to do this!" George said. "Go ahead and buy the time. What did you say it would cost?"

The four Democratic Congresswomen in 1945 were Mary T. Norton of New Jersey, dean of Congresswomen and one of the most humane and honest women I've ever known; Chase Going Woodhouse of Connecticut, who looked like a Dresden china shepherdess; Emily T. Douglas of Illinois, whose husband, Paul Douglas, later was elected to the U.S. Senate; and Helen Gahagan Douglas, former stage, screen and opera star who brought more glamour to the House of Representatives than usually is seen there. She is the wife of Melvyn Douglas, also a stage and screen star, who during World War II was a major in the U. S. Army. Paul Douglas was a major in the Marines. It was Helen Douglas whom Richard M. Nixon defeated for the Senate in California in 1950, with some of the dirtiest tactics ever used in a campaign.

The cost of the broadcast was very little compared to the amount of money that is thrown away during every campaign. The men never will learn that there is truth in the slogan of the old Women's Division: "Elections are won between campaigns." FDR and Mary Dewson, his righthand female political adviser in 1932 and later the vice chairman of the DNC and director of its Women's Division, knew that telling the people what the Administration was doing, what its goals were and what the opposition was doing day by day to thwart their achievement, would build a foundation upon which a victory in the campaign could be built. Through *The Democratic Digest* and the Reporter Plan, Democratic women told the story of the New Deal, not just in campaigns but all during the year. Rainbow Flyers, each dealing with one issue, were distributed by the hundreds of thousands during a campaign. They were on colored paper, one page each, with plenty of unprinted space so that they were not too formidable looking even for what we in Washington called "the precinct mind." It is the smart politician who knows that it is the people with "precinct minds" who elect Presidents, not just those of erudition.

One of the most effective Rainbow Flyers on an issue ever distributed was printed in the 1946 Congressional campaign when the Republicans were attempting to defeat Democrats by blaming President Truman for the meat shortage that was causing sky-high prices. The flyer simply and squarely ". . . put the blame where it belonged, on the shoulders of the Republican members of the 79th Congress who in June and July of that year voted five to one to cripple price control and so upset the meat supply. When controls were ended on June 30, the price of meat soared up—and up—and up— until by August 20 when the Decontrol Board decided that ceiling prices on meat must be reinstated, prices on desirable cuts had gone up 70 percent. This skyrocketing in prices brought cattle to the slaughterhouses in droves; cattle that weren't ready for the market, cattle that normally would not have been slaughtered until September or October." The flyer urged voters to "Sit Tight in This Emergency But When You Vote on Nov. 5 Remember That It Was the Republicans in the 79th Congress Who Crippled Price Control and Gave the 'GO' Sign to Inflation." Our facts were obtained from the Department of Agriculture, which President Truman had quoted as saying, "The present level of livestock ceilings is a fair and equitable one, and one which should be sufficient to bring forth the maximum production of meat. An increase in prices or the abandonment of price control on meat now would, in the long run, add to rather than solve our difficulties."

We distributed as many of these flyers as our budget would permit, probably several hundred thousand, and immediately upon their receipt men leaders as well as women in various key States telephoned to ask for them by the millions. The Women's Division budget, although generous, would not cover printings of this magnitude, so I suggested they print their own. In those days State committees were accustomed to having the National Committee supply them with campaign materials. It was not until the 1952 campaign that the National Committee began expecting State committees to pay for every piece of material they received from the DNC. In my opinion, and that of many other national leaders of both sexes who preceded me, the National Committee is a service committee. It is sad that television has brought the costs of campaigning so high that the DNC no longer is able to distribute literature to the States, where the voters are.

The National Committee constantly was soliciting funds or giving big fund-raising affairs in the States, so it seemed fair to us to return some of the money to the States where it was needed desperately.

When the National committee was strong and worked cooperatively with State committees, there was a cohesion in the party that has been lacking since the power of the National Committee was diminished by Presidents who chose weak chairmen and did everything possible to reduce the committee's role in the party's life. One might say a strong President did not need a strong committee, but in my opinion that would show an ignorance of the facts of political life. Presidents such as Roosevelt and Truman realized the necessity for national committee chairmen, treasurers and vice chairmen to build organizations that could produce votes and funds.

When every candidate is forced to have his own local organization there is chaos and everyone suffers. Neither Jack Kennedy nor LBJ really understood national politics, in my estimation, in spite of good qualities that made them successful candidates for the Presidency. LBJ underestimated the real assistance a strong DNC could give him or any Presidential candidate. He told Chairman John M. Bailey once that he, LBJ, could run the National Committee with one secretary. That LBJ needed little help in 1964 against Senator Barry Goldwater could not be disputed, but if he had needed such help it could not have been forthcoming, for by then the National Committee had fallen—or been pushed—into a state of desuetude. Only the Office of Women's Activities, headed by the vice chairman, the late Margaret Price, functioned with any degree of efficiency. Margaret was a lovely woman with imagination and a good solid foundation of political experience, but she had little chance to exhibit anything more than a pleasing and imposing platform presence and a ladylike acceptance of the crumbs of cooperation thrown to her by both Presidents and the committee chairmen with whom she served.

When Stephen A. Mitchell, the man Adlai E. Stevenson had chosen to be chairman after the Chicago Convention of 1952, integrated the Women's Division into the DNC shortly before I left in 1953, it became the Office of Women's Activities, in theory a step up for women but actually a step way down.

To return to the meat flyer, some of our most astute men leaders told me both before and after the elections it might have kept many Democratic congressional candidates from defeat in 1946. Shortly after the flyer was issued, I took a telephone call from Jack Arvey, the Illinois national committeeman, in the office of the DNC treasurer, George R. Killion, when I was telling him of the great demand for more of the flyers. When my secretary switched Jack's call to George's office and George heard Jack tell me he needed five million of those flyers, George allowed me to order all that were requested from anyone. "We'll worry about who pays for them later," George said, knowing full well that in case of a Democratic victory there would be no problem about who paid.

Fortunately for the DNC treasury, before I telephoned the printer news came over the ticker that President Truman had done away with all meat price controls and ceilings. Instead of following what I am sure was his own inclination—to fight for what was for the people's good, as he did in the campaign of 1948—he had taken the advice of some of the more timid of his advisers. Actually, as bitter as it was to us then, the election of the Republican 80th Congress helped mightily to give President Truman his victory two years later. I felt so sad at his action in eliminating controls on meat, wrongly giving in to the opposition in my opinion, that I put my head down on my desk and cried. The only other political incident that moved me to tears of sadness was Alger Hiss's conviction for perjury. I was taking a brief, much needed rest at the Virginia Hot Springs when I heard of Hiss's conviction. It will take years to recover from this, my common sense and inner political instinct warned me. Surprisingly, I returned to Washington and found that practically no one in the DNC headquarters agreed with me.

I consider it one of the greatest privileges of my life to have been in a position to work with Harry Truman from the day in April, 1945, when he took the oath of office for the Presidency to the day in January, 1953, when he departed for his home in Independence.

I vividly remember the day President Roosevelt died. At the National Committee we were preparing for the Jefferson-Jackson Dinner, which was to take place in a few days. Fannie Hurst was to be the woman speaker and I had brought her speech to the chairman's office just as his secretary received the phone call from the White House. The committee offices in the Mayflower Hotel literally were awash with tears, not only because of grief but also because they all seemed to think the death of FDR would bring the government to a standstill: losing FDR was only half the tragedy, they felt; having Truman try to succeed him was the other half.

I went up and down the corridor, stopping in every office and saying, "Stop behaving like this. Of course, we all are heartbroken to lose FDR, but we belittle his memory to doubt that Harry Truman is capable of being a good President. Roosevelt chose him. Never forget that." I truly felt that way, but I did not know the former Vice President, now the new President, at all.

As the months passed and I had the opportunity to watch him work, I knew our country was in safe hands. Truman was not well-known around the country, but in Washington his work as chairman of the special committee investigating the national defense program had brought him to the favorable attention of everyone in the Congress and in the higher echelons of government, including President Roosevelt. Truman's name was synonymous with an old-fashioned honest, no-holds-barred method of seeking to keep the expenditures of the federal government in its vast defense and war programs to a minimum and to avoid duplication of effort and expense whenever possible. It was a backbreaking and mind-boggling job but Senator Truman handled it with calm courage that won him the respect of his fellow Senators.

My admiration for him increased every time I saw him, which was fairly often, because he used the Women's Division for getting the facts to the voters about his programs and plans.

In the administration of foreign affairs the man from Independence insured his place in history as one of our strongest Presidents. Following World War II, it was evident that this nation must become the leader of the free world, whether or not we wanted that responsibility. Aid to Greece and Turkey, the Marshall Plan for economic cooperation with Europe, programs of mutual defense such as the North Atlantic Pact, the Point Four program, now the Technical Assistance Program of the United Nations—these were some of the innovations in the Truman Administration. The strength of these programs prompted Winston Churchill in 1962 to say in Washington to Harry S. Truman, "You, more than any other man, have saved Western civilization. When the British could no longer hold out in Greece, you, and you alone, sir, made the decision that saved that ancient land from the communists. You acted in a similar fashion with regard to Azerbaijan when the Soviets tried to take over Iran. Then there was your resolute stand on Trieste, and your Marshall Plan which rescued Western Europe wallowing in the shallows and indeed easy prey to Joseph Stalin's malevolent intentions. Then you established the North Atlantic Treaty Alliance and collective security for those nations against the military machinations of the Soviet Union. Then there was your audacious Berlin Airlift. And, of course, there was Korea.''

I had not known the vast amount of knowledge of history of all civilized countries he had stored in his mind, nor of the basic integrity and humanitarian principles in his heart. He was an uncommon man, even though he appeared to be as common or as ordinary as any shopkeeper on any main street in America. There was no pretence to him. His word was his bond, he said what he meant in direct words, he never shilly-shallied. He faced facts as they were or as he saw them. He had great courage. He was considerate, kind and tolerant of human frailties. He had true humility about himself, but high regard and respect for the office he held. "I don't care what history says of me. I know what I've done," he said. He knew that he gave every problem just consideration, and when his decision was made he was able to sleep soundly without regret. He always did what he thought was right and he knew the difference between right and wrong.

One of my most vivid memories of President Truman's understanding concerns something I did in 1952. Senator Estes Kefauver of Tennessee was running as hard as a man could for the Democratic nomination for President, but he never had told the President as the head of our party that he was running. I considered this regrettable, especially because I knew the President did not like Estes. Whenever I had the chance I urged Estes to call on the President and tell him of his plans. Lawrence Westbrook, who was on the committee staff then, was one of Estes' closest friends, so I enlisted Larry in the campaign to get Estes to observe what I considered proper protocol. One morning Larry told me Estes was to see President Truman at 5 that afternoon. As the day progressed I began to worry that the President might be a bit short with the Tennessee Senator at the end of a busy day and that the meeting would not bring about the détente I had hoped it would accomplish between those two very different men.

Finally in the late morning I made up my mind I must see the President before Estes did. I called Matt Connelly for an appointment "a brief, off-the-record one," but Matt said "No chance." I then did something I never had done before nor ever did again; I called Mrs. Truman and requested her to ask the President to see me for a few minutes that afternoon. She called back to say he would see me at 4:45. I went in the side door so the press did not observe me and was ushered by Matt into the Oval Office. The President shook my hand, seated me with great courtesy in the chair beside his desk, as he customarily did when I called upon him, and asked, "What can I do for you today, India?"

I almost had heart failure. How dare I be there to give the President of the United States advice as to how to treat a member of the United States Senate? I was so appalled at myself that I mumbled, "Nothing really, Mr. President. I would not blame you if you never saw me again. I am here to ask you to be as pleasant as you can to Estes Kefauver when he calls on you in a few minutes. He will be asked by all the reporters what you and he said when he leaves. If he acts the least bit aggrieved, it will be bad for party unity. I know you do not like him, but please be nice to him and forgive me for having the nerve to come to see you about this. It is a dreadful thing to have done."

"It is not, India," that great man said with a smile. "Don't you know I know your only concern is with the good of our party? I always welcome your advice. Don't ever hesitate to give it."

He must have taken it or, more probably, he was simply his usual gracious self when he talked to Estes, for the papers the next day carried pictures of a smiling Senator who said the President had told him he would put no obstacles in the way of his getting the nomination. Estes' supporters felt that the President did not live up to this. At the convention, the President did not support the man, who had won many spring and summer primaries, but I am sure he did not put obstacles in the way of a Kefauver nomination. He just preferred Adlai Ewing Stevenson as our nominee, as I did.

"Who are you for?" a prominent national committeeman asked me shortly before the convention.

"I have to be neutral, you know," I replied.

Whereupon my friend said, "Yes, I know but who are you neutral for?"

President Truman really did not become the Chief Executive, running the government in his way rather than in the way FDR had done, until after the 1946 Congressional elections. That year the Democrats lost enough Senate and House seats to give control of Congress to the Republicans. From that time one, there was a change in the President. He seemed more sure of himself. Some pundits felt there was a decided change in his method of operation after he was elected President in 1948, but I began to notice it in him after the '46 elections.

If the Watergate scandal brings more women into politics—as I hope it will—we will have achieved something worthwhile from that sordid mess. If this sounds as though I think women are more honest than men, I do. They may not continue to be so after they have been in the arena longer, but as of now I truly believe that women basically value the truth more highly than men.

Trying to get more women interested in politics was part of my work when I was with the Democratic National Committee. I often thought after 1952 that I had succeeded too well because all the experts said it was the women who elected General Eisenhower. After 1948 I was asked to speak to dozens of non- or bi-partisan groups, and I always urged the women to participate in politics. "I hope you will be a Democrat," I would say, "but if you believe in the other party, work for it." Work for it they did, thousands of them who never before had lifted a finger to help any candidate. Some of "my" men used to warn me that I was not helping Democrats when I spoke to these non-partisan groups, but even if they were right I still am glad I preached participation, for in our form of government a citizen should do whatever he or she can to elect people of principle and high quality.

Voting is the most basic essential of citizenship and I think that any man or woman in this country who fails to avail himself or herself of that right should hide in shame. I truly wish there were some sort of badge of dishonor that a non-voter would have to wear.

Chapter 12

"Congratulations, Mr. President. But before I talk to you I want to let a person who has been certain all along that you would be elected, and who has worked very hard in this campaign, speak to you. Here she is." And with those words, Senator J. Howard McGrath, chairman of the Democratic National Committee, handed the telephone receiver to me. And what did I do?

I said feebly in an unnatural voice, "Dear Mr. President," and then I burst into tears.

Not being a woman given to crying jags either in personal or professional life, I was ashamed and astounded, but I was overcome by the tension of the campaign and especially of that election night of November 2, 1948, when practically no one but I at the "Victory Party" at the Biltmore Hotel in New York City thought the party would live up to its name.

"Dear India," that master politician, Mary W. Dewson, whispered as she kissed me goodnight about 11 p.m., "I know you cannot be as confident as you appear, but you are a good sport and I admire you for it." Molly, as she was known to all Democrats, was Franklin D. Roosevelt's righthand woman in politics—next to Eleanor, of course—when he was governor of New York and when he ran for the Presidency in both 1932 and 1936.

Any woman who ever has worked in politics in either major party will realize that Chairman McGrath's giving me the opportunity to speak first to the President when the Republicans finally conceded victory around noon of November 3, 1948, was a most unusual and generous tribute from a male politician to a female one. Such generosity is infrequent on all levels of political life, but I have been fortunate in finding it in quite a few men, notably President Truman, Howard McGrath, Bill Boyle, and Averell Harriman.

In the years since 1948 I have read in several books and heard countless persons tell how certain they were that Harry S. Truman would be elected that year, but few were vocal during the campaign. Even among the White House staff and the committee personnel, only a handful actually believed that the Man from Independence had a chance to defeat Thomas E. Dewey.

"The Boss," as Harry S. Truman called his wife, told me she always was pessimistic before an election. In New York City just a couple of days before November 2, Mrs. Truman remarked to me, "I am beginning to think Harry will win." I begged her not to say such a thing. I was much too superstitious to welcome optimism from one who twice had not thought her husband would be elected to the United States Senate from Missouri, be elected Vice President in 1944, and who, until his reception in New York, had been her usual pessimistic self. Pessimistic, that is, about the outcome of a political campaign, not about life in general. "The Boss" was a good term for Bess Wallace Truman. Harry S. Truman consulted her about small and great matters (except his stinging rejoinder to Paul Hume, the Washington *Post* music critic, who had written an unfavorable review of Margaret's singing).

In modern times there never has been a First Lady who was as little known to the general public as Mrs. Truman. She is one of the best educated and most cultivated ladies who ever has presided as mistress of the White House. She is a lady in the old-fashioned sense, belonging to the school who believed that it was permissible to have one's name in the paper only when one was born, married and died. She was politically realistic enough, however, to know that she had to have a certain amount of publicity because of her husband's position, but she kept it to the minimum and never gave interviews. I have worked with thousands of women and I've never known one for whom I had more affectionate respect than Mrs. Truman.

President Truman's platform talks from the Whistle Stop Train were exactly what the voters wanted to hear. If the press who were on the train had taken the trouble to leave the club car and mingle with the audiences, they would have known that Harry S. Truman was winning votes all along the way. It was easier, however, to sit in the club car and hear the speeches over the loudspeaker. And they had all been told by their publishers that Dewey would win, so why bother? When I entered the club car after a stop and told the reporters that Truman was getting across well, they would smile and ask me to have a drink.

I seldom had time for the proffered refreshment with the press, for it was my job to look after the women who rode the train. That had been the purpose of my taking the trip. The advance men would see that there were plenty of women at every stop and that they would be invited to ride the Presidential train to the next stop. I saw to it that the women met President and Mrs. Truman, although sometimes I had to be quite rude to visiting men politicians who were unaccustomed to having women treated like first-class citizens. I never had any trouble with the White House assistants, since they all knew I was aboard by the President's order and that women were to be given equal treatment with men on the Harry S. Truman Campaign Train.

In previous campaigns no women except wives, daughters, daughters-in-law and secretaries had accompanied Presidential candidates on campaign trains, so I was the first professional to see that women, who did much of the political work in their home communities, were given the chance to meet the candidate and his family. This strategy paid off well, for in many places where the heads of our party were doing nothing to promote the national ticket I was able to enlist the aid of dedicated women.

I bypassed the state and county leaders, if necessary, and sent material for distribution to these women, who got it to reach the voters instead of mildewing in some stable or warehouse. These women were called "IE's Gals" at our headquarters, and their names and addresses were in a separate card file—one, incidentally, to which we turned for support later when telegrams or letters were deemed necessary to help line up enough votes to pass a measure in the Congress.

Many of these women have been my friends ever since 1948. One was Terrell Maverick, wife of former Congressman Maury Maverick, who met us somewhere in Texas. She became so enthused with the idea that her old friend Harry Truman had a chance to win, that she spent a couple of nights with me in my train bedroom (built for one) to plan what she could do in Texas to help the Truman-Barkley ticket.

Several years after Maury's death, Terrell married Walter Prescott Webb, the well-known historian, whose article "How the Republican Party Lost Its Future" inspired better and more erudite speakers than I. I quoted from Professor Webb's article often and always gave him credit. I was intending to do so once at a Jefferson-Jackson dinner in Indianapolis in early 1952 until I heard the then governor of Illinois, Adlai E. Stevenson, use virtually the entire Webb article without attribution as the main speech at the dinner. In fairness, I must report that Adlai was filling in on a few hours' notice for the Vice President, Alben Barkley, who had been delayed in Washington by a crisis in the Senate. That probably was the first and only time Adlai ever used a speech written by someone else without changing it or rewriting it entirely. One of his campaign weaknesses was that he was still polishing a speech when he approached the platform or prepared to go on radio or television.

One day on the Whistle Stop trip I got a "morningcap" that almost choked me. After a prebreakfast stop—and it was amazing how many persons there were at every station when we made those ghastly stops—I asked the President's doctor, Wallace Graham, if he could give me some soda mints. "I seem to have had indigestion for several days," I said. "No soda mints for you," he said. "I've been watching you and have wondered how long you could stand the pace you have set for yourself. Come into my room and I'll give you something."

The "something" turned out to be a fairly large glass of brandy, and he prescribed a day of complete rest. "Rest for a whole day!" I exclaimed. "Why, that would be impossible." I suppose I thought the election would be lost if I were out of circulation for a day. Somehow or other, I'll never know how, they managed from San Diego to Phoenix while I slept off the effects of the early morning brandy dose and incidentally got a good rest.

"Take it easier from now on. We're only half through the campaign," the President warned the next morning.

I did not want to be away from the New York headquarters too long at a time, so every now and then I would leave the train and fly back East. Gladys Tillett or Dorothy Girton, editor of *The Democratic Digest*, would take over the train chores and Katharine Elkus White, my deputy, would go to her home in Red Bank, New Jersey, for a little rest. My main concern in New York was the Democratic Record Show, which was on the ABC radio network every Monday, Wednesday and Friday afternoon for fifteen minutes, from October 11 until the day before the election. We sought to carry the record of the Democratic party right into the homes of millions of housewives in the most painless way possible. The show had plenty of music and lots of gimmicks such as were popular on commercial shows. Each show carried a political wallop, and, as *Variety* wrote, "The Democrats may not be matching the Republicans in air-time coin, but they came up Monday with the most novel radio pitch in election campaign history."

The conservative Washington *Star* gave us an editorial which said our show was "as American as apple pie—or pinball machines and bubble-gum," and that as silly as it might be, "it is one of those phenomena that make this land of the free and home of the brave seem considerably more attractive, if perhaps less sober-sided, than places like Russia, where political jokes are as scarce as free elections." I must confess, however, that in this editorial the *Star* doubted that the show would be of value in swinging the election away from the GOP. I would not claim that the series of shows was of as much value as Truman's "Give 'Em Hell" train platform speeches but they were of great value, as were the "Housewives for Truman" trailers.

In many states groups of housewives traveled in house trailers, automobiles and station wagons through cities, towns and villages, stopping often to talk to the people about high prices, the big issue in the campaign. There were exhibits illustrating the differences between 1946 food prices, official figures collected by the U.S. Bureau of Labor Statistics on June 15, two weeks before the Republicans amended price controls to death, and current prices, which invariably were about twice as much as they had been two years before. That the "No Good Republican Congress," as President Truman had labelled the 80th Congress, was responsible for high prices was the main theme of our campaign.

Most Democratic leaders were convinced that President Truman stood no chance of winning, even the chairman of the National Committee, Senator J. Howard McGrath, who said to me one day in his headquarters' office in the Biltmore Hotel in New York City, "Everybody knows that Truman doesn't stand much chance of being elected. We're operating a holding operation, so you're foolish to be killing yourself the way you are." Since I did not agree with him, I continued at the pace at which I was working. I must say Howard was a wonderful person to work with. Although he did not think Truman was going to win, he never kept me from doing all I felt was necessary to round up the women's vote for Truman. In those days the Women's Division of the Democratic National Committee had its own budget, but we needed much more money for the campaign than had been alloted to us. In spite of the shortage of funds, Howard was most generous in making it possible for us to operate efficiently and effectively.

He okayed the expenditure for the Democratic Record Show. It was my idea to have this series, so I rebelled against the idea of the public relations director of the committee, Jack Redding, and the Warwick & Legler advertising company running the show. I insisted upon having Margot Gayle, a woman radio writer whom I chose, put on the payroll of the advertising company and, furthermore, I insisted upon having final approval of what went into each show. There were several battles of the sexes over my stubbornness or insistence (depending on one's point of view) upon the best possible shows, but I won, and the shows were tremendously effective. Later the advertising company executive told me they were proud to have been in charge of this highly successful series of ten political broadcasts.

The men kept prodding me about the content of the last show. I admitted I did not know, but said I knew something would come along to give us a good show and that until it did, we would plan nothing. This made them wild. My faith was rewarded when I read Milburn P. (Pete) Akers' political column in the Chicago *Sun* after Truman's visit to Springfield, Illinois. "This is our show," I said. "And we will get Melvyn Douglas to read it." Mel, the *Sun* and Pete agreed, and we had exactly the right final show.

Pete Akers' column, which carried the headline, "If Harry Truman Walked at Midnight" follows:

Perhaps Mr. Truman, who spent Tuesday evening in this city, should have remained another hour or so. For Abraham Lincoln, so the poet

Vachel Lindsay wrote, walks the streets of Springfield at midnight. And, had the two chanced to meet, Old Abe, who made no more of a success of his New Salem general store and grog shop than Mr. Truman did of his Kansas City haberdashery might have had a few friendly words for him.

The two, with Secret Service men and newspaper reporters at safe distance, could have strolled down 8th Street toward the old Lincoln home at the corner of Jackson. And there, sitting on the porch, Old Abe, busy whittling, would have said: "Harry, I'm struck by some parallels. You and I both come from old Kentucky stock, you know. We both went to storekeeping, and as they say, we didn't make a go of it. Fact is, I was right happy to get that job as deputy surveyor; just the same as you were happy when you had to close your store to get on the payroll as a road commissioner.

"And we both were in the Army, too, of course. I never said much 'bout that. The Blackhawk War wasn't much. But one day, after I'd served awhile in the legislature, I got elected to Congress; just like you went to the Senate.

"You did better, after you went to the Senate, than I did after getting elected to the House. One term was all I could get. But you got re-elected. Once, after they'd organized the Republican Party, some of the fellows wanted me to run for Vice President too. But I didn't. I hear they made you take it. Anyway, four years later, with the Democrats split three ways—just like they are now, Harry—I got elected President. I had troubles with the South, too.

"No sooner did I get down to Washington than folks were talking appeasement. They wanted me to appease the South, Harry; let the erring sisters depart in peace, some folks said. But I didn't, I figured my job was to save the Union. So I provisioned Fort Sumter, and the war started. It's not much different today, Harry. Some folks want you to get out of Europe; to appease Russia. But you're doing just what I did; you are provisioning those Western democracies. You've got to do it; you've got to save Western civilization just as I had to save the Union.

"Of course, a lot of folks didn't like it. They used to say I was inept; that I didn't have the capacity to be President. And maybe I didn't. What man has? That young fellow Dewey (maybe I shouldn't talk that way about a Republican, Harry) that young fellow Dewey— well, if he gets into the White House he, too, may find the job isn't easy. I hear tell, Harry, the newspapers say a lot of mean things about you. Shucks. Get out the books and read what they had to say about me, when I ran for re-election.

"Now about this election, Harry; you're doing right in getting out and talking with the people; after all, this is still the people's country. Keep it that way.

"Harry, I got to go; Mrs. Lincoln's calling me. Just let me say this: Our fathers brought forth on this continent a new nation, conceived in liberty, and dedicated to the proposition that all men are created equal. It's the President's job to preserve that liberty and to establish equality. Remember that, Harry; if you do, the job's not too big— even for a couple of once bankrupt storekeepers."

The radio shows highlighted the sad records of the "No Good Republican 80th Congress." Written in the style of soap operas, the shows combined music and humor as well as hard facts. A well-known Democratic woman took part in each show, among them Mrs. J. Borden Harriman, FDR's Minister to Norway; Helen Gahagan Douglas; Mrs. Katherine Elkus White, my deputy and later to be named ambassador to Denmark by President Johnson; Miss Gladys Dickason, vice president of the Amalgamated Clothing Workers of America, and assistant director of the CIO Southern Organizing Committee; Mrs. Mary McLeod Bethune, a cotton farmer's daughter who became one of the nation's most distinguished educators and leaders, founder-president of both the Bethune-Cookman College in Florida and of the National Council of Negro Women; Miss Frieda Hennock, prominent Wall Street attorney whom President Truman just had appointed the first woman Federal Communications Commissioner; Mrs. Dorothy Vredenburgh (now Mrs. John Bush), secretary of the Democratic National Committee; Mrs. Mary Norton, the first woman to chair an important Congressional committee, the House Labor Committee; and Mrs. Tillett and I.

Also in each show was a typical housewife, voicing her and her family's reaction to the legislative record of the Republican 80th Congress. Our researcher had no trouble finding quotes from prominent Republican leaders indicating their scant concern for the average family. For instance, the late Senator Robert Taft of Ohio had advised that in order to cut down on food bills people should *Eat Less!*

Senator Kenneth S. Wherry of Nebraska had bragged, *"I'm the fellow that knocked out meat control."* Representative John Taber of New York State had been against the Marshall Plan because he did not believe Europe needed help. He said he would fly to Europe to see for himself. After visiting the war-ruined cities and observing the gaunt and starving faces, he came home and said, *"I didn't see any hungry people in Europe."*

"It is time for the Republicans to take over. We are the best stock—we are the best people and represent the real grit, brains, and background of America," declared Pennsylvania Representative Hugh Scott, then chairman of the Republican National Committee and later Senator, now retired. The Republican candidate himself, Governor Thomas E. Dewey of New York, was quoted in two shows. In one the quotation was of a statement he made upon returning from a nationwide tour in which he tried to woo the voters in all States but when he got home he said, *"It is nice to be back in New York State, where you don't have to explain in words of one syllable what good government means."*

The other Dewey quote was, *"That's the first lunatic I've had for an engineer. He probably should be shot at sunrise, but we'll let him off this time."* This generous comment was uttered after an engineer had made the mistake of rumpling the Dewey dignity by suddenly backing up the train. Later the engineer said, "I think just as much of Mr. Dewey as I did before—and that's not very much." When Tallulah Bankhead told this story at the Madison Square Garden rally for President Truman the Saturday night before the election, she convulsed the audience by ending it with the words, "And then the train backed up—with a jerk."

I dramatized the issue that I was sure would be of great interest to the women voters that year in the speech I made in Philadelphia on the convention's opening night. Never having been a public speaker, having no desire to become one and certain I would be a poor one, but determined to speak out to the best of my ability for Harry Truman, I decided to use the bread and butter issue of high prices for my maiden effort at a convention. Using a hat box prop, I released a large balloon to depict inflation, jerked out a streak to illustrate soaring food prices, and then, with a tow-headed tot on the stand, dissected every item of expense in her feeding and clothing.

I cannot claim credit for more than the topic and the delivery of the speech. My husband suggested the props, and one of my staff, the late Ella G. Roller, took on the responsibility of getting them together. Ella and I wrote the speech together, and she brought in two friends from the infant television industry who rehearsed me every time they could snatch me from some of the many activities that kept me running from early morning until late at night during the week before the convention. They did their job well, though, for they succeeded in making me feel sure enough of myself so that I was not a bit nervous as I looked out at the sea of faces yawning in front of me when my time came to be introduced by the temporary chairman, Senator Alben W. Barkley, who had just finished giving an eloquent and long keynote address.

My speech brought the tired delegates and press to life and created quite a furor. The photographers yelled so loud and so often for "just one more" that I must have waved that steak under the television lights long enough to cook it.

It was a pound of round steak that we had bought in Philadelphia for $1.10. Two years before the same piece would have been 46 cents, which meant that the price of round steak had more than doubled in two years.

I stressed that the cost of living had gone up 28 percent in the last two years; that of food 45 percent and clothing 26 percent. I told the audience that the Federal Reserve Board predicted one out of every four families would spend more than it earned that year. I compared the prices of the other items in my market bag; margarine, 48 cents a pound that day, 24 cents two years ago; butter, 52 cents before price controls were killed, 95 cents that day; milk 23 cents a quart for grade A that day, 15 cents before.

When the little tow-headed tot was lifted up to the lectern, I gave the prices we had paid that day for her clothes and told what they would have been two years before. Her sturdy brown leather oxfords had gone up from $4.75 to $6.00; her little cotton percale dress had shot up from $3.98 to $4.98; and her slip, which would have cost $1.00 in 1946, had cost $1.69 that day.

The closing words of my speech were, "President Truman has asked not once but many times for stand-by price controls with which to bring down the cost of living. In November we must elect a Democratic President and a Democratic Congress. The Democratic Party is the friend of millions—not of millionaires. . . . Just as I am pulling the cord that is at the end of the price balloon, so the Democrats will pull the cords of legislation to halt inflation. We can pull the price balloon within reach. We can force it back into the box. And, finally, we can put the lid back on prices . . . I appeal to all American women to join together to bring down the cost of living. You can do it! Register! Vote! Elect Democrats!"

Chapter 13

President Truman was kind enough to say to me some years later, when my husband and I were seeing him and Mrs. Truman off for their first trip abroad together, that I had made the actual keynote speeches at the '48 and the '52 conventions. "High prices for which the 80th Congress was responsible was your '48 theme and it was one of mine, too. In '52 the candidate did not come within a mile of using your theme." Of course it was the Korean War.

High prices was the only issue I used in the speeches I made when traveling with the Whistle Stop Train. Very often when we left the train I was called upon to make a five-minute speech before the President appeared on the platform. At first this was very embarrassing for me, but after a few speeches I thoroughly enjoyed being part of the program. If I were going to have to say anything, I would ask that the driver of the car in which I was riding stop some place where I could buy a cake of Ivory soap. It was my one and only prop for a five-minute speech about high prices.

Sometimes one brief statement can help a candidate more than a dozen speeches. At a press conference in our Washington headquarters a few weeks before the election, a reporter asked if Dewey's World War II draft status or lack of military service would become an issue in the campaign. I answered that President Truman had asked us at the committee to make no reference to it. When the reporter persisted and asked why President Truman had made such a request, I said it was the President's innate decency that made him not want the draft question raised. I think every newspaper in the country used that little item, most of them in front page boxes. I found out later that Fred Blumenthal in our p.r. division had planted the question and I think he took quite a chance in doing so, but he paid me a compliment when he said, "I knew you would give a newsworthy answer."

I wrote a letter from the Whistle Stop Train to my staff, some at New York headquarters and some in Washington. They were marvelous women, all of them, and each one who received the letter made a great contribution to our victory in 1948—

Dear Katherine (White), Mary (Tobin), Kayse (Blackburn), Venice (Spraggs), Dorothy (Girton), Lynn (Nichols), Ella (Roller), Natalie (Spingarn), Barbara (Larkin), Agnes (McGrath), Marian (Dennehy), Marylee (Buckley) and everyone else in the W.D. . .

Mary Tobin was the high-powered press woman who finally persuaded me that I must have my picture in the papers. Every former newspaper woman feels there is nothing more undesirable than seeing one's face reproduced in the press. But, as Mary pounded into my ears, "I can get publicity for you, who represent all Democratic women, but I cannot get it for Mary Zilch from Podunk. You know that."

Here is my letter:

This will be a round-robin letter for I never find time to write. This is a hectic trip and I am busy from early morning (and I mean as early as 5:45 a.m. many mornings) until midnight. Groups of people get on the minute we hit a state and ride through the state with other groups joining us for shorter rides between so I am busy "hostessing" all the time. I dash back and forth between the front car (really the end one with an observation platform) where the President and Mrs. T. and Margaret hold forth, to the diner eight cars ahead where I entertain the ladies when and if they need solid refreshment. The setup of the train is as follows (No. 1 is last):

No. 1 car, the Ferdinand Magellan, where the Trumans sleep, eat and sit all day when they are not off the train. Not very palatial accommodations so it is crowded when there are six guests but I try to keep the guests moving ahead so there will be room for others.

No. 2 car—the Secret Service lounge, where no guests are allowed to stop but I am permitted to so I stop there for a breather now and then. The S.S. boys (20 of them) are my pals. Charlie Ross, Clark Clifford, Matt Connelly, etc. have compartments in back of the Secret Service lounge.

No. 3 car—guests' lounge. In the rear are the work room and a couple of compartments for Dr. Graham, etc.

No. 4 car—compartments for the rest of the W.H. gang, including me. There are two to most compartments but I have one to myself. Practically the only recognition that I am an executive!

No. 5 car—recording room. 2 poker rooms for press and press lounge in the rear.

No. 6 car—work room for press.

No. 7 and 8—diners.

No. 9, 10, 11, 12, 13, 14, 15, 16, 17 compartments for press and probably Secret Service.

The Trumans are wonderful people, considerate and sweet. They couldn't be nicer to me. Occasionally I eat with them but most of the time they have to entertain guests. Their dining table only seats six. They are good sports and the President is amazing for he is the first up and the last to go to bed. The crowds are magnificent; enthusiastic and friendly. The press boys say it is only because he is President that the people are turning out in such numbers but I am inclined to doubt this. I am sure this trip is doing him much good and it is grand for me to meet so many women, even though I cannot tell whether I am just excess baggage. All three of the Trumans say they are very glad I am along and they all talk as if they expected me to be with them until election day. I shall have to be in New York part of the time, but that will give others the chance to go on the campaign train; it is a real treat.

I find many people to whom I talk do not know all of the House is up for reelection every two years—many afraid Democrats will lead us into another war—many have been impressed by opposition's repeated statements that government is wasteful and too bulky—feel that it would be good to clear out dead wood in Washington. I mingle with the crowds every chance I get and since I wear no badge they talk freely to me.

I pass on to Clark Clifford the comments I hear that seem important and he uses many of them; he is so nice and cooperative.

Thanks for the wonderful job you all are doing.

It saddens me to realize that recipients of this letter, Kayse, Mary, Dorothy, Lynn, Ella and Venice all are dead, although all but

Kayse were younger than I. We had a splendid group of women in the Women's Division in 1948 and I give them all full credit for helping me accomplish what we did.

Although it really was not my job to work with the press, I did a great deal of it. I flatter myself to think I had something to do with Margaret's losing her fear of the press. During the early part of the trip she acted as if every representative of the media was an enemy, a feeling fostered no doubt by her father's old friend, Charley Ross, who was a grade A newspaper man, the head of the St. Louis *Post Dispatch* bureau in Washington when he was tapped by his old schoolmate to be press secretary in the Truman Administration. But Charley was not in the same class as a White House press secretary with Steve Early, FDR's press man, or Jim Haggerty, Eisenhower's press liaison.

After watching Margaret for several days, I saw her one morning being a little snippy to a *Life* correspondent who, I knew, was a great admirer of Truman. Margaret had manners as charming as any young girl I ever knew, due to her mother's training, so I did not hesitate to advise her that she should not treat all of the press as if they were against the Truman family. "Many of them personally admire your father and they will give him every break they can in stories, so you must be your usual sweet self with them. Don't be afraid of them. Be natural and you will find they will respond well."

I never shall forget speaking to a large group of men and women at the Democratic clubhouse on Madison Avenue in New York City several nights before the election and hearing them laugh uproariously when I said they would be sorry and ashamed the next Wednesday that they had not worked hard enough to enable Truman to carry New York State. During later years I never appeared at a gathering of Democrats in New York City or its environs during which someone did not say, "I remember well your prediction of Truman's victory in 1948. We all thought you were crazy." When we recall that Truman had as adversaries not only the Republicans but also Henry Wallace's short-lived Progressive Party and the States' Right Dixiecrats led by Strom Thurmond, now a Republican, it is remarkable that Harry S. Truman retained the White House. It is doubtful if any other Democrat could have achieved such a miraculous victory.

One additional observation on the Truman-Dewey race:

Postelection analyses by persons with experience and a knowledge of politics make good reading, but it is my firm opinion that preelection polls should be abolished, by legal means if necessary. They are totally unreliable; they can be slanted by the way in which the question is asked; and they do immeasurable harm to all candidates. The small segment of citizens who participate in a poll may try to be truthful, but how many persons know ahead of time for whom they will vote when they are in the voting booth? All but the little band of faithful, devoted to one candidate, may change their minds several times during a campaign. Many do not make their final decision until just before voting. Political polls are pernicious. I wish reputable newspapers and other publications would ban them. To me, they belong in the same category as those stories in the second-rate magazines with lurid headlines on the covers. The stories inside are nothing but stupid gossip with little or no basis in fact.

I cannot write truthfully that I ever enjoyed inaugurations. I received three real invitations to the Truman inauguration (not the handsomely engraved ones that go out by the thousands and are nothing more substantial than souvenirs, although many who receive them suppose they are bona fide invitations to all the events surrounding the actual inauguration. It was pitiful how many women appealed to me shortly before January 20, 1949, for tickets to the various affairs, to find that upon their arrival in the nation's capital they had nothing but a hotel-room reservation.

The main events included a dinner of the Truman-Barkley Club (large contributors) at the Mayflower Hotel Tuesday night; reception for the governors at the Shoreham Wednesday in the late afternoon; the Electoral College dinner that night at the Mayflower, at which the President did his famous mimicry of radio commentator H.V. Kaltenborn; the Inaugural Gala at the National Guard Armory the night before the inauguration; the inauguration Thursday at noon at the Capitol Plaza; the parade that afternoon; a reception at the National Gallery of Art for the Trumans and Vice President Barkley in the late afternoon; the Inaugural Ball at the National Guard Armory that night; and a reception given by the Secretary of the Treasury and Mrs. Snyder at the Wardman Park Hotel Friday, followed by a reception given by Senator J. Howard McGrath, chairman of the DNC, and Mrs. McGrath at the Shoreham Hotel.

The only tickets I had in a quantity to give to disgruntled visitors were to a meeting I had planned for women on Friday morning at the departmental auditorium, but I also gave away all the dinner and reception tickets I had, so Herbert and I only attended the National Committee party for the Trumans. I was heartsick to miss the President's entertainment at the Electoral College dinner but—I could not have enjoyed myself knowing how many wanted to be in my place. Of the three sets of invitations, one came directly from the White House, so I asked that it be kept separate in order to use it for myself and Herbert. Through an understandable mixup, for my office was like Grand Central Station, the three sets were put in the same drawer and it was impossible to tell which came from the President. My secretary tried to find out from various sources which set of tickets for the inauguration was for the best seats but no one knew, so I kept one set for Herbert and myself; gave one set to my daughter and Patty Bruen, who had been engaged to my son and was visiting us for the inaugural festivities; and the third set to my sister, Grace, and her husband, who had come on from Detroit for the week. Dick Bourke had been active in Democratic politics in Detroit but he and Grace were looking to me to provide them with tickets.

We went our separate ways to find our places for the inauguration. Herbert and I were seated in the Capitol Plaza, not near but not too far from the Presidential stand to make out its occupants without the aid of the opera glasses and binoculars with which we had provided ourselves. We knew who had *our* tickets when, to our surprise and dismay, we saw the Bourkes standing on the inaugural platform along with the Truman and Wallace and Barkley families!

The Women's Inaugural Meeting attracted many men, although leaflets announcing the meeting, distributed at all the hotels and the committee headquarters, read: "Gentlemen admitted if accompanied by ladies." We had not publicized the fact that President and Mrs. Truman would attend the meeting, but even so, we had to put the SRO sign outside long before the program started. When I first broached the idea of having such a meeting so that the women visitors could take home some tangible ideas to pass on to other women leaders in clubs and in civic and political organizations, the chairman had said I was crazy to think anyone would attend, particularly the morning after the Inaugural Ball. I asked if he would agree if I were able to plan an interesting program. He said he would, but that he was sure I could not get a single Cabinet officer to speak.

I lined up Attorney General Tom Clark, Secretary of Labor Maurice Tobin, Assistant Secretary of State George V. Allen, Federal Security Administrator Oscar R. Ewing, and Congresswoman Helen Douglas. The President also agreed to put in an appearance together with Mrs. Truman. Howard was flabbergasted when I told him about the plans and, of course, said he would be there himself. I gave him the honor of presenting to the President a bronze bust by the noted sculptor Felix de Weldon. The artist donated it to us so that the DNC could present it as a personal gift. Official gifts presented to the President become the property of the government, but I asked Howard to make it clear that the de Weldon bust was a gift to the Truman family. The President not only brought his wife but all the members of their families who were in Washington that week and introduced them one by one to the audience. My women's meeting, which the chairman had thought would be a dismal failure, turned out to be one of the stellar attractions of the week.

The President and Mrs. Truman always were nice about appearing when I asked them to be somewhere, except I never could get her to a political meeting without him. She would accept invitations extended through me to fashion shows and other affairs for women but she drew the line at a political meeting. "You do not understand, India," she once said, "I am not like Harry and Margaret. I find it hard to go to a meeting of that sort since I will not make a speech and I do not like just being on display." She really is a very reserved person.

The President "crashed" a reception that was given for me shortly after his election in '48, which surprised and delighted me as well as all the hostesses and guests. Esther Van Wagoner Tufty, the duchess as she is known to her press confreres, and Tallulah Bankhead headed the list of women who planned the party and were the hostesses. If I remember correctly, Mrs. Truman and Margaret joined the receiving line when they arrived early at the lovely party, which was given at the Carlton Hotel. When the President appeared through a side door he made a little speech, giving women credit for the great part they had played in helping him to be elected.

I regret that I was not more of a pack rat. For instance, why did I not have enough sense to buy a tablecloth from the Shoreham Hotel upon which former President Herbert Hoover had drawn for me the foundation of the White House? At the National Reorganization Conference Dinner in 1949 he was the principal speaker and I also spoke. A lectern was on the table between President Hoover and the master of ceremonies, so I was the only person sitting next to the former President. Not long before, the Trumans had had to move from the White House to Blair House so that the White House could be gutted and put into safe condition. It seemed natural for me to ask President Hoover if he had known when he lived there that the house was unsafe. He said that he did and that the reason it was going to be so expensive (the rebuilding job cost about five and one-half million dollars) was that "that skinflint Coolidge would not use the money [I think he said it was $90,000] appropriated by the Congress during the Coolidge Administration to reinforce the foundation." Having been an engineer, he knew all about the reasons why the mansion was falling to pieces, and taking a pen from his pocket, he made eleborate drawings to illustrate what he was telling me. It was extremely interesting, although I did not understand all of what he said and I stupidly did not think of buying the cloth from the hotel until the next morning. I feel sure I could have obtained it, if I had asked the maitre d' about it immediately after the dinner. By the time I telephoned the next morning, I was told the cloth probably already had been laundered but that even if it had not been, it would be impossible to locate it. I think it would have been something to be preserved.

President Hoover had been forgotten by both political parties from the time he left the White House in 1933 when Franklin D. Roosevelt entered it until President Truman asked him to head a commission to study the reorganization of the federal government. A national citizens committee to support the Hoover Commission, as it became known, was established with Dr. Robert L. Johnson as chairman. It was at a two-day conference of this committee that President Hoover and I were dinner speakers.

The day after the dinner I was having luncheon at La Salle de Bois with a couple of women and I noticed that three men at a nearby table kept looking at us with great interest. Since we all were past the age when we ordinarily excited undue interest from the opposite sex, I wondered what the reason was. Finally one of them got up and came to our table and speaking to me said, "Aren't you India Edwards?" I said I was and then he went on, "Please excuse me, but my friends and I are so curious about something that we decided we just had to ask you what you talked about last night to former President Hoover. He is a friend of ours and we all admire him very much, but we know he is a man with no small talk and usually he never speaks a word to a strange woman sitting next to him. Have

you known him a long time or what was it that made him talk so ani-
matedly to you and even draw something on the tablecloth?'' I
laughed, of course, and said, "No, I never met President Hoover
until last night but I started talking to him about something he knew
about—the condition of the White House underpinnings, and then
there was no stopping him. He told me in detail how it was built,
what was wrong from the beginning and why the foundation had
deteriorated the way it has. I had a very interesting time but I do not
think he had any dinner.'' The man seemed relieved, thanked me
and rushed back to tell his two companions why President Hoover
had been so chatty with a Democrat.

Writing that my luncheon guests that day and I were past the age
to excite undue interest in the opposite sex reminds me of an amusing thing that happened one night when I spoke to a large group of
college students in Washington for a summer seminar. There were
only males in the audience, which must have numbered several hundred. We had dinner and then I spoke for about an hour after which
they were to spend another hour asking questions. Herbert was to
call for me at a certain time but when he arrived the question and answer period was going so fast and furiously that I could not break it
up for about another hour. I always enjoyed those sessions with
young people more than anything so I was happy when a session
could be prolonged.

Herbert stood in the rear and waited and when the affair finally
broke up he waited for those who crowded around me at the table to
leave before letting me know he was there. He was chuckling when
we finally got together to leave. "Well, old girl, what do you think I
just heard about you?" he asked. "One boy said to his companion,
'She certainly knows her stuff,' whereupon the other said, 'Yes, she
would have to, to be in the position she is in,' but the other one added, 'No, she wouldn't, you know how women get ahead in everything; it's probably the same in politics.' So then the one who
thought you would have to know your stuff in order to be in the position you are in said, 'But not her. She's too old for that.' '' Herbert
said the boys turned scarlet when he said to them, "You're wrong.
I'm her husband and she isn't too old, but that's not how she got
where she is.''

President Truman felt strongly about Agriculture Secretary
Charles Brannan's farm plan and the health plan, both presented to

Congress in April of 1949. The President had asked Oscar Ewing to make a comprehensive study of the possibilities of raising the health level of the nation. Mr. Ewing, better known as Jack than Oscar, reported facts similar to those contained in a proposal for better health care for Americans made by the President to Congress in 1945 and again in 1947.

The American Medical Association each time increased the fury and size of its attack upon the health program. The AMA had opposed public health departments, proposals for county and community hospitals, and the Hill-Burton Act for constructing hospitals and clinics all over the country. Much of what the President proposed after his commission on the health needs of the nation issued its report and recommendations was passed in the Johnson Administration. Health insurance for all still is an unmet need. It will come, though, in spite of the AMA.

Charles F. Brannan, Secretary of Agriculture for President Truman after his first Secretary, the late Clinton P. Anderson was elected to the Senate, made a study of the farm situation, at the President's request. He made specific proposals for a program that would assure the farmer a stable income. The President had discussed various plans and ideas with Charlie, for Mr. Truman had been a farmer and he knew intimately the problems of families dependent upon the soil for their livelihood, so the Brannan plan was a program very close to the President's heart. He knew it would be controversial, because it sought to help the small family farmer rather than the agricultural corporations that were operating vast acreages and forcing thousands of small farmers to leave the land. My assistants and I wrote and spoke many, many times on behalf of the Brannan plan.

As soon as the Secretary of Agriculture made public the new farm plan in the spring of 1949, the American Farm Bureau Federation led the protest that it was a form of socialism and subsidization. The attacks were much the same as those made under the sponsorship of the AMA, which proclaimed the President's health insurance plan "socialism" and worse. "Industry and business have demanded—and received—subsidies from the federal government for generations—in the form of mailing permits, freight rates, tariffs disguised by the word 'protective' for special-privilege use, tax privileges for plant construction, and other fields," the President wrote in his memoirs, but neither the National Association of Manufacturers nor any Chamber of Commerce, local or national, ever branded these things socialistic.

I always considered it a great compliment to the women of the nation that President Truman felt, if the Women's Division of the Democratic National Committee explained his plan, our efforts would help to enact it into law. Not that we addressed only women in our talks and writing to point up the needs for such a program. We usually had many men in our audiences. I wonder now how I had the audacity to debate doctors on several occasions, but at that time I was familiar enough with the health plan to feel capable of telling the truth about it and pointing out the deliberate untruths the opposition was circulating.

Chapter 14

The year 1950 was one in which the Republicans—and some Democrats—played politics dirtier than usual. The pattern was not regional, for it was followed from coast to coast, not in every State but in far too many for there not to have been a main theme underlying the tactics of all those who felt that any means, no matter how scurrilous, justified the end of victory. Senator Joseph R. McCarthy of Wisconsin was responsible for the tactics some unscrupulous politicians used to win in 1950.

Representative George A. Smathers of Florida engaged in this sort of smear campaign to defeat Senator Claude Pepper, whose protégé the handsome young man had been. In the May Democratic primary, Smathers defeated the liberal Pepper, who had been in the Senate since 1936; this was tantamount to winning in the general election at that time in Florida. Claude ran successfully for the House later and still is one of the finest legislators in that body. Smathers, still a young man, did not run when his third term expired in 1968.

In North Carolina another fine man, Frank P. Graham, who had been appointed to the Senate in March, 1949, was smeared as soft on communism and integration by his opposition. Although he won

the highest number of votes in the May Democratic primary, he had
to face the next highest candidate, Willis Smith, in a run-off June
primary, in which he was defeated. Dr. Graham had been president
of the University of North Carolina for nineteen years and was one
of the leading educators of the South. He was the American representative on the good offices commission of the United Nations
which arranged the truce between the Netherlands and Indonesia.
He was one of the nation's leading defenders of academic freedom
and a staunch supporter of equal job opportunities for all. Both he
and Claude Pepper were great losses to the Senate.

Another Senatorial campaign that reeked of McCarthyism was in
California, where Representative Richard M. Nixon—whom I la-
beled a "housebroken McCarthy" in a speech because he had
served in the House and McCarthy had not—ran against Representative Helen Gahagan Douglas. I was in California many times during that campaign after Helen won the Democratic primary in June
and I was horrified and shocked at the manner in which Nixon and
his cohorts were seeking to make the voters believe Helen was at
least a "fellow traveler" if not a "card-carrying commie." Nixon
cited instances when her votes in the House of Representatives
were identical with those of Vito Marcantonio, an American Labor
Party member from New York and considered definitely "pinko."
Leaflets distributed by the Nixon campaigners were on pink paper
and he called her "the Pink Lady" all during the campaign.

I had not campaigned in Florida or North Carolina because as an
officer of the Democratic National Committee I could not support
either candidate when two Democrats were running against each
other. Hearing and reading about the foul methods used by the
McCarthyites did not prepare me for actual contact with their in-
nuendos and slimy tricks.

I went into Nixon's congressional district to hear a debate between the Republican who was seeking to take Nixon's place in the
House and the Democrat who was running against him. The Democrat sought to discuss the issues, but all the Republican did was to
call his opponent a communist. I never had heard a politician be so
open in slandering his opponent in a face-to-face encounter, so I was
not surprised when I went backstage (the meeting was in the auditorium of a high school) immediately after the debate and heard the
Democrat say, "How dare you call me a communist? You know per-

fectly well that I am not.'' The Republican replied nonchalantly, "I know you're not but I've raised doubts about you in the minds of everyone in that auditorium and there's not a thing you can do about it.'' The young man to whom he was talking was purple with rage and so choked up he could not utter another word. I had to rush onto the stage for I was to close the meeting. Although I do not remember one word I said, I know it was one of the fieriest speeches I ever gave, but it did the young Democrat no good. Only he could offset what his opponent had said and as far as I know he never did that. He was defeated, of course.

There was something he could have done about it, something requiring courage and money, but well worth it if there were no basis for the charge. I remember earnest conversations I had with Chet Huntley, and I always thought my persistence and insistence helped him decide to take legal steps to prove he was not a disloyal American. Chet was a very popular young local commentator for a Los Angeles radio station when Herbert and I spent ten months in 1954 in and around that area. We often saw Chet socially and always made it a point to hear his broadcasts. As we got to know him, we often discussed the fact that a story was being circulated to the effect that he was a communist. I am sure that many of his friends were urging him to find out who had started the story and then to sue. We joined that group. Eventually Chet or his lawyer found out that the story had been originated by a Rae Suchman (Mrs. John), described in the Los Angeles *Times* as a "wealthy clubwoman.'' It was my understanding that she was a prominent member of the Liberty Belles, a far-right organization. Chet sued on the grounds that by calling him a communist she sought to "pull'' sponsors from him by telling them he was "a dirty, low-down skunk who was giving comfort to the enemy.'' I think he sued for two hundred thousand dollars. When the case was tried in November, 1954, he was given what mattered most to him, a public apology from this woman who admitted she had no basis for the story she had circulated widely. He was awarded ten thousand dollars, which he gave to charity. I feel sure that he would not have become part of the Huntley-Brinkley NBC star team if he had not legally cleared his name.

The Maryland Senatorial election of 1950 was of special interest to me, for Herbert and I lived in that state and voted there. Millard E. Tydings was running for reelection, with John Marshall Butler his

Republican opponent. Senator Tydings could not by the wildest stretch of imagination be called a liberal, much less a pinko or commie, but he was a Democrat and so a certain group of McCarthyites was determined to defeat him. It was the dirtiest of the 1950 campaigns. It seemed absolutely necessary that the campaign be investigated by the Senate, especially since there were concrete actions and materials that could be exhibited. I talked to some of my good friends on the Committee on Rules and Administration, which would have the authority to conduct such an investigation if the Senate ordered it to do so. They all agreed that this was a campaign that should be investigated, but they all doubted that the Senate would vote to hold the necessary hearings.

A few days before Christmas in 1950, Ella Roller of my staff—a Maryland resident—lunched with me. We became so incensed as we talked about the Butler-Tydings campaign and what seemed to us the Senate's lack of courage in not investigating the campaign that we determined to urge the Senate to hold hearings after the Christmas recess. I talked the matter over with Senator Clinton P. Anderson of New Mexico, and he agreed to bring it up in the Democratic caucus that would precede the convening of the Senate early in January if by that time I could assure him that a majority of Senate Democrats were in favor of an investigation. I must admit I had very little more confidence than he did but I thought it worth trying.

I talked to every Democratic Senator during the holiday season. A few were in Washington but most were at their homes, so I had to call them long distance. There was no wide area telephone service line at the committee in those days—there may have been none anywhere—so our telephone bill must have been huge, but as DNC vice chairman I did not need anyone's OK to make whatever long distance calls I deemed suitable. I did not tell the President or Bill Boyle about what I was doing, in fact, I never told anyone about it except my husband. I did not tell Eleanor Tydings until long after her husband's death in 1961, so Millard himself never knew who was the sparkplug that got the Senate into action after his defeat. He received the nomination for the Senate again in 1956, but because of ill health withdrew before the election.

I certainly did not get a positive answer from every Senator. I had to argue quite a bit with some of the Southerners before they gave any indication that they might vote yes on a resolution to bring the matter to the attention of the whole Senate. My most effective argument was that if this sort of corrupt practice was allowed to go uncensured the Senator to whom I was talking might soon find himself in the same sort of predicament that Tydings was in. One of the most dishonest things that the Butler team had done was to distribute throughout the State a four-page tabloid entitled *From the Record* that included a photograph that made Senator Tydings and Earl Browder, the head of the Communist party, appear to be standing side by side in a very chummy position. This was a cropped photograph that eliminated quite a few men who actually were between Tydings and Browder on a platform at some meeting. The tabloid itself was paid for by the Butler campaign headquarters but allegedly put out by a front organization of so-called Young Democrats for Butler.

When Clint returned from New Mexico I told him I was certain he would have support enough to carry his proposed resolution in the Democratic caucus. I never dreamed it would be endorsed unanimously, as it was. The Senate directed the Committee on Rules and Administration to appoint a subcommittee to hold hearings. Senator A. S. Mike Monroney, Democrat from Oklahoma, was chairman and the other members were Democrat Thomas C. Hennings of Missouri, and Republicans Robert C. Hendrickson of New Jersey and Margaret Chase Smith of Maine. They held public hearings from February 20 until April 11 and made their report in August. The report did not recommend the unseating of Senator Butler—none of us expected that—but it did state that this recommendation ". . . is not to say that we approve or condone certain acts and conduct in his campaign. To the contrary, we vigorously denounce such acts and conduct and recommend a study looking to the adoption of rules by the Senate which will make acts of defamation, slander, and libel sufficient grounds for presentment to the Senate for the purpose of declaring a Senate seat vacant." As a result of the investigation and hearings, Jon M. Jonkel, Senator Butler's campaign manager, pleaded guilty to violation of the Maryland election laws for failure to properly report contributions and expenditures in the Butler campaign and was sentenced. The rest of the devastating report involved Senator McCarthy, his staff, and the *Times-Herald* (a Washington morning paper, now defunct) and some of its top executives.

This was the first time McCarthy's name had been included in a

Senate report in a derogatory way. Soon after the report was made public, Senator William Benton of Connecticut criticized the senator from Wisconsin in a speech on the floor of the Senate, saying ". . . in the light of the report on the Butler election, McCarthy should resign." Benton introduced a resolution calling for an investigation to determine whether explusion proceedings should be instituted. The resolution pointed out certain findings relating to McCarthy's activities in the 1950 Maryland Senatorial election and suggested further investigation of them as well as of other acts of Senator McCarthy since his election to the Senate. This resolution, introduced on August 6, 1951, brought about a hearing, but McCarthy was not censured. That action by the Senate did not come about until 1954, when Senator Ralph Flanders, Republican of Vermont, introduced a resolution which read: "Resolved, that the conduct of the Senator from Wisconsin, Mr. McCarthy, is unbecoming a member of the United States Senate, is contrary to senatorial traditions, and tends to bring the Senate into disrepute, and such conduct is hereby condemned."

To the average citizen a censure of this sort may seem a mild rebuke, but to a Senator it is almost "the kiss of death." The Senator from Wisconsin—who by his "use of indiscriminate, often unfounded, accusations, sensationalism, inquisitorial investigative methods, etc. ostensibly in the suppression of communism" added the word "McCarthyism" to the dictionary—did not survive long after being censured. He died in 1957.

I always felt a great sense of pride in having had the determination—audacity one might even call it—to persuade the Democrats to do their duty by investigating the Butler election and McCarthy's part in it.

I am sorry I never told President Truman about the role I played in this. I am sure he would have approved, for he had as low an opinion of McCarthy as I did.

I think that the only time I ever have refused to shake hands with a person was when McCarthy rushed at me with outstretched hand at the conclusion of the first morning's session in the Army-McCarthy hearings in 1954. We were not living in Washington at the time, but I happened to be there for a meeting of the Defense Advisory Committee to the Secretary of Defense on Women in the Services. My friend Senator Stuart Symington of Missouri gave me the one guest ticket each member of the committee had because his wife Evie was out of the city. I was sitting behind Stuart in a place where McCarthy could not see me, but I noticed during the hearing that Katie Malone, the wife of Republican Senator George Malone of Nevada, called a page and sent a note to McCarthy. He turned after reading it and looked in our direction. I attached no importance to that until, just as the session was about to end, he jumped out of his chair and made straight for me. The news and television cameras were on him constantly, so if I had taken the hand he outstretched, I am sure that there would have been pictures in many papers of the vice chairman of the DNC shaking the hand of the infamous Senator from Wisconsin. I rushed out of the room. I had not the slightest intention of shaking hands with a man whom I considered despicable.

General George Marshall had appointed me to the Defense Advisory Committee on Women in the Services when his Assistant Secretary for Manpower and Personnel, Anna Rosenberg, had assembled a group of women from all over the country to serve on this newly formed committee. The committee is still going strong and has done a good job over the years in helping to upgrade the women's services and to recruit for them. Anna had not told me of any trouble in having me cleared for this committee. When the former governor of Florida, Millard Caldwell, director of civil defense, wanted to name me to his advisory committee, he was told there was a file on me in the House Committee on Un-American Activities. He and his deputy, Sara Whitehurst of Maryland, were sure there was some mistake or explanation, so two men from the Security Division of the agency or the FBI (I never was sure where they came from) called and made an appointment to come to my office to discuss the matter. I told them exactly what I had told Fulton Lewis, Jr., the radio commentator popular with right-wing listeners when he had called me one day in 1949 and asked me why my name appeared in a ". . . 1948 listing as one of the sponsors of the notorious Congress of American Women and not in the 1949 listing?" When Lewis asked me about this, I was alarmed, because he might have said that I had been a dupe of a communist front organization although that was not the truth. My opinion of Lewis rose considerably when I listened to his broadcast that evening, November 14. He could not have been more fair and objective in reporting what I told him. He said, "Mrs. India Edwards, director of women's activities for the Democratic National

Committee, said today that the reason her name appeared in a 1948 listing as one of the sponsors of the notorious Congress of American Women is that the name was used without her authorization and as soon as she found out what had been done she insisted that it be removed. . . . The way Mrs. Edwards got into the picture was that the 1948 report of the California Legislature's Committee on Unamerican Activities lists Mrs. Edwards as one of the original sponsors and founders of the organization. But the recent special report of the organization which I just mentioned—the report by the Congressional Committee—does not include her name. Mrs. Edwards told me this afternoon that Mrs. Gifford Pinchot [whose husband had been a Republican governor of Pennsylvania] asked her to go to Paris in 1948 as one of the original organizers of the movement; also invited her to a preliminary meeting in this country. She said she attended the meeting because, having lost a son in the war, she felt it was her duty to try to do what she could for the cause of world peace and that was the purported aim of this group of women. She did not, however, make the trip to Paris, and, indeed, heard nothing more about the movement until some months later when, on the invitation of Mrs. Elinor Gimbel, vice chairman of the organization, she attended another meeting in New York. On this occasion, she said, she made a contribution of $10.00. Later, she told me, she was surprised to find that her name was being published as one of the sponsors of the group, whereupon she wrote the organization a letter and demanded that her name be dropped immediately. She said that a special emissary came to Washington from New York to try to persuade her to change her mind, but that she persisted in her refusal and, so far as she knows, her name was dropped."

I asked that my name be removed not because I had any inkling that the organization was a communist front, but because I never let my name be used by any organization about which I knew as little as I did about this one, especially when I was with the Democratic National Committee. My friend Elinor Gimbel (Mrs. Louis, Jr.) did affiliate herself with some questionable organizations over the years and was one of those who supported Henry Wallace in his bid for the Presidency in 1948. She is a loyal, patriotic American woman, who uses her wealth to support many worthy causes and philanthropies. Louis Gimbel, Jr. and both of their two sons served in the Air Force during World War II in which the father was killed.

I showed the men investigating me for the civil defense committee the transcript of Lewis' broadcast which he had been kind enough to send me. They suggested that I ask President Truman or Attorney General Tom Clark to have the file on me removed from the House Committee on Un-American Activities, whereupon I ordered them to leave my office at once. I was insulted to think that they would suggest that I use influence to have something removed that certainly could do me no harm, no matter how many times it came up. And it did reappear three more times: First, when the Republicans took over the government in 1953 and I was interviewed by the Security Division of the Department of Defense because I was on the Advisory Committee; second, when Governor Harriman appointed me director of the Washington office of the New York State Department of Commerce in 1957; and third, when President Johnson appointed me in 1964 as a National Defense Executive Reservist. Each time I was questioned and each time I showed the questioners Fulton Lewis' transcript and that was that.

Family picture taken in Nashville, Tennessee, in 1898. Front row, left to right: Mrs. John W. Thomas—grandmother; India Walker; Mrs. Charles Fish—paternal aunt; James Walker—paternal uncle, holding Helen Frances Fish. Standing: Mrs. Archibald Walker; Miss Eleanor Hall; Miss Grace Thomas; Babby—the Walker children's nurse, holding Virginia; Dr. Fish.

India dancing with Robert Carter in St. Louis when she was about 17. After winning a few prizes in country clubs, they hoped to become professionals, but they had only one professional engagement: a week at the opening of a ballroom in the West End of St. Louis.

India Moffett (later Mrs. Herbert T. Edwards) and her children, John and Cissy.

India Edwards stops by the city room of the Chicago *Tribune* and sits behind her old desk as she talks to two of the young women who worked with her when she was women's page editor, Dorothy Schmidt (left) and Eleanor Page (right).

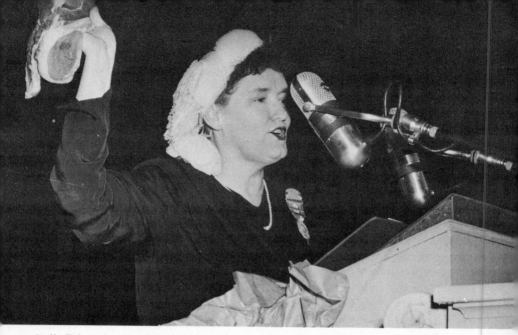

India Edwards speaking at the Democratic national convention in Philadelphia, July 12, 1948. Her speech was hailed as the first political speech prepared for television. *(Wide World Photo)*

President Harry Truman and India Edwards in San Francisco at a "party harmony" luncheon. *(Acme Telephoto)*

India Edwards speaking at Democratic national convention in Philadelphia, in 1948. *(International News Photo)*

India Edwards at her own campaign headquarters in Chicago, July 18, 1952. *(Wide World Photo)*

Cover photo of *The New York Times Magazine,* September 12, 1948. Left to right: Senator J. Howard McGrath, of Rhode Island; Joseph Blythe, of North Carolina, chairman and treasurer of the Democratic National Committee; India Edwards. *(George Tames/NYT Pictures)*

Reception for Perle Mesta, minister to Luxembourg, and Georgia Neese Clark, treasurer of the United States. Left to right: India Edwards; Bess Truman; Mrs. Mesta; Mrs. Clark; Mrs. Charles W. Tillett. (One seldom sees a picture of Mrs. Truman laughing so uproariously.) *(Carlton Hotel Photo)*

Left to right: Eugenie Anderson, ambassador to Denmark; India Edwards; Judge Burnita Shelton Matthews; Frieda Hennock, first woman on the Federal Communications Commission. Anderson, Matthews and Hennock were three of the many women appointed by President Truman to high posts in the U.S. government. *(Michael Rougier, Life magazine © Time Inc.)*

Mrs. James McGranery (left), Perle Mesta, Adlai E. Stevenson and India Edwards at Democratic headquarters in Washington, D.C., during 1952 campaign. *(Wide World Photo)*

President John F. Kennedy leans across several rows of unoccupied chairs to greet India Edwards and thank her for her help in the 1960 presidential campaign. *(Chase Photo)*

President Lyndon B. Johnson and India Edwards in Oval Office of White House, June, 1968. *(Lyndon Baines Johnson Library)*

Candid shots of India Edwards and President Johnson in Oval Office, June, 1968 *(Lyndon Baines Johnson Library)*

India Edwards celebrates her 70th birthday at a party given by the Woman's National Democratic Club in Washington, D.C., in 1965.

Chapter 15

In 1951, the Republicans were screaming Corruption, Communism and Korea as reasons for "getting the scoundrels out." The corruption in the Truman Administration was so infinitesimal that it seems almost ridiculous today to realize that Republican speakers and press had done an astounding job of selling the public on corruption in Washington.

I do not think anyone ever questioned Harry Truman's integrity any more than that of the popular general, Dwight D. Eisenhower, who succeeded Truman in the White House. Some of those serving in the Truman Administration were publicized as being venal and no doubt there were some—but they were few in number. We Democrats were unusually stupid in the years between 1948 and 1952, for we underestimated the effectiveness of the Republican program to persuade citizens that corruption was rampant in the Truman Administration and a main reason to vote against Democrats in 1950 and 1952.

President Truman asked me to take over the chairmanship of the DNC in mid-October of 1951 after Bill Boyle had resigned because of poor health. The press indicated that Bill resigned at the President's request because he or his law partner Max Siskin were under investigation on charges of improper political influence on the Reconstruction Finance Corporation. I never questioned Bill Boyle's honesty and I believe President Truman shared my faith in him, but it is possible that the Chief Executive doubted the integrity of some of Bill's associates, just as I did. Bill had been in poor health for some time and often was unable to be in his office for weeks at a time. During those weeks I, as the elected vice chairman, was acting chairman. There were deputy chairmen, appointed by Boyle, who I suspected were far from being the loyal, honest men they should have been. I refused to have any dealings with them and informed Bill of this when he was in the hospital.

Fortunately, I always had access to President Truman and was able to ascertain his ideas about the Women's Division's efforts to inform Democrats around the country about his domestic and foreign programs. Boyle's deputies were determined that we should never mention the President's health plan or the Brannan farm plan, but every time I discussed these with the President he would say, "Go right on, India, exactly as you are doing. This is what I want you to do."

President Truman offered me the chairmanship in a novel way. We talked about the necessity of having a chairman who understood organization and issues and who knew our leaders throughout the country. Finally he said, "I am thinking of asking a woman to be chairman. What would you think of that?"

"I would not think very highly of it," I replied.

"But when I tell you the woman is yourself, would you feel differently?" he asked.

"No, Mr. President, I wouldn't," I said.

"Why not?" he queried; "you would be a good chairman. You have been acting chairman for some time and you know the ropes. Also, I would like you to have the distinction of being the first woman ever to head one of our two leading political parties; you deserve this honor."

"I appreciate more than I can tell you that you have this confidence in me," I said, "but I do not think the men of our party are ready to have a woman chairman. They would not work with her the way they would with a man."

"They would work with you that way after they discovered as I have, that you operate like a man," he replied.

"There isn't time before the 1952 Presidential election for them to discover that," I said, and then added, "Mr. President, you know *I would be so busy protecting my rear* I never could move forward."

That clinched it. He laughed heartily and then told me that he was glad in a way that I would not accept his offer because the next campaign would be dirty and he would hate to see any woman for whom he had high regard mixed up in it. "You would hold your own," he said, "but it would be very unpleasant for you."

Not accepting his offer was one of the great mistakes of my life, but I did what I thought at the time was the best for the Democratic Party.

It was amusing and also very touching to me to have three Senators, the late Brian MacMahon and William Benton, both of Connecticut, and the late Blair Moody of Michigan, each call me around the time the papers were carrying rumors that the President was considering me for chairman to say he had suggested this to the President. I also was happy to have Monroe Sweetland, national committeeman for Oregon, send me a copy of a wire he had sent to the President. It said: "We are enthusiastic at prospect of casting Oregon's two votes at October 31 meeting for Mrs. India Edwards as national chairman. This would be dramatic earnest to the nation of our determination to maintain good housekeeping in our party and of willingness to recognize competent leadership of an outstanding Democratic woman." I heard from only a few other national committeemen and not a single national committeewoman at this time, although many newspaper columnists and radio commentators reported the rumor and later confirmed it when the President in a press conference said he had offered me the chairmanship but that I had refused it.

Not all the press items about this matter were complimentary, but many of them applauded the idea. The late Bill Henry of the Los Angeles *Times,* a respected political commentator, devoted an entire column focusing on my role as a woman in politics:

Chicago—If, against her announced wishes, the members of the Democratic National Committee should, this week, choose Mrs. India Edwards as their chairman, this town would stick out its collective chest and say, "That's our girl."

Queenmaker—Sober thinkers in the Democratic ranks are inclined to believe that the tremendous success of Mrs. Edwards in building up the women's strength of the party is the best reason for not electing her as national chairman. Plenty of people can be found, they say, who can handle the general problems of the ruling political party, but where could anybody be found to do what Mrs. Edwards has done among the women? They give this square-jawed, determined and forceful woman credit for all sorts of miracles, not the least of which has been the feat of procuring key government posts for women for the first time in history. Women have controlled 50% of the voting strength of the country for quite a long time, they say, but it took Mrs. Edwards to convince the male politicians that the girls were entitled to recognition.

System—You don't get full agreement on Mrs. Edwards—there are two schools of thought. One group, friendly, says that she is smart, hard-working, persistent—and a very clever operator, politically. The other group, numbering among it a lot of disgruntled male politicians who object to being outsmarted by a mere woman, say that she is "the exposed nerve of the female sex" and that by the simple process of annoying the top-ranking Democrats from the President on down the line and making it plain that she regards any rebuff to her as an insult to the whole female sex, she bludgeons her way to accomplishments. As for the lady herself, she says that she is just a hard-working grandmother. Best description—formidable!

As a footnote to Bill Henry's column I might add that J. Loy (Pat) Maloney, managing editor of the *Tribune,* told me one time when I was visiting old friends at the paper on a political trip to Chicago, that he thought I was wrong never to call on Colonel McCormick when I was in the Tribune Tower. I explained that the Colonel and I had parted friends in spite of our political differences and I did not think it would be a good idea to see him now that I was so deeply involved in Democratic politics; he might say something that would upset me and that I did not want to occur.

"He wouldn't do that," Pat said. "He's so proud of you it is funny. Why, just today at the editorial conference he said it looked to him as if our India is running things in Washington. He would like to see you." I never took Pat's advice, though. I will never forget that when my son was killed Pat Maloney called and said the Colonel would like to have me return to the paper on my own terms if going back to work would help to alleviate the sorrow of losing John.

A profile of me appeared in *Coronet*, a little magazine published by *Esquire*. Tristram Coffin wrote an article titled "India Edwards: Queen-Maker of Washington."

One of her male admirers says appreciatively, "India is a man's woman. She tells you exactly what she wants and doesn't waste time being coy." India has only three "musts" for her protégés. First, they must be capable. She assured Don Dawson, the President's personnel manager: "the greatest humiliation of my life would be if one of my candidates turned out sour." Second, they must be presentable. Mrs. Edwards is not interested in the Phi Betta Kappa or a diamond-in-the-rough type. She also bars those who rely on willowy hips and side-long glances to win friends and influence people. India does not rule out sex as a handy weapon, but she figures that man, being a contrary creature, does not like heavy doses during office hours. Third, the candidate must be acceptable to their Senators—and this for a very practical reason.

Tristram ended with these words:

Many women ask India how they can break the male hold on politics and government. Invariably she replies: "Get in on the local political level. If more women would volunteer to ring doorbells, they would get greater recognition." All those who meet Mrs. Edwards inevitably pose the same big question: "When do you think a woman will be nominated to the national presidential ticket?" She puts a finger pensively on her cheek and replies solemnly: "It will be a long, long time. There is still too much feeling against our sex. Anyone who predicts that a woman will be nominated for President or Vice President in this generation is going in for wishful thinking."

If that is right, and India usually is right, she is living a generation too early for her own good. For, as the politicians in the smoke-filled rooms say, India Edwards is "a natural for the ticket."

Chapter 16

I remember when President Truman told me of his intention to relieve General Douglas MacArthur of his command in the Far East during the Korean War. It was on Monday, April 2, 1951. The public announcement was not made until April 11. He had reached this momentous decision before April 5, when General MacArthur challenged civilian control of the military.

The President outlined to me on the 2nd the reasons for his decision and showed me documents and memoranda pertaining to the times the general had ignored orders of the Commander in Chief. He told me he had come to the conclusion that he must relieve the independent and arrogant general, who had shown over and over by word and action that he was in disagreement with the policy of the government and had no hesitancy in challenging this policy in open insubordination to his Commander in Chief. President Truman had great respect for the military. While he talked, there seemed to be a strong undercurrent of sadness in his mind as he contemplated what he was going to do to uphold the principle that civilian control of the military is one of the strongest foundations of our system of free government. There was no meanness, no smallness in his words or the thinking that instigated these words. There was no anger, just sadness.

I said I thought he had every cause to pursue the course he had indicated he was going to take but that it would cause a tremendous uproar in the country and probably would hurt him politically. He quickly said he could not allow political considerations to enter into a matter of such gravity, so fundamental to the foundations of our constitutional form of government. He went on to say he did not know when he would take action, but that when he did, it would be after consultation with and the approval of his top advisers in foreign policy: Secretary of State Acheson, Secretary of Defense George Marshall, General Omar Bradley, (chairman of the Joint Chiefs of Staff), and Ambassador Averell Harriman.

Truman did not know then that MacArthur's next and final challenge would come just three days later on April 5. Joseph W. Martin, the Minority Leader, read a letter in the House of Representatives which General MacArthur had addressed to him. Martin, an isolationist with a long record of opposition to the foreign policy of the Roosevelt and Truman administrations, no doubt was happy to read MacArthur's letter of March 20. MacArthur not only challenged the foreign policy of his Commander in Chief but deliberately disobeyed the order sent to him on December 6, 1950, that all public statements by MacArthur be cleared with the department concerned.

The President warned me not to tell anyone, even Herbert, what he was planning in connection with General MacArthur. I almost burst with excitement when news of Martin's reading of the MacArthur letter appeared in the newspapers. Each day I expected the announcement that Truman had fired MacArthur, but it was not until April 11 that the earthshaking words were made public. President Truman told me later that he waited to have assurances from his four chief foreign policy advisers that MacArthur had gone too far and that he was right in relieving MacArthur (some thought he should have done it two years before) at this crucial time.

The plan was for the orders of dismissal to be transmitted through an intermediary to Secretary of the Army Frank Pace, Jr., who was in Korea. Pace then would deliver them in person to the general in Tokyo. Truman was anxious to handle this sticky matter in the most correct way possible, but unfortunately the plan could not be carried out. General Bradley rushed to the Blair House at dinner time to tell the President that the story had leaked and that a Chicago paper was planning to use it the next morning. Secretary Pace was at the front with Lieutenant General Matthew Ridgway, the commanding general of the Eighth Army in Korea, who was to take over General Mac-Arthur's United Nation command. Pace could not be reached in time for him to give the general the order of dismissal. In view of this, the President had Joe Short, his press secretary, call a press conference for 1 a.m. on April 11, so that all the papers would have the story. He dared not wait for the orders to be delivered in a courteous way for fear General MacArthur would resign rather than wait to be fired if he read about the loss of his command in the newspaper.

It was not until I read Merle Miller's oral biography of Truman, *Plain Speaking* that I learned that it was my old paper, the Chicago *Tribune,* that was ready to use the story as a "scoop." Miller wrote that Truman's eyes blazed with fury as he told about his troubles with MacArthur, but he was calm and deliberate when he spoke to me. When we later talked about the event, he did not mention the Chicago *Tribune,* I think because he respected my lingering fondness for that paper and its publisher and editors despite political disagreement.

In 1951 I visited a number of European countries after attending the World Health Organization meeting in Geneva, Switzerland. All the ambassadors and the high commissioners in West Germany and Austria entertained me handsomely. Every high-ranking Truman appointee with whom I visited told me the scuttlebutt was that Truman was going to nominate Eisenhower for the Presidency at the 1952 Democratic convention. They were much surprised when I said I never had heard anything at home to make me believe that was true. The first thing I did when I returned to Washington was to ask the President if he planned such an action.

"I may be presumptuous in asking you this," I said, "and if so, I apologize but I would like to know now if you are planning to do that, for I never would work to elect a military man President and I will resign from the DNC now if General Eisenhower is going to be our candidate next year." President Truman assured me he never would support a military man for President either, so I never put any credence in the stories put out by the general and his friends that Truman wanted Eisenhower to run on the Democratic ticket in 1952.

I had been shocked earlier that year when my friend, the estima-

ble Senator from Illinois, Paul H. Douglas, had said in a press conference in Los Angeles that he thought General Eisenhower might
be the candidate on both the Democratic and Republican tickets. I
always thought, from what persons close to the general told me
about his political ambition and beliefs, that he himself entertained
the idea that both conventions might nominate him, but I was
horrified to hear a Senator make such a suggestion. It would be a sad
day for this nation if we ever gave the nomination for President in
two major parties to one man, for then it would be quite easy for him
to become a dictator.

President Truman and I heartily disliked one Senator and we disagreed with him on most subjects. Occasionally we would express
our sentiments about this Senator from Nevada to each other in
terms that were anything but complimentary. I was delighted, therefore, when Harry Truman wrote in his memoirs what he thought of
Senator Pat McCarran: "The McCarthys, the McCarrans, the Jen-
ners, the Parnell Thomases, the Veldes have waged a relentless attack, raising doubts in the minds of people about the loyalty of most
employees in government. It is one of the tragedies of our time that
the security program of the United States has been wickedly used by
demagogues and sensational newspapers in an attempt to frighten
and mislead the American people ."

Admiral Chester Nimitz had been chosen by the President to head
a small group of distinguished men and one distinguished woman,
Miss Anna Lord Strauss, early in 1951 "to make a comprehensive
and basic study of the whole loyalty program and to make recommendations on what the government needed to provide greater protection to the rights of individuals and at the same time maintain
zealous watch over its security."

Senator McCarran was chairman of the Senate Judiciary Committee with a record for obstruction and bad legislation. Blocking the
bill to have a commission make a nonpartisan study of the government's loyalty security program, McCarran succeeded in his efforts
to kill this legislation and to keep the Nimitz Commission from making a nonpartisan and honest study of the government's loyalty-
security program. In Truman's words, "This was another move by
McCarran calculated to check the administration's program and to
encourage the demagogues in the Congress."

In September of 1951 we held a regional conference for the Western States in San Francisco. Since President Truman was there to address the opening session of the Japanese peace treaty conference, he took time out from his Presidential duties to deliver a rousing political speech to one of our luncheons. I presided and introduced him. Senator McCarran was there, so we put him at the President's right and I sat at his left. Certain the Senator disliked the President's fiery speech, which I liked, I was greatly amused at the picture that appeared in some newspapers. As the President wrote me after he had returned to the White House, "I don't know whether you have seen the picture of the noonday luncheon or not, but I have one of McCarran and myself standing up. He looks exceedingly unhappy while you look exceedingly happy. It was a great meeting."

(Incidentally, the President's address in the Opera House that opened the peace treaty conference was the first time television spanned the United States from coast to coast.)

Just following that Western conference, Senator McCarran urged the White House and the committee chairman to get rid of me. I am sure he would have liked to do away with President Truman also. Some of the reporters in writing about the speech that the President gave at that luncheon said that it indicated he would run for reelection the next year in spite of the fact that he had said he did not know who the Democratic candidate would be in 1952.

In October, 1952, I debated Mary Pillsbury Lord (Mrs. Oswald B.), co-chairman of Citizens for Eisenhower, at Town Hall in New York City at one of America's "Town Meetings of the Air," which were broadcast by three hundred stations of the ABC network. Our subject was "Why Change?" In one way she had a great advantage, because the Democrats had been in office for twenty years, but in another I had the bigger advantage because I had the twenty-year record of the Democratic Party about which to talk. I truly thought I won the debate, but what did it matter? Her candidate won the election.

I agreed to debate Clare Boothe Luce several times during the 1952 campaign, but each time our television executive responded to say I had the requested date open, the man who had asked for me would say, "Sorry but Mrs. Luce has found it impossible to be here for that program."

After this happened about five times, our man thought something was fishy, so he asked a close friend of his at one of the network headquarters what the story was. "Well, to tell you the truth," his friend said, "Mrs. Luce won't debate India Edwards or Helen Gahagan Douglas. She accepts, thinking she will have a man opponent and when she finds out it is Mrs. Edwards she backs off."

Some years later, in 1970, I read in Stephen Shadegg's book that Clare Luce felt a debate between two women was treated by the press as a "catfight." She had announced this opinion after the 1940 campaign, in which she supported Wendell Willkie and Dorothy Thompson supported Franklin D. Roosevelt. Shadegg also wrote that Clare Luce met with Helen Gahagan Douglas when she came to Congress in 1941 and persuaded her that it would be wise never to discuss the same subject on the same day, and under no circumstance to comment on what the other had said.

I never found that any of my debates with women, including Bertha Adkins, who headed Republican women during the Eisenhower Administration, ever degenerated into a "catfight." Neither did Helen Douglas, who, ever since she was defeated by Nixon in as dirty a campaign as ever has been waged in this nation, has maintained her dignity so admirably that I have wondered how she could do it. I am afraid I would have burst out at some time with my true opinion of Richard Milhouse Nixon if he had done to me what he did to Helen. She is one of our very great women and I am proud to call her my friend.

I enjoyed a delicious dinner at Twenty-One in New York one night in 1949 as the guest of two prominent Republicans who were so embarrassed by the way one of their women leaders behaved at that afternoon's session of the *Herald Tribune* Forum that they insisted upon taking me out for a scrumptious dinner. My hosts were Governor Val Peterson of Nebraska and Victor A. Johnston, campaign director of the Republican National Senatorial Committee. Governor Peterson had been a speaker at the Forum the night before. Mr. Johnston, Mrs. Elizabeth Heffelfinger—Republican national committeewomen from Minnesota and usually a very bright, controlled person—and I were three of the seven politicians who were to debate with national leaders of nonpartisan civic groups the responsibility of the individual citizen, and whether he or she could exert a more effective influence on the formation of national policy by working through nonpartisan organizations or through a political

party. Mrs. Heffelfinger apparently became so excited at the prospect of speaking to an audience that filled the ballroom and balcony
of the Waldorf-Astoria Hotel (and I think the program was broadcast, at least locally) that she forgot the subject we were to discuss
and launched into a tirade against the Democratic party, FDR and
HST. She addressed her remarks mainly to me. Her fellow Republicans were terribly embarrassed, but I only laughed and shook my
head and declined to answer her when Helen Hiett Waller, the moderator, asked if I wanted to respond. We were not there to have a
political debate and I thought it unwise to indulge in one.

I cannot refrain from quoting what Vic Johnston said about me at
the Forum that afternoon: "On the stage today we have an example
of prestige value in political activity. It is Mrs. India Edwards, who
belongs to our rival party. She has certainly achieved a position in
America that is very powerful, and more powerful probably than
any woman could achieve in any other respect. Her counsel is
sought by the President. She recommends people for very high
offices. And they get the jobs, too. And I would think that what she
has done for women has been of very great benefit to women in politics. And yet I differ with Mrs. Edwards in political activity, and we
will try to beat her candidate for public office probably, and she will
try to beat ours. But I do respect the work she has done."

Once I did so badly in a political debate that I wished I had not
taken part in it. It was in 1948, when Mary Donlon, a prominent
New York Republican, and I debated the domestic planks of our respective party platforms in an ABC radio moot court series, "On
Trial." John Harlan Amen, eminent New York attorney and associate trial counsel for the United States at the Nuremberg trials, was
Miss Donlon's attorney, and James Lawrence Fly, former chairman
of the Federal Communications Commission and general solicitor of
the Tennessee Valley Authority, was mine. Mary Donlon was an attorney herself and later was appointed by President Eisenhower to
the U.S. Customs Court, and I do not mind admitting that I was out
of my class when I debated her that night. My lawyer did not arrive
at the station in time to have the planned conference with me, so I
found myself in as unhappy a situation as I've ever been in publicly.
No one was unkind enough to mention it to me—perhaps no one had
listened to the program!

I never was afraid to debate a man, but I did not like doing so because I always felt that a male politician wore kid gloves when he debated issues with a woman. I resented this, although I understood it. At various times I debated Senator Clifford B. Case of New Jersey, Senator Jacob K. Javits of New York and "Ab" Herman of the Republican National Committee.

My speech at the 1952 convention was about Korea. For I knew by then that it was an unpopular military action and that it was going to do our party no good in the elections of that year. I was unhappy that we had troops in Korea, but I did not question the wisdom of President Truman and his advisers in sending them to that country, which had been invaded and which the Security Council of the United Nations had voted must be defended. I knew for weeks, of course, that I was scheduled to speak at the convention and I had both of my speech writers, Gladys Uhl and Kay Armstrong, trying to write something that I could use. For some time I had written all my own speeches, because I could not use anybody else's words, but the time came when I had to have help. I was too busy to do more than rough out an outline. Then Gladys or Kay did the research and writing. Venice Spraggs often worked on speech material for me also. Some suggestions she had given me inspired me at 5 a.m. July 22, 1952, to write the speech I gave that night. I was not satisfied with anything that Gladys or Kay had given me and I did not seem to have an idea in my own head about what I wanted to say. But something Venice had written about Emperor Haile Selassie of Ethiopia standing alone before the League of Nations in 1936 to warn that in the unchecked aggression against his homeland worldwide consequences were involved had stuck in my mind. As I lay awake the night of July 21 worrying about what my speech the next day would be, I suddenly knew that I must talk about the importance of the Korean War to us. I had to speak as a woman—a wife who wore a Gold Star in World War I and a mother who wore a Gold Star in World War II. A very different sort of speech than the one I had made in 1948, it was not very partisan, although I was critical of the fact that the United Nations had not been mentioned in the amphitheater in which I was speaking when the Republicans held their convention there two weeks before. Nor did the Republicans pay tribute to the brave men who were fighting in Korea under our flag and that of the United Nations. I tried to make the women listening to me realize why we were in Korea.

The words I spoke came from my heart and they reached at least one listener in Washington, D.C., who wired me as follows: "Congratulations on your wonderful fighting speech last night. I am sure that it will do a great deal to awaken the women of our country to their terrific responsibilities in the coming election. Warmest regards. Harry S. Truman."

This was the second speech to which the President referred when he said I had made the keynote addresses at both the 1948 and the 1952 conventions and that he had embraced the earlier one, but that the 1952 candidate—Aldai Stevenson—did not follow through on the latter.

Chapter 17

There are few politicians who agree with me that Adlai Stevenson could have won in '52 with a shrewd, well-planned and well-executed campaign. By '56 Stevenson had lost the South by seeking to appease the Dixiecrats and many of his staunch supporters in '52 had lost their enthusiasm for him because of his attitude towards the Dixiecrats. I tried to tell him that the Dixiecrats were like the communists; they only understood force and strong opposition. Compromise and tolerance were signs of weakness to them and would get him nowhere. I felt as if I were talking in a foreign language which he did not understand. Probably he was right when he said to me in Istanbul, Turkey, in 1953, that he was a philosopher, not a politician.

I think he would have made a great President if he had had the chance to become one in 1952. And I think Kennedy chose unwisely when he did not make Stevenson the Secretary of State in 1961. As useful as he was as the Ambassador to the United Nations, he would have been a great Secretary of State, in my opinion. Who knows? Perhaps we would not have become involved in that most useless war of our history—Vietnam—if Adlai had been Kennedy's and then Johnson's Secretary of State.

I have always felt that I had a little to do with President Truman's choice of Adlai Ewing Stevenson to run as his successor. I began talking to the President in 1951 about what a fine man Adlai was and what a good candidate he would make if President Truman decided not to run again, which I strongly suspected would be his decision. As he wrote in the second volume of his memoirs, he first talked to Stevenson about seeking the nomination early in January, 1952, and also in March of that year, when Adlai told him definitely that he was committed to run for reelection as governor of Illinois and that he did not want to seek the nomination for President. "But," the President wrote, "I felt that in Stevenson I had found the man to whom I could safely turn over the responsibilities of party leadership. Here was the kind of man the Democratic party needed, and while I would not pressure him, I felt certain that he would see it as his duty to seek the nomination."

On the night of March 29 at the annual Jefferson-Jackson Dinner in the National Guard Armory, as the head table guests walked down the stairs from the reception room to the vast banquet room, President Truman indicated that he wanted to speak to Vice President Barkley and me. As we walked along, he said in a whisper, "I am going to announce tonight that I am not going to run for reelection. It will be a surprise to everyone but the family and some of my staff. I wanted you two to know about it before the announcement." I do not know what was the matter with the Veep and me, but we both laughed and treated it as a joke. I suppose we both thought that he would not tell us such an important fact in that offhand manner.

I do not know how the Veep felt when he heard the public announcement, although I expect he immediately thought he would have a chance at the nomination. I know how I felt. Adlai was sitting next to me so I turned to him and said, "You have to run. There is nothing you can do now to get out of it." There was not much opportunity to talk then. I suggested that Adlai must make up his mind what he was going to say, so he said he would come to my apartment before breakfast the next morning to discuss the matter fully, since he was going on "Meet the Press' the next afternoon.

Herbert and I lived in Maryland, twenty-five miles out of Washington, but kept a small apartment in town to avoid the long ride home after a late party. I knew Adlai would not talk freely if Herbert were with us, so I did not tell him Adlai was coming. The next morning I slipped out of bed without awakening my spouse, dressed in the bathroom and was ready to receive Adlai when he came at 8. He stayed about an hour while we went deeply into the subject of what he would say on the press interview that afternoon. I wanted him to make it clear that he was available and not to close the door on his nomination.

His inclination was to say definitely that he was committed to re-election in Illinois and that he did not want to seek the nomination. When I asked him to be frank and tell me whether or not he really did not want to run for the Presidency, he admitted that he was ambivalent about it. He mentioned his divorce and the ages of his two younger sons as being reasons for his not wanting to be in the White House.

The he said, "India, I am not as liberal as you and Mr. Truman are. I am sure you could find someone else more liberal than I who really wanted to be President."

My reply was that we did not want a knee-jerk liberal and that his record as governor of Illinois indicated that he always made the right judgment, so he was liberal enough for me. I knew President Truman had talked to him and was disappointed that he was not more eager to try for the Presidency, but I did not know all the details of their conversations. The main thing I wanted to get across to Adlai was not to be coy that afternoon; to say definitely that he would not accept the nomination if that were the truth, but otherwise to say nothing that would make his audience feel he was unavailable.

Some of Stevenson's critics used to say he was influenced too much by the last person to whom he talked. He did not tell me with whom he was having breakfast when he left the apartment, so I do not know what advice he received, but I know he followed mine. No one who heard him that afternoon was in any doubt as to whether he would accept the nomination if it were offered to him. Jack Arvey said later that he did not think Stevenson ever would have had grass-roots support enough to be drafted as the Democratic nominee if it had not been for that "Meet the Press" program. Stevenson did not enter any Presidential primaries nor did he have an open organization seeking to get the nomination for him, but he was not drafted. An enormous amount of work was done by quite a large number of people who believed in him, wanted him to get the nomination, and worked arduously, if quietly, both before and at the convention. I do not believe any man ever has been drafted to run for the Presidency.

There were several men seeking the nomination that year. First and foremost was the able Senator from Tennessee, Estes Kefauver, who won a large number of the State primaries he entered and was served by unusually loyal and admiring men and women. As I have written earlier, President Truman did not like him and naturally did not support him, but also did nothing to put obstacles in his way.

Averell Harriman of New York (whom I supported in 1956), Senator Robert S. Kerr of Oklahoma, Senator Richard Russell of Georgia, the Veep and a few others also tried to be nominated in 1952.

Before I went to Chicago, about two weeks before the convention was to convene, I asked President Truman if there were any truth to the rumors that he was supporting Barkley instead of Stevenson. He told me emphatically, "Barkley is too old to run for President." In his memoirs, however, he wrote that he had told Barkley that he would support him because Stevenson had refused to run. I do not know what happened to make Truman believe that Stevenson would not run, but I must say that Adlai made it easy for persons to feel he did not intend to run. He was very wishy-washy about the whole affair.

I could not contact delegates for Adlai because of my position with the DNC. In Chicago I kept my ears open and reported to him daily on how I thought things were going. He would be pessimistic about being nominated, although he never said he did not want the nomination, and every day I would say he was closer to getting it. Finally I told him on Friday, July 25, that I was sure he would be nominated on the third ballot that night.

I said I hoped he was ready to name the man he wanted as Vice President and he said he was thinking of Senator J. William Fulbright of Arkansas. I protested that although Bill Fulbright was a scholar and a great authority on foreign affairs, he would add nothing, in fact, would be a hindrance, on the ticket because of his voting record on civil rights.

"But don't you think a Southerner would be good?" asked Adlai.

"Yes, indeed," I replied, "but not such an out-and-out segregationist as Bill Fulbright. Consider John Sparkman, Senator from Alabama." Adlai said he did not know him as well as he knew Fulbright but he would consider him.

In his memoirs President Truman wrote, "The convention recessed again after Stevenson had made his speech of acceptance. Meanwhile, Sam Rayburn, Stevenson, McKinney and I retired to a small private room behind the stage in the hall and discussed possible candidates for Stevenson's running mate. I left before a decision was reached, but before leaving I suggested that Senator John Sparkman of Alabama would be the best asset to the ticket. He was nominated by acclamation on a voice vote without a ballot being taken, and the thirty-first Democratic National Committee was adjourned."

President Truman was mistaken in writing that the convention adjourned after that Friday-night session, for Sparkman was not nominated until the final session on Saturday, when first I and then Judge Sarah Hughes had our names placed before the convention. Our nominations were purely gestures as far as we were concerned, but, believe me, there will be a woman Vice Presidential or even Presidential candidate on both tickets before many more years have passed. I hope to live long enough to vote for a woman.

After Judge Hughes was nominated, people asked me why I allowed another woman's name to be placed before the convention. I was actually delighted that there were two women nominated. The more women recognized in public affairs the better.

This was and is my true belief. I've never felt so insecure that I wanted to be the only woman involved in planning or acting. Katie Louchheim, who succeeded me at the DNC, once asked me why I was always so anxious to have more women at the head tables at banquets. "Don't you realize," she said, "that more women only diminish your importance?" "On the contrary," I replied, "the better our sex is represented the more important we all are."

Judge Sarah Hughes was not one of my favorite people, but nonetheless I was happy that the National Association of Business and Professional Women, of which she then was president, put her name in nomination.

When I told President Truman that former Congresswoman Mary Norton was heading a group of women determined to nominate me, he said he thought it was a fine idea and that I might be nominated if I really wanted it. I assured him I did not. Stevenson, on the other hand, said to Olive Remington Goldman, a well known Democratic woman leader in Illinois, "It's all right to have her name put in nomination if she understands that she must withdraw." He made this comment several weeks before the convention when Olive, one of my supporters, was telling him about the plan.

Stevenson would have had trouble with the woman libbers. When he met Herbert for the first time at a private dinner party during the 1949 inaugural festivities for President Truman, they had quite a long talk. Adlai then walked over to me and said quite seriously, "India, what are you doing in politics with such an attractive man as a husband?" He thought only frustrated housewives or lonely spinsters could be interested in politics.

Joseph P. Lash wrote in *Eleanor: The Years Alone* that Mrs. R. preferred Stevenson, but that she did not think he would accept the nomination. Mrs. R. worked hard for Stevenson in both campaigns, and in 1960 tried very hard to get him the nomination. Annoyed with him in 1960 because of his indecisiveness, she surely knew him well enough to know that he was no different then than in 1952 and 1956. He was unwilling to fight for the nomination but refused to stop those who were working to get it for him.

Mrs. Roosevelt once said that she had not gotten Stevenson in time to make him aware of how "the other half" lived, as she had done with Franklin. When Franklin was courting, she said she always had him call for her at the settlement house where she was doing volunteer work instead of at her home. She said she always arranged for him to wait twenty or more minutes for her. That would give him a chance to see the poor people going in and out. "This taught him a great deal," she said.

Mrs. R. was passionately devoted to and fiercely defensive of her four sons. The first time I saw her after Franklin, Jr., was elected to the House of Representatives was at a theater in New York City when I had to climb over her to reach my seat. "Why didn't you support my Franklin in the primary?" she asked in an unfriendly way, although she knew perfectly well why I could not support anyone in a primary race. I always thought she was more sympathetic to her sons than to Anna, her only daughter who died last year, but that may have been because the boys, even when they were men with wives and children, looked to her for help of every sort. Anna, on the contrary, was independent and handled whatever problems she encountered in her own indomitable and courageous way. Of course, I did not know them when FDR was alive, so it may have been that Anna was her father's favorite.

Once Mrs. Roosevelt had her secretary call to say she would like to see me the next time I was going to be in New York. I said I would be there one day the next week on my way to Vermont, where Herbert and I were going to attend Cissy's graduation from Bennington College. Since we would be driving, we arranged to stop over in Hyde Park. We arrived as planned around noon at her Val-Kill cottage for a "small, family luncheon." Tommy (Malvina Thompson, her secretary) opened the door and invited us in. She informed us that Mrs. R. was out seeing about the picnic she was giving for the residents at the Wiltwyck School, a place for New York boys who had gotten into trouble with the juvenile court. She had one-half the boys and some of the counselors one day and the other half and the rest of the counselors the next.

The fact that one of Mrs. R.'s cousins and his wife and some of Elliott's sons and his stepson, Faye Emerson's child, were there made it a "family" luncheon but "small" it was not. We all ate hot dogs, baked beans and ice cream cones out on the lawn, with Mrs. R. not just superintending but actually cooking the hot dogs. Then she supervised games and gathered the dozens of boys around her and read to them a book about FDR's childhood. I kept looking at my watch and finally reminded my hostess that if she wanted to talk to me, we would have to do so soon for we had to be on our way to Vermont. We dashed into the living room, talked briefly, and then Herbert and I were on our way.

Herbert asked Tommy who were Elliott's sons and she said, "All the white ones, we think."

I thought we in the Women's Division had done a good enough job of organization between 1949 and 1952 so that our candidate in '52, especially such an attractive one as Stevenson, would surely win if he ran on the achievements of the Roosevelt and Truman administrations and his own potential. But the whole campaign was dismal. There was so little coordination between Adlai's people in Springfield, Illinois, and the DNC in Washington that it was almost as if the two factions were fighting each other instead of the real opposition. Americans have never been prone to reward their military heroes with the Presidency, so I did not think General Eisenhower was a "shoo-in" as many did. The size of Stevenson's popular vote, the largest until then of any Democratic Presidential candidate except FDR in 1936, gives validity to my insistence that Stevenson could have won with a well-run campaign.

I may be unfair, but I think Stephen A. Mitchell was such a poor chairman that he contributed greatly to Stevenson's defeat. As the vice chairman and director of the Women's Division, I must share the blame, although Steve worked hard to keep me from doing my job. His idea of what a woman politician should be coincided with that of Ed Flynn, former chairman of the committee and later national committeeman in New York, who said to me once that New York's national committeewoman represented the ideal. "She is a lady, she presides gracefully at meetings, she can introduce the President properly, she never differs with my opinion, and she can be counted on to make fat contributions when they are needed." I asked Ed how we managed to get along so well, and he admitted that we probably couldn't if we worked together too closely.

I was the only person who had been with Truman four years earlier who was traveling with Stevenson in 1952. Consequently I alone was aware of the differences in the size of the crowds and their reactions to the two Presidential candidates. Most of Stevenson's traveling was done by plane. I insisted that the governor's sister Elizabeth "Buffie" Ives accompany him. I knew the fact that he was a divorced man was hurting him in certain parts of the country and I thought it would be helpful for people to meet his sister. I also had urged that Mrs. Truman and Margaret accompany the President on all his trips during his campaign. Buffie was kept so busy greeting relatives all along her brother's Whistle Stop tour that she had little time for the political women who came aboard. It appeared Adlai was certain to be elected if all his relatives voted for him!

Ernest Ives, her husband, a retired Foreign Service officer, was aboard the train also, and he was a delight to all who met him, not living up to the jingle Helen Sioussat of CBS wrote about him. It occasioned much mirth, however, when it was distributed throughout the train as a Western Union press message:

> I'm the husband of the sister of the candidate
> I'm a most unnecessary chap
> Just the husband of the sister of the candidate
> Who never gets the praise nor takes the rap
> Every fellow in the train
> Has a duty clear and plain
> At each whistle stop
> He'll hop
> For fear he will be late.
> It makes no difference what I do
> For the reason, sad but true,
> I'm just the husband of the sister of the candidate.

Jane Dick (Mrs. Edison) of Lake Forest, co-chairman of Citizens for Stevenson, was in the campaign party also, to look after the members of that organization who boarded the train. Having Jane aboard was a definite asset and so were Betty (Lauren Bacall) and Humphrey Bogart, whom the train visitors were as anxious to meet as they were the candidate. Katie Louchheim, who was working for the Labor Division of the National Committee in that campaign, occasionally joined the train.

Stevenson had a new and attractive style of campaign oratory and a delicious brand of humor, which some seemed to think was a detriment but which I think delighted his audiences. Humor has always been a politician's strong ally. Though Adlai's wit was sharper and more sophisticated than that of any other politician I ever have heard speak, his special brand of humor was not less acceptable as a political asset. Some said he talked over the heads of his audiences, but I never found this to be true.

After the first campaign speech I heard him give, I repeated to Carol Evans, his secretary, my oft-given advice: Never type more than two-thirds of the way down a page. I had noted he was dropping his head in order to read the last third of each page, exposing his balding pate and growing increasingly inaudible. "I learned from watching President Truman deliver a speech that you can give it as though you were not reading it if you do not have to drop your head." I shared this tip and fully expected it would be welcomed. It wasn't. Adlai wanted each sheet of a speech to start at the top of the page and go to the bottom. The hole in his shoe which endeared him to people undoubtedly stemmed from the same thrifty characteristic that made him want not to waste paper.

Chapter 18

Georgia Neese Clark, the U.S. Treasurer, met me in Geneva at the conclusion of the World Health Organization meeting. She was not able to accompany me on the first part of the trip we had planned because the inoculations she had to take before leaving Washington made her so ill that she stayed in Geneva until she felt able to travel further. She would not hear of my giving up visiting Rome, Florence and Venice, as planned, so I went to those places alone. Having sprained both ankles in Geneva—where I was hospitalized for treatment for a week—I hobbled through Italy on two canes.

I had not left Georgia to the mercies of strangers, for Ed Ward, the consul general, and his wife saw that she was well cared for and had everything that she needed. She joined me in Bonn, and from there we went to Berlin, where we were entertained in the guest house of the High Commissioner and Mrs. McCloy. It was a concrete fortress built beside a sparkling lake. The butler told us that it had been the home of a high-ranking Nazi. It looked as if he had built it to withstand an army and a long siege. We moved on to Vienna, which even so soon after the end of World War II was a city of such warmth that it gave us a *gemütlich* feeling.

I suppose it was my years of newspaper work that made me so

anxious to see everything, even places that were off-bounds to visiting Americans. In Berlin I persuaded an old *Tribune* friend of mine, then the chief of the New York *Times* bureau in Berlin, to take me to East Berlin to see the immense war memorial the Russians had built. I had been told in McCloy's office that it was not possible to visit East Berlin, but I managed to see as much of it as I wanted to, for it was a gloomy, forbidding city. The war memorial was something to remember with its numerous carefully tended flower beds and its impressive size. If I remember correctly, it was the crypt of hundreds, perhaps thousands, of Russians who had fallen in battle in Berlin.

In Vienna I spoke to a Russian soldier to ask if I were going in the right direction for a certain address and to find out if any of the many Russian soldiers parading around the city could speak English. His reply that I was heading in the right direction caused his two companions to look as if he had committed an unpardonable sin. High Commissioner Donnelly made me feel ashamed of myself when he told me at dinner that night that Russian soldiers were not permitted to speak to Americans and that it was quite possible that the soldier to whom I spoke was already on his way to Siberia if his companions had reported him to superior officers.

In Venice my curiosity paid off. My second day there was the most important national festival of the year. The consul tried to get a ticket so I could see the ceremonies in the cathedral and St. Mark's Square, but he failed. That morning I started out for a walk, turning right after leaving the Royal Danieli Hotel. When I reached St. Mark's I was stopped by a uniformed guard who asked if I had a ticket for the ceremony. I did not, of course, but I stood for a moment watching the crowds of people who did. I turned around and went in the opposite direction.

As anyone who has visited Venice knows, there are not many places to walk, for it is a city of canals and most people go from one place to another by water instead of on their legs. I leisurely wandered along, turning from one little street into another until I was well lost. But I saw many interesting things, including glass blowers and kid glove seamstresses. I was beginning to feel quite tired, so when I saw a little green garden with a low metal fence and an unlocked gate I went in and sat on one of the several metal benches. It did not seem to be a private garden. In one corner there was a door leading into what I thought might be the Doge's Palace. I walked over to the door, opened it and immediately a man in a long black gown took me by the arm and said, "Hurry, you are almost late," and he ushered me into the cathedral. I joined a group of people standing very near the altar and there I stayed while the magnificent procession entered and the service commenced. The assemblage filled the vast church, hundreds standing. The ceremony was all in Italian and Latin, so I understood nothing but I think it was a combination of civil speeches and a mass. It was one of the most dramatic and colorful ceremonies I ever have seen.

I spent most of the afternoon in bed, so I was fresh and ready for the delightful evening the consul and his wife had arranged for me: dinner at La Fenice and an orchestral concert in an outdoor theater. When the consul said how much he regretted that I had not been able to witness the spectacular festivities of the morning, I told the story of how I was ushered into the cathedral with nary a word about a ticket. He said it undoubtedly was a sacristan who pulled me in, thinking I was someone who belonged because I had come in from the bishop's garden. "You were closer to the altar than you would have been if I had secured a ticket for you," he said, "but you would have had a seat if you had had a ticket."

We enjoyed visits with President Truman's two women diplomatic appointees, Perle Mesta in Luxembourg and Eugenie Anderson in Copenhagen, Denmark. They both had been appointed in 1949, so were very much at home in the countries to which they had been assigned. We ended our European tour in Paris, where Margaret Truman and her companion, Reathel Odom, were visiting the David Bruces at the American embassy. We were fortunate enough to be included in some of the beautiful parties that were given for Margaret, the most elegant and largest of which was a dinner dance at a gorgeous chateau which was the Bruces' country residence.

Georgia was a delightful traveling companion, so we had a wonderful trip, made glamorous by the fact that the Department of State had alerted every embassy and legation in the places we visited that we were to be there. After our glorious week in Paris, we sailed home on the *France.*

Someone once sent Herbert a copy of *Le Jour,* a Paris newspaper, which listed the ten most influential women in America, and we were greatly amused to see that my name was third on the list, preceded only by Mrs. Franklin D. Roosevelt and Mrs. Harry S. Truman. Mrs. Margaret Chase Smith (Senator from Maine) came next, and the others were Mrs. Helen Gahagan Douglas, Mrs. Robert A. Taft (wife of the Ohio Senator), Mrs. Ruth McCormick Miller (publisher of the *Times-Herald*), Madame Bonnet (wife of the French ambassador), Mrs. Ruth Shipley (director of the Passport Bureau of the Department of State) and Mrs. Betty Darling (administrative assistant to Leslie Biffle, Secretary of the Senate).

When I was in Austria and Germany in 1951, the Department of State asked me to make a number of speeches to the women of those countries who were just beginning to become involved in politics. The groups generally seemed interested, but I soon found that the interpreter accounted greatly for the enthusiasm or nonenthusiasm of the audience. When I was speaking in a Viennese theater, I noticed several women enter at the rear. As they walked down the aisle, I recognized my friend, Edith Sampson. I did not know she was in Europe, so I was really surprised. I interrupted my speech and asked her and her companions to come to the stage. She and I embraced and I introduced her to the audience in glowing terms. I asked her to talk to the women for a few minutes. Then we had to say good-bye for she was on her way to another meeting. The Austrian women could not get over the warmth of our greeting—Edith was black—and it did more to convince the Austrians that nonwhites were not treated badly in the United States than any words could have done.

I first heard of Edith Sampson after George V. Denny, moderator of the "Town Meeting of the Air," and a number of distinguished representatives of various organizations had returned from a good-will trip around the world. Mrs. Sampson, one of the two black people included among the thirty or so travelers, had done such a spectacular job that when the group returned to Washington and decided to form themselves into an organization to keep in touch and meet occasionally, she unanimously was chosen chairman, in spite of the fact that some of the Southerners on the trip had started out being prejudiced against her because of her color. The other black was the late Walter White, executive director of the National Association for the Advancement of Colored People.

* * *

Chester S. Williams, who had acted as George Denny's co-director on the trip, and who later was with the Department of State and then the United Nations, told us of this remarkable black woman who had created a favorable impression not only on her fellow travelers but on everyone with whom they came in contact on the trip. He described the time the Begum Ali Khan arranged a meeting of the All Pakistani Women's League in Karachi and invited the four or five women in Denny's group to speak to the thousands at the meeting. Edith Sampson made a great impression on the women by narrating her struggle to be educated and then to be trained as a social worker and a lawyer. She told them how Mary McLeod Bethune, founder-president of the National Council of Negro Women, had telephoned her from Washington and asked if she could afford to spend five thousand dollars to represent the council on the round-the-world trip. After the meeting had adjourned and they were having refreshments, the Begum went to the platform, called Edith to join her, and said the league wanted to give her a present. It was a lovely purse with five thousand dollars in it. This posed a delicate problem. The Pakistani women would have been insulted if she had refused to take the money. She, of course, could not accept such a gratuity. She solved the problem in a tactful and diplomatic way by saying she would like to accept the money in the name of the council and then return it to the league so that all of them could become dues-paid members of the National Council of Negro Women.

In Delhi, India, Mrs. Sampson's retort at a large meeting to an Indian who asked why she talked only of the advances blacks were making in her country and not of the humiliations and discrimination they suffered was one that made every other American there immensely proud and the Indians in the large audience humble and ashamed. "Yes, my people have been slaves. They have suffered discrimination and humiliation but their lot is improving every day and I would rather be the lowliest, most downtrodden Negro in the United States than one of your untouchables," Mrs. Sampson answered the questioner.

After meeting and talking with her, I did not find it difficult to persuade President Truman that this woman would make a contribution to our U.N. delegation. Again he gave me the privilege of calling her and telling her of his decision to appoint her. "God has been preparing me for this job all my life," she said. "I will not let President

Truman or our country down.'' She served so well that Secretary of State Acheson asked that she be included in our delegation a second time. She was assigned to work with the committee handling the prisoners of war problem. I have been told she did a superb job and never allowed the Soviet to outmaneuver her, as they often sought to do. Not all of her race were pleased with her appointment. Although she was a good lawyer and negotiator, she did not have the facade of a trained diplomat.

Several black women leaders asked Mrs. Tillett and me to invite them to the first dinner the Woman's National Democratic Club gave for Mrs. Truman. We did so although we knew it would cause consternation among certain prominent members of the club. Our guests all sat with Herbert and me because Mrs. Tillett was at the speakers' table. When Senator and Mrs. Walter George of Georgia and Senator and Mrs. Tom Connolly walked into the banquet room and saw the five or six black faces they stopped just inside the door, then the Georges and Senator Connolly turned and left, not to return, but Mrs. Connolly went to her table and stayed throughout the meal and program. How I admire that woman! I had tried to persuade the women in charge of the affair not to put all the blacks at the same table, feeling it would be better if they were scattered over the room. Feeling was running so high and there was so much antagonism to our entertaining Mary McLeod Bethune, a great human being, and several other black women, that the committee on arrangements seemed to want to make the dark-skinned guests as conspicuous as possible. The club, incidentally, has had quite a few black members for many years and many black speakers, so they have outgrown their narrow prejudices of 1946. In March, 1975, they honored that marvelous woman, Representative Barbara Jordan of Texas, with a dinner.

Katie Louchheim, who succeeded me as vice chairman of the Democratic National Committee, was prominently identified with the group that first persuaded the club to admit a black to membership. I was not in Washington at the time but several years later when I had returned and there still was only one black member, Emily Taft Douglas (Mrs. Paul), Daisy Harriman (Mrs. J. Borden), Constance Casey (Mrs. Joseph E.), Polly Shackleton (Mrs. Robert W.), Nathalie Spingarn (Mrs. Jerome) and a few others and I made a concerted effort to open up the membership to our black sisters.

Dear Daisy Harriman was always in the forefront of all liberal and progressive movements even in her eighties and nineties.

My lack of racial bias can be traced back to my mother, who, although she was brought up and lived during her early adult life in Nashville, Tennessee, always was opposed to the Jim Crow way of life. Mother once took a trip from Detroit, where she then was living, to Florida to see a sister who was ill. It was during the depression and she had to make the trip in the most inexpensive way possible. She found it interesting, she told me later, and not too uncomfortable, until somewhere in Georgia a very elderly black woman boarded the bus. Seeing that there were no seats unoccupied in the rear, where the Jim Crow law legally forced blacks to sit, but that there were several vacant seats in the front, the old woman sat down in one of them. It happened to be next to Mother. The driver, watching in his rear view mirror, shouted, "You can't sit there, nigger, you know that." "Where is she to sit?" asked Mother, "you surely do not expect a woman of her age and infirmity to stand."

"She'll stand or she'll get off," the driver retorted. "If she has to stand, I will stand with her," Mother said, and stand she did all the way to the old woman's destination. "Quite a long distance," Mother said, in telling me of the incident.

Chapter 19

If President Truman had been willing to override the less favorable opinion some of his Cabinet officers had of professional women, he would have made more appointments—policy-making ones included—than the many he did make. But he always consulted the man for whom the woman would work. If that man did not want a woman in a particular post, and I was not able to change his opinion, the woman lost out.

For instance, when there was a vacancy on the Supreme Court, I begged President Truman to consider appointing Judge Florence Allen of Ohio, whom President Roosevelt had nominated and the Senate had confirmed to be the first woman on a federal district court. President Truman assured me he thought it a good idea to have a woman, especially one of "Sister" (as her fellow judges called her) Allen's reputation and capability as a Supreme Court Justice, but that he would have to consult Chief Justice Fred Vinson to find out how he and the other Justices would feel about having a woman in their august group. My disappointment and unhappiness were great when the President sent for me a few days later to tell me that the Chief Justice and his confreres would not willingly have a woman as a Justice. She would make it difficult for them to meet informally with robes, and perhaps shoes, off, shirt collars unbuttoned, and discuss their problems and come to decisions. I am certain the old line about there being no sanitary arrangements for a female Justice was also included in their reasons for not wanting a woman, but President Truman did not mention this to me.

Walter Scott in his "Personality Parade" column of September 8, 1974, which purports to answer questions with facts, slipped up when he wrote that Perle Mesta's main qualification was money when Harry Truman appointed her to Luxembourg in 1949. She had money, there is no doubt of that, but she never was a big contributor to the Democratic Party and it was I, not President Truman, who thought of making her a diplomat. Perle acknowledged this in the book about her life which she wrote after returning from Luxembourg.

My husband Herbert always called Perle "Perlie Whirly." Although I am sure she did not object to the Perlie, for two of her best friends, Ike Eisenhower and Speaker of the House Sam Rayburn, affectionately called her that, I do not think she liked the Whirly. She always gave Herbert a cold look when he said it. Probably realizing that the name fit her, she never admonished him. She did like activity and if something was not happening, she would stir up a party. She liked her own parties best and why not? She spared neither effort, money nor time to make each memorable, whether her guests were VIPs or GIs.

In 1974 we read about Perle's quiet departure from Washington to her girlhood home in Oklahoma in clippings sent to us by friends to the desert oasis where we lived after Herbert's retirement from the United States Information Agency and mine from politics. And now she is dead. The finale of Perle's half-century reign as a hostess of international fame saddened me and revived memories of the days when she was "the Hostess with the Mostest," a title she cherished even more, I think, than that of "Madam Minister" when she was President Truman's representative to the Grand Duchy of Luxembourg. However, if she ever had achieved the title of "ambassador to the Netherlands," I think that would have outranked the title Irving Berlin, Howard Lindsay, Russell Crouse and Ethel Merman had conferred on Perle in the musical comedy *Call Me Madam*, that opened on Broadway in 1950.

The height of Perle's ambition was to be named ambassador to the Netherlands when that post was available in the early fifties. She did everything possible to persuade President Truman to fulfill that ambition. Poor Perle, little did she know that the Dutch were so upset when it was rumored in the press both here and abroad that she might be the next ambassador, that I received a personal letter at my home from a prominent newspaper publisher in The Hague, whom I had met several times when he had visited Washington, urging me to persuade President Truman not to appoint Perle. The man, an aide to Prince Bernhard, Queen Juliana's consort, wrote that Perle would not be acceptable. I knew his advice came from the royal family. I showed President Truman the letter, which he read carefully and then tossed back to me with the remark that he never had the least intention of moving Perle from Luxembourg, where she was doing a good job. He then admitted that he and "the Boss" had been astonished when I had suggested in 1949 that he appoint Perle as minister to Luxembourg. She was their friend, they liked her, but they never would have thought of her as fitted for a diplomatic career, nor would they have supposed that she would be willing to leave her glamorous and busy life in Washington to be a diplomat in one of the smallest countries in the world. "But you were right," he told me, "she considered it a challenge and in her own way she met it and has made good."

Ambassadorships were not for sale in the Truman Administration and neither Perle Mesta nor Eugenie Anderson were given their posts because of huge financial contributions to the Democratic party. Perle had helped to raise money for the Truman campaign in 1948 and Eugenie had done her share to raise funds in Minnesota when she was the Democratic national committeewoman in her State, but neither was rewarded for those activities. Their appointments, as well as many more that President Truman made of qualified women to high posts, were in recognition of the loyal and hard work I and many other women had done during the campaign. When Bill (William M. Jr.) Boyle, who coordinated the Truman Whistle Stop Train, asked me after the successful election what I wanted as a reward I replied, "Nothing for myself but a lot of jobs for a lot of women. I'd like to stay with the National Committee if the President and the chairman [Senator Howard J. McGrath of Rhode Island] want me here."

Those two gentlemen and Bill, who replaced Howard as chairman in August, 1949, were agreeable to having me remain and all three, especially the President and his assistant, Donald S. Dawson, gave me great cooperation in achieving my goal to get more women into high Presidentially appointed jobs. Perle was the second of the several dozen Truman appointees, her predecessor being the first woman Treasurer of the United States, Georgia Neese Clark, Democratic national committeewoman for Kansas.

There was no doubt that Perle was a good diplomat in the post to which President Truman had assigned her. Everyone who visited Luxembourg while she was there was enthusiastic about her. The Luxembourgers themselves responded to her warm friendliness and sincere admiration for them and their little country. When I visited her, I asked a waitress in a picturesque old country inn where the minister was entertaining a luncheon how she and her friends liked having a woman as the American minister. "Ah, we love it," the rosy-cheeked, buxom young woman replied; "it makes us feel good in here," firmly patting her ample chest.

Eleanor Roosevelt made it a point to see me when she returned from a visit to Luxembourg, for she, too, had not been sure until she saw Perle in action in the little Duchy that she would be the credit to our country and our sex that she was. In an article in *Flair* magazine, then published by Cowles, Mrs. Roosevelt wrote,

When Perle Mesta was appointed to Luxembourg I am sure that many people thought as I did, that it was a personal appointment, since she had been such a warm friend of the President and Mrs. Truman. . . . I shrugged and smiled a little as I wondered whether all the people of tiny Luxembourg could not be entertained in one week, and then what would be left to interest our Madame Minister? How little I really knew and how shallow were my observations. Luxembourg is the seventh-largest steel-producing country in the world, and when the President appointed Mrs. Mesta he knew she ran her own steel business and that she was familiar with the iron mines that belonged to her. It was no surprise, to him, then, that immediately on arrival at her post she accepted an invitation by the miners in southern Luxembourg to come and see their mines. . . . He knew that she wanted to be useful. . . . I want to say here about this particular Madame Minister that she will not be found wanting in devotion to duty.

* * *

I doubt that officers of the Department of State were among Perle's admirers. She did not earn her laurels as a traditional diplomat but as a warm, thoughtful hostess not only to VIPs but to thousands of GIs stationed in the nearby countries for whom she held open house on the first Saturday of every month while she was in Luxembourg. Around twenty-five thousand young men in uniform enjoyed her hospitality at these open houses, which had to be held in a hall she rented instead of the residence when the crowds outgrew the house. Perle paid for these parties herself, as she did for most of those she gave in Luxembourg, for she was allowed only $6,000 a year for entertainment, and that would not go far for the sort of parties and the large numbers of guests who visited Perle. Her salary was $17,000 annually, so it is not surprising that she spent $60,000 additional during the time she was in Luxembourg.

The press had nicknamed Perle "Two-Party Perle," because she had been a Republican—and a hardworking one—for Hoover in 1928, for Landon in 1936 and for Willkie in 1940. Before 1944 she had switched her registration in Arizona, where she was living on a ranch, to Democratic because, in her own words, she thought, "The Democrats were doing more to meet the needs of the people."

Perle was one of the speakers at the convention campaign school we held two mornings of the 1948 convention week in Philadelphia. I chose as her subject "Why I switched from the Republican to the Democratic Party." A member of the staff of the Women's Division worked with her in preparing her speech. The day before she was to give it for the first time, she had luncheon with an old Republican friend, Louis Bromfield and told him how nervous she was. He offered to read the speech and perhaps improve it. Perle, shrewd usually but certainly naive that day, accepted his offer and gave him her only copy typed on our speech typewriter. He admitted to her months later that he had become so incensed at what she was going to say that he had torn up the speech and flushed it down the toilet. At the time he told her he had lost it. This was only a few hours before she was to speak. After a hurry-up call to me, I located a copy, but the speech typewriter was unavailable and Perle had to read from small type as she told several thousand women why she had switched political parties.

Mrs. Hugh Butler, a professional public speaking teacher who was putting on a streamlined course in effective campaign speaking for us on the other two mornings of the convention, gained one of her most noted pupils at that time. Perle decided, if she were to become a public speaker, she should take some lessons from a professional. They stood her in good stead, for in later years she put herself into the hands of a lecture manager and received four-figure sums as recompense for her efforts. She used these fees for Luxembourg scholarships to this country. This was after she had returned to this country from Luxembourg in 1953, after a trip to Russia at the invitation of the government of the USSR.

Well do I remember suggesting that Perle give a party in Los Angeles during the 1960 Democratic convention for all the delegates, alternates, and their spouses with Lyndon Baines Johnson, the Majority Leader of the U.S. Senate, and Lady Bird as guests of honor. I was supporting Lyndon for the Presidential nomination and so was Perle. She was planning an elaborate supper-dance similar to those she had given at the 1940, '44 and '48 conventions, both Democratic and Republican, with the guest lists limited to VIPs.

"It would help Lyndon more if you were to invite all the delegates and alternates than just the governors, publishers, congressmen and society dames and writers," I told her. She demurred, saying such an affair would cost too much, but I countered by saying that if she gave a brunch with no liquor, it would cost no more than a fancy supper with champagne flowing freely, something that Perle always had at her parties even though she never drank anything alcoholic nor smoked since she was a strict Christian Scientist. "Just think how pleased Joe Doakes from Podunk, and especially Mrs. Doakes if she is with him, will be to be invited by Perle Mesta to a party," I said. I had little trouble persuading her to give this party for Lyndon and Lady Bird, but I stressed that the invitations must include cards of admission, plainly stating that they were not transferable and were good only for the member of the delegation and his or her spouse. "You will have to be in charge of seeing that there are no crashers," she said and I agreed to this, although I realized it would be a colossal job, considering the fact that there might be about five thousand guests.

I enlisted the assistance of some of Lyndon's aides to be with me at the entrance to the huge room at the Ambassador Hotel Perle had engaged for the brunch. We were being firm but tactful, we hoped, in refusing to let Joe Doakes and Mrs. Doakes bring in their two teen age children and four relatives who lived in Los Angeles. Perle suddenly appeared at the entrance and said, "Let them all come. The more the merrier." So the party became practically a mob scene. The food ran out and, although the hotel was able to supplement the menu Perle had selected, not all the guests enjoyed as nice a meal as their hostess had planned for them.

"Migawd, Perle," I whispered to her as I saw waiters serving daiquiris, bloody Marys, and whiskey sours from huge trays, "I thought you weren't going to have any liquor. That will run your bill up astronomically." "I know," she replied, "but Marguerite said we must serve liquor." Marguerite Tyson, Perle's sister—because she and her husband George shared residences often with Perle—took most of the burden of managing the households off Perle's shoulders. Marguerite also was a Christian Scientist and a level-headed person, beautiful and intellectual and always anxious to stay in the background and give Perle the limelight she enjoyed. Marguerite's death about ten years ago was a loss that Perle never seemed to get over.

After the 1960 brunch, Perle told me how many thousands of dollars the affair had cost—I seem to remember it was nearly forty thousand. She was quite unhappy about it, especially as our man had not won the Presidential nomination. She really was a trifle miffed with me about the party, but since she came out in support of the Republican candidate, Richard M. Nixon, and raised money for him, we did not see much of each other during that campaign. I felt no guilt in connection with the cost of the party, for it was the drinks that were served and the many thousands of crashers who enjoyed them along with the invited guests that ran her bill up so high.

President Truman's second appointment of a woman in the diplomatic field took a little longer to achieve than did Perle Mesta's. Eugenie Anderson was not known to the Trumans nor to Secretary of State Dean Acheson. In fact, she was not well-known outside her home State of Minnesota, but every one of us from national headquarters who worked with her after she became interested in politics was impressed with her political perspicacity, erudition, charm, hardheaded common sense and sensitive awareness of the changing world and the important part the United States had to play in it.

Eugenie Anderson, née Moore, was born in Iowa, the daughter of a Methodist minister. After her marriage to John Pierce Anderson of Red Wing, Minnesota, an artist, they lived in New York for several years and then settled down at Tower View, the Anderson farm in Red Wing. Eugenie had been trained as a pianist, but after the birth of two children she gave up preparation for that career and devoted herself to her family. In 1937, after an extended trip to Europe, she began an intensive study of democratic government.

I worked very closely with Mrs. Anderson in 1946 and 1948. Since her husband's artistic career left him free to live abroad if his wife should be given a diplomatic post, I determined that I would try to secure one for her. I did not know what mission would be in need of a chief, but I began suggesting to President Truman the advisability of considering a qualified woman for the next available post. It required delicate, persistent negotiation on my part and a grade A performance on hers to persuade the President and the Secretary of State that she was the best choice for Denmark. Dean Acheson told me later that Eugenie Anderson was one of the two best political diplomatic appointments that President Truman ever made. The other was David K. E. Bruce, who has served in so many important posts that it usually is forgotten that he started his brilliant diplomatic career as a political appointment.

I suggested that Eugenie come to Washington early in 1949 to have conversations with the President and the Secretary of State. Both were impressed by her knowledge of foreign as well as domestic affairs and by the charm of this modest, soft-spoken woman, who was only forty at that time. The Danish ambassador in Washington went to New York to meet her while she was there for a brief stay. The ambassador's report was satisfactory, so his government indicated they would accept this qualified woman to represent this country in Denmark. When there had been rumors earlier that another woman might be given the American embassy in Denmark, there had been a furor in that country because she was not wanted.

Denmark, although a small country both in area and population (about 64,000 square miles and in 1949 four million people) was— and is—of genuine strategic significance to the United States and

NATO. Accepting a woman not trained for diplomacy was a very great compliment to Eugenie Anderson. I am proud of the fact that I was able to bring this comparatively unknown feminine political leader to the attention of the President and the Secretary, so that they were able to discover she was a woman to whom they could entrust such an important post. Hubert Humphrey, elected to the Senate in November 1948, helped with his enthusiastic endorsement.

President Truman nominated Eugenie October 12, 1949. She was confirmed by the Senate on the 19th and took the oath of office on the 28th. She, her husband, and their fifteen-year-old daughter Johanna and eleven-year-old son Hans sailed for Denmark aboard a Danish ship early in December.

Two *Time* reporters went to Denmark and interviewed Danes in schools, taxis, restaurants—and even at random over the telephone. They said the results were remarkable indeed; they could not remember a single adult questioned who did not know Mrs. Anderson. A taxi driver, when asked what he thought of her said, "I think all Danes like Mrs. Anderson. She's a reasonable woman, isn't she?"

As an indication of what Mrs. Anderson's accomplishments meant, I quote a letter that Dean Acheson sent to Herbert Humphrey to be read at the testimonial dinner given in Minneapolis for her when she returned from Denmark in 1953.

> MY DEAR SENATOR HUMPHREY:
>
> Since unhappily I cannot be present in person, may I send words of greeting to Mrs. Anderson and her friends who are honoring the magnificent service which she gave to her country as our Ambassador to Denmark.
>
> All of her colleagues in the State Department and all of her fellow countrymen who saw her work in Denmark were proud of and grateful to our Ambassador. The ideal ambassador should today represent all that is best in our country. Mrs. Anderson did that because that is the sort of person she is. Our ideal ambassador should also faithfully and well promote the interests of the United States. This also Mrs. Anderson did by bringing to her task the capacity for the hardest work, for taking infinite pains, and the highest qualities of mind and spirit.
>
> But something more than even the highest competence is required—what Conrad calls that unmistakable touch of love and pride

beyond mere skill. This Mrs. Anderson brought to Denmark. In her relations with her staff, with Danish officials, and—vitally important—with the Danish people she inspired because she gave understanding, respect, affection. When King Frederik IX decorated her with the Grand Cross of the Order of Dannebrog, he was expressing warm esteem which both the Government and the people of Denmark felt for her.

In the field of intergovernmental relations Mrs. Anderson handled for us matters of the greatest difficulty and importance with firmness, tact, and efficacy. It is worthy of note that when she signed, on April 27, 1951, the Greenland Defense Agreement, and on October 1, 1951, the Treaty of Friendship, Commerce, and Navigation with Denmark, she was the first woman to sign an executive agreement or a treaty as an Ambassador of the United States.

Soon after her arrival in Denmark, she gave her first party. It was not as the conventional or the readers of society columns might suppose for officialdom. It was given for the workmen and their wives who had worked so hard to prepare the residence for her arrival. From that day on the Danes opened their hearts to her, and to their great delight she learned Danish and spoke to them in their own language.

So I come back again to the description of the ideal ambassador, and say to you, if you seek one, look at your guest of honor.

With every wish for her happiness in new fields of service.

Eugenie Anderson's next "field of service" in the world of diplomacy was Bulgaria, to which President Kennedy in 1962 appointed her Minister, a post where she served three years. During her time there, she negotiated and concluded the Financial War Claims Agreement and resolved a number of long-standing cases so that certain American citizens detained in Bulgaria were permitted to return to the United States. She began studying Bulgarian after her arrival, and on July 4, 1963, became the first Western diplomat to speak in Bulgarian on the state TV and radio.

I am certain the Andersons' stay in Bulgaria was not as pleasant as that in Denmark. Living behind the "Iron Curtain" was very different from being in Scandinavia. John's activities in and around Sofia were restricted as far as photography was concerned. He had his own motor car, which he felt sure was not "bugged," so when he wanted to have a confidential conversation with his wife they had to take a ride into the countryside around Sofia. When Esther Murray and I visited them in the autumn of 1963, we often had picnics. We would drive in John's car to the mountains in order to discuss openly the many things Esther and I wanted to know about this beautiful country, so different from any other we ever had visited. Eugenie knew her official limousine, the office, and the residence were wired so that the Bulgarian government could keep watch on her. John, Esther, and I would sometimes carry on conversations that must have puzzled the Bulgarians who heard them. We were doing it for devilment.

The Bulgarian government soon discovered that the charming and utterly feminine-appearing woman representing the American President had an "iron fist in a velvet glove." She was as firm and tough in handling official business as any strong man would have been.

In the fall, President Johnson appointed Eugenie a member of the U.S. delegation to the U.N. with the rank of ambassador. She became our representative on the U.N. Trusteeship Council as well. Resigning from the U.N. in September, 1968, she was appointed special assistant to Secretary of State Dean Rusk. Since then she has done some lecturing, especially on the problems of the Middle East, a region she has visited five times since 1964. She also has traveled extensively in Eastern Europe, Africa, the Far East and India. Not confining her interests to places far from her home, she was active in civic affairs whenever she was in Red Wing. From 1955 to 1960 she was chairman of the Minnesota State Commission for Fair Employment Practices, the first Minnesota woman to head a State commission. In 1971 she was elected as the first woman member of the Board of Directors of the First National Bank of Minneapolis, a post she still holds. She also serves on the State Commission on Minnesota's Future and on the Minnesota Humanities Commission.

Chapter 20

I did not feel too friendly to Judge Sarah Hughes in 1952 when her name came up with mine for the Vice-Presidential nomination. In 1950, when the death of a commissioner caused a vacancy on the Federal Trade Commission, I asked President Truman if he would consider her for appointment. She had been made judge of the 14th District Court in Texas in 1935 by Governor James V. Allred, and, since then, had been elected four times to that post. The President agreed to consider her if I produced the necessary political endorsements, which I worked hard to secure. She had wholehearted support from her junior Senator, Lyndon B. Johnson, but the senior Senator from Texas, Tom Connolly, was bitterly opposed to any woman receiving a Presidential appointment.

"It looks to me, Miss India," said this venerable Senator when I talked to him about Judge Hughes, "that you want to get a woman appointed to every federal commission."

"How perspicacious you are, Senator," was my reply, "that is my exact goal, but I must have your help to get the first woman on the FTC and I am sure you would like to have a Texan—and a highly qualified one—be that woman." He finally agreed, but not until Senator Johnson and Mr. Sam (Speaker Rayburn) had added their pleas to mine. Before seeking any endorsements, I had called Judge Hughes in London, where she was vacationing with her husband, to ask if she would accept the appointment if it were offered. She said she would. The very day that I had assembled all the written endorsements and had sent them to the White House, Judge Hughes returned to New York and called to say she had decided that she would not accept anything less than a full six-year term. Since the vacancy she was to fill had only two more years to run, she feared she would not be renominated in the event of a Republican victory in 1952.

I was furious, of course, and almost frantic when I called Donald Dawson, the special executive assistant to the President in charge of patronage and appointments. He told me they were sending Judge Hughes' name to the Senate that afternoon along with other nominations for posts that required Senate confirmation. We decided that if I could come up with another woman lawyer with the proper qualifications and political endorsements by the time the list was ready, President Truman would agree to substitute her for Judge Hughes. How I worked that day, telephoning dozens of persons all over the country, seeking a candidate for this post which seemed so eminently fitting for a woman to occupy. At last I came up with the name of an attorney—Mrs. Louise Grant Smith of St. Louis. We did not have a Democratic Senator from Missouri then, so I had to clear her name only with the National Committee members of that State.

Imagine my dismay when the national committeewoman absolutely refused to endorse Mrs. Smith. She had no real reason for withholding endorsement, only that she did not like Mrs. Smith personally and saw no reason why she should be honored with a Presidential appointment when there were "plenty of women like myself who have worked longer and harder for the Democratic Party than Louise Smith has." This is one characteristic of too many women that has kept women out of public service in the past. Loyal and hard work in a political party does not necessarily carry with it the experience and training required for appointment or election to public office. And in my opinion personalities never should influence a leader to withhold endorsements of qualified persons.

I endorsed Chase Going Woodhouse to President Truman for appointment to the Federal Power Commission in 1951 and to Governor Chester Bowles of Connecticut when he had to name someone to fill Brian MacMahon's term in the Senate after that fine man died in 1952. She seemed to find it extraordinary that I should be willing to endorse her for these posts (neither of which she was given) because she and I had not had a pleasant relationship during the brief time we served together as executive and associate directors of the Women's Division of the Democratic National Committee in 1947. That I found her impossible to work with did not blind me to the fact that she had been a good House member in the 79th Congress or that she had support for the Federal Power Commission appointment from many members of the House and Senate and many spokesmen for organized labor. I would have been happy if she had received either appointment.

I doubt that President Kennedy's appointment of Judge Hughes to the Federal District Court at the behest of Vice President Johnson meant as much to the women of Texas as the earlier appointment to the FTC would have, although the later appointment was a much bigger plum and would mean much more to Sarah Hughes herself. It was she who administered the oath of office to Lyndon B. Johnson in Air Force One on that tragic day in Dallas in November of 1963 when he succeeded John F. Kennedy as President of the United States. Incidentally, President Johnson appointed the first woman to the Federal Trade Commission, Republican Mary Gardiner Jones.

There were many garbled accounts in the papers about how Burnita Shelton Matthews' name was included at the last moment in the list of twenty-seven new judges the President nominated October 15, 1949; her appointment was to the Federal Circuit Court. I would like to clear up the record. I had sent the names of four women to the DNC chairman Bill Boyle and to Attorney General Howard McGrath to be recommended to the President for consideration when he made the new judicial nominations. I knew we would not be fortunate enough to have more than one woman included, but as I told them I thought law schools should be closing their doors to women, rather than opening them more widely, if not one woman was among the twenty-seven.

I found out on the afternoon of October 14 that the list to go to the Senate from the White House the next day did not include a single woman. I barely knew Mrs. Matthews, but she was the only candidate with an impeccable combination of professional and political endorsements. I abandoned my other three suggestions, all of whom

I knew fairly well and who I had been assured by trusted persons
were competent to be federal judges. I wrote a letter to the chairman
in which I said, among other things:

> I know there will be unfavorable reactions if not one woman is
> among the twenty-seven new judges nominated by President Truman.
> The feeling around the country among literate and less literate women
> is that the President is giving women a Fair Deal for the first time and
> there is rejoicing . . . but I hear often the criticism that most of the
> women's appointments are window dressing, not on the policy level
> . . . you and I know this is somewhat true, for only Federal Com-
> munications Commissioner Frieda Hennock, Civil Service Commis-
> sioner Frances Perkins and War Claims Commissioner Georgia Lusk
> are on the policy-making level.
>
> Burnita Shelton Matthews, who is fifty-five years old, has lived in
> the District of Columbia since 1918. She was the only woman en-
> dorsed by the D.C. Bar Association for the U.S. Court of Appeals. I
> am not asking that she be given one of these judgeships for I know
> they are gone but couldn't she be given one of the others? She is from
> Mississippi and is endorsed by Senators Eastland, Stennis, Myers,
> Kefauver, Kerr, Kilgore, McMahon, Sparkman, George, Anderson
> and Pepper, all of whom have written to the President and to the At-
> torney General concerning her. Many women's organizations have
> endorsed her. She is not the Matthews whose appointment to the Fair
> Employment Practice Board by the Civil Service Commission was
> protested because of her discrimination against Negroes, that is An-
> nabel Matthews. . . . I know you can swing it if you decide it is wise
> politically. Please, please, please!

To Howard I said among other things, "I could not sleep tonight if
I felt that I had not done everything I could to have at least one
woman among the twenty-seven," and I sent him a copy of my letter
to Bill. Both these letters were sent special delivery to their homes.

To the President I sent copies of both letters along with the following:

> Is the woman never satisfied? I wouldn't blame you if you asked
> yourself that question upon receiving a letter from me begging that
> one woman be included in the twenty-seven new judges whom you
> will nominate soon, considering that you just have nominated the first
> woman Ambassador [Eugenie Anderson of Minnesota] that this coun-

try ever has had. But, as I explained to Bill Boyle and Howard McGrath in the letters I have written to them and copies of which are enclosed, I do feel that there will be a bad reaction to the naming of so many new judges and not one woman among them.

To write that I was happy when Don called me around noon the next day to ask if I could bring Mrs. Matthews to the White House that afternoon is to express my emotion mildly. Hardly taking time to explain to her why we had to rush, I took her to the White House. Apparently the President was satisfied by his interview with her. Her name appeared on the list of the twenty-seven new judges that went to the Senate Judiciary Committee that afternoon.

After Mrs. Matthews was nominated and confirmed by the Senate, I sat next to a leading attorney in Washington at a dinner party. He told me the D.C. bar association probably never would endorse another woman for, said he, "we only endorsed Burnita Matthews so as not to be considered antifemale." Judge Alan Goldsborough, a venerated federal judge of Maryland, sent word to me several years later that he wanted me to know he was bitterly opposed to Judge Matthews' appointment because of her sex, but that she was a good judge and he felt her work in the Court was a credit to the legal profession.

Getting anyone appointed to high office is such a complicated and difficult procedure that few persons understand it. When a woman is involved, the appointment is even more complicated and difficult. For every post there are many names presented by state political leaders, Congressmen and interested organizations. The Cabinet member, who will make the recommendation to the President, the White House staff personnel and the chairman and vice chairman of the National Committee must make every effort to see that anyone accepted by the President as a nominee is able to convince the Senate committee empowered to turn down the nominee or present his or her name to the full Senate for confirmation, that he or she is well qualified for the post and politically acceptable to the political leaders of his or her state. Anyone who has not been concerned with this kind of patronage work finds it hard to understand why it is so hard for a woman to be named to a high-ranking post. Someone interested in her appointment has to work day and night, sometimes subtly and tactfully, sometimes in an aggressive way, and always with patience. This effort must be backed up by the knowledge that until the appointment has been confirmed by the Senate it may not materialize no matter how certain it seems along the way.

I felt ghoulish when I rushed to the White House a June morning in 1949 after I had read of the accidental death of the U.S. Treasurer, William A. Julian, to find out if the President would be willing to give consideration to a woman for this post. He said he would if the Secretary of the Treasury agreed and if I could produce someone qualified. The Treasurer's post always had been a sinecure, with no special experience or ability in finance necessary for eligibility—loyal and effective party work alone had been the criterion for choice. In the case of picking a woman, however, President Truman insisted upon having one who understood banking. I think he was correct. I was happy that one of the best national committeewomen—Georgia Neese Clark of Kansas—was a banker, albeit a very small town one. When Chairman McGrath and I presented her name to the President and Secretary of the Treasury John W. Snyder, they were delighted to appoint her. The President in his usual thoughtful way suggested I call to notify her of the prospective honor. I did so with pleasure. When I called her in Richland, I asked her if she were sitting down. When she said she wasn't, I said, "Well, sit down before I talk to you, for you are going to be shocked almost to death." And she was when I told her the President wanted her to be Treasurer of the United States. She was the first woman to serve in that post, which has been occupied by a woman ever since, but there never has been a banker in it since she left in 1953.

Oscar (Jack) Ewing of New York, a vice chairman of the DNC, and Paul E. Fitzpatrick, chairman of the New York State Democratic Committee, had been telling Frieda Hennock for months they would support her for the first Democratic vacancy on the Federal Communications Commission. I had consulted Paul Porter and Charles Denny, former chairmen of the FCC, about what sort of woman would be best suited to serve on this commission. They both agreed that she must be a top-notch attorney, preferably one with experience in a well-known Wall Street firm. They said Miss Hennock would fill the bill, so she and I lined up support for her. She called me one day in July, 1948, to say she had heard there was to be a vacancy soon, but Jack and Paul had assured her that there need be no haste in approaching the President about it. Jack was so busy with a case in New York that he could not come to Washington just then, and Paul was going on a fishing trip.

"Ridiculous," I said, "you come down here tomorrow and I will take you to see the President at the earliest moment I can get an appointment with him. There will be a line from here to Baltimore seeking that job as soon as it is definite that there is to be a vacancy. Our only chance is to be there first." She came; we went to the White House the next morning and before long her name had been sent to the Senate.

There were three nasty incidents connected with President Truman's appointment of women that are almost unbelievable. Undoubtedly there have been many such incidents from the first time a woman was appointed to high office. There always have been men whose objection to women serving in high posts was so ingrained they would do anything to keep a woman from an office in which they could "do business" better with one of their own sex. While women are so busy performing their duties, they do not recognize the dirty infighting that can go on when an unscrupulous man decides to try to get rid of a high-principled, efficient woman. I trust there is always someone powerful enough in every administration to fight for women in high office.

Marion J. Harron of California was appointed in 1936 by FDR to the U.S. Board of Tax Appeals, which became the Tax Court in 1942. She was ending her twelve-year term in 1948 and anticipated no trouble in being reappointed because she had a splendid record. When I spoke to President Truman about her, he told me it would be impossible for Treasury Secretary John W. Snyder to recommend her reappointment because of certain charges made against her. He said if I could prove these charges to be untrue he would be happy to reappoint her. He knew her record as a tax judge was excellent. I talked to John to find out what the charges were. From what he said, I suspected they stemmed from some of her fellow judges. When I told her this, she was shocked and inclined to think I was wrong, but after some investigation she was forced to agree that my suspicions were right. When John Snyder became aware of the truth, he recommended her reappointment to the President, who sent it to the Senate for confirmation.

In the hearings held before Senator Walter George's Finance Committee, spokesmen for the American Bar Association testified against Marion Harron's reappointment by saying that in a poll of lawyers in the ABA's tax section, 104 voted against her reappointment and only 57 were for it. Some said she lacked judicial temperament. There were unprovable charges of an ethical and moral nature. Everyone who knew Marion was certain that they were fabrications that would have been laughable if they had not been so serious. Many lawyers testified in her favor. Finally Senator George, who was against her before the hearings started, was forced to report that despite the complaint about her temperament, the record showed her to be a competent and impartial judge. Her reappointment was confirmed. Judge Harron retired from the court when her second term expired, but was called back the next year and served until 1970. Still deserving of the tribute paid her in 1940 by a group of woman educators who named her one of the ten most outstanding young American women of that year, along with such notables as Helen Hayes, Alice Marble and Clare Boothe Luce. She died of cancer in 1972.

The second nasty incident involving male chauvinists' attempts to keep a woman from a high post in government occurred when President Truman named Dr. Kathryn McHale of Indiana to be one of three members of the newly established Subversive Activities Control Board. The two men named were confirmed quickly, but the Judiciary Committee, headed by Senator Pat McCarran of Nevada, did not even make plans for a hearing on Dr. McHale's appointment. The White House inquired time and time again as to what accounted for the delay. At length Senator McCarran revealed that Dr. McHale would not be confirmed without public hearings and that, if they were held, information would be brought out that she was a lesbian. Senator McCarran advised the President to withdraw her name. President Truman was horrified that Senator McCarran would make such a charge against a woman of Dr. McHale's reputation and prominence.

Dr. McHale, who was unmarried, had been a member of the faculty at Goucher College for fifteen years; she also had taught at Columbia University, the University of Minnesota and Carleton College. From 1929 to 1950 (the year she was appointed by President Truman) she had been executive director of the American Association of University Women. She held B.S., M.A. and Ph.D. degrees from Columbia University in the fields of education, psychology and philosophy as well as many honorary degrees. She belonged to numerous organizations and societies in the field of education and was a member of the board of trustees of Purdue University.

Saying he would not withdraw the name unless Dr. McHale wished him to do so, the President asked me to talk to her about the situation. It was a very hard thing for me to do—remember, this was 1950—and a dreadful decision to ask a woman to make. If she asked the President to withdraw her name it might appear she was guilty, even though she merely did not wish to have her name dragged through the dirt of Senator McCarran's proposed hearing. I went to see Dr. McHale, who was serving before her appointment had been confirmed, and bluntly told her of the Senator's statement to the President and the need for her to make a decision regarding the President's future action. "Does the President wish to withdraw my name?" she asked.

"No, he does not unless you want him to do so," I assured her, "he will stand by you, for he is that sort of man. Do you want to take time to make a decision?"

"No," Dr. McHale replied emphatically, "I can make the decision now. If the President is willing to stand by me, I will not ask that my name be withdrawn. I will fight such a vicious lie with all the strength that I have. You can assure our President that it is a lie." I relayed her decision to the President and that was the last we heard of a public hearing. Senator McCarran's Judiciary Committee recommended that she be confirmed by the Senate, which was done. She served until she died in 1956.

When President Truman nominated Frieda Hennock for a judgeship, she had given up a very large income as a Wall Street attorney to serve on the Federal Communications Commission and was doing a spectacular job for the public. Without her watchful eye and constant reminder to her fellow commissioners that the airways belonged to the public and not the networks, channels for noncommercial broadcasting (now public broadcasting) never would have been set aside. I strongly advised her against seeking a judgeship, however, because I knew she had had a love affair with a prominent married judge in New York. I was sure Senator McCarran would use the affair in public hearings before the Judiciary Committee. My prediction proved to be correct. Frieda's name was not sent by the committee with approval to the full Senate. A similar indiscretion in a man would have gone unnoticed but never in a woman.

Thank God the double standard of morals is being destroyed by the women's liberation. Feminists are on the right track in demanding equality of opportunity, equal pay for equal work, and the abolition of sex discrimination in all business and career fields. I consider myself to have been a liberated female all my life. I've always been willing to fight for equality when necessary for myself and other women but I've never wanted to give up my femininity and the privileges being a woman has given me in my personal life. I have expected none in professional life, neither in the newspaper nor the political worlds. I do not believe any man with whom I have dealt has ever pulled his punches because I was a woman. President Truman stressed to reporters on several occasions that he treated me exactly as he would a man. He also gave me what men always have considered the ultimate compliment to a female: that I operated like a man. This was all I ever asked from the men with whom I worked in politics or journalism. But I always have wanted to be treated as a woman in private life.

In talking to Donald Dawson about Merle Miller's book based on interviews with President Truman after he had returned to Independence, I remarked that I loved the book because it brought back so many wonderful memories of the many conversations I had had with the President. "But, of course, he never used four-letter or swear words in my presence," I said, and was surprised when Don said, "Neither did he in mine nor in that of any of the other White House assistants. He had too much respect for the Presidency to use such language in the Presidential office."

Listening to Merle Miller talking with David Susskind on television one night, I was amused to hear him say President Truman was afraid of women. President Truman was afraid of nobody, woman or man. He just was not a baby-kissing politician nor the sort who kisses and hugs women as easily as if he were shaking their hands. I never will forget the time a woman grabbed him and tried to kiss him when he returned to Washington three days after his historic victory at the polls in 1948. There was quite a large picture on the front page of the now defunct *Times Herald* showing the President with a big smile, bending backward, a fur-coated, sharp-faced woman bending toward him, and me in the background. The caption read: "This unidentified woman is shown as she boarded the Presidential train at Union Station today in an unsuccessful attempt to bestow a kiss on President Truman."

Adlai Stevenson wasn't as successful in avoiding the kiss of an unknown feminine admirer in 1952 when one of the women who had boarded the train some place in Ohio threw her arms around him and gave him a big smack. I was standing next to him, so I pulled and he pushed and we started her on her way out of the observation car.

Chapter 21

Clark M. Clifford, the distinguished Washington lawyer who was President Truman's first counsel, and I had occasion to work together closely until he left the White House to go into private practice. I always found him most cooperative, just as I did his successor, Charles S. Murphy. They both have served as advisers to every Democratic President and Presidential candidate since the Truman Administration, and Clark was President Johnson's Secretary of Defense after Robert McNamara resigned.

When I wrote Clark that I finally had started writing my memoirs he replied in a letter that I cherish, for he is a knowledgeable, experienced politician as well as a top-notch attorney: "You were the most effective woman in politics I ever knew. Your understanding of the political process and the importance of it to our democratic form of government was superb. In addition, you were one of my favorite public speakers. You have the rare quality of being able to stick to the subject and engage in a logical progression of thought. Your devotion to President Truman and your unflagging support for his cause in those dark days of 1947 and 1948 were indefatigable. I have always felt that you played a very important part in President Truman's spectacular victory in 1948." As a public speaker with neither training nor natural aptitude, which never was evident during the years I was often asked to speak as society editor and then women's editor of the Chicago *Tribune,* I think I managed fairly well. I tried never to speak over fifteen or twenty minutes and I always managed to seem to be speaking without notes, even if I were reading the speech.

One speech I worked hard over was prepared for a big Jefferson-Jackson dinner in Boston. Vice President Barkley was to be the principal speaker, and I had been asked to talk for five minutes. As I was dressing for the dinner, which I expected to enjoy, there was a knock at my door. The State chairman asked if I could expand my speech to thirty minutes. The Veep was detained in Washington on Senate business. I agreed to expand my speech to fifteen minutes. During the cocktail party, I stayed in my suite and wrote a new speech. At the dinner, all the famous sons of Massachusetts were introduced "for a few remarks." There were so many of them and their "few remarks" all became such lengthy speeches that when I was introduced as the principal speaker at a quarter to twelve I arose and said, "Fellow Democrats: I have enjoyed hearing from all your great leaders and now I am sure the only words you want to hear from me are good night." And I sat down.

The next morning when I entered my office in Washington my secretary said, "The President called you himself and wants you to telephone him as soon as you come in." When I reached him, he said Secretary of Labor Maurice Tobin, who had attended the dinner, had called the President early that morning to tell him about my speech and how it brought the house down.

I received another direct call from President Truman on the day he returned to Washington from Independence after he was elected in 1948. All of us at the committee were among the huge crowd that welcomed him at the Union Station. Driving down to the station in a chauffeur-driven limousine with Gladys Tillett and Mary Salisbury, I took it for granted we would continue to the White House in the same car. When we tried to find it, we discovered it had been commandeered by General Harry Vaughan and some friends of his. I remonstrated with him and claimed my car. He refused to give it to us and was exceedingly rude to me. If Milton Kronheim had not come along and offered us a ride in his Jeep, we might have had a hard time getting away from the station.

I was so angry I refused to go into the White House. Seeing Don Dawson as Gladys and Mary were getting out of the Jeep, I explained to him why I was too angry to join a festive throng. When the telephone rang at home later that afternoon, I said to my mother, "Please answer it and no matter who it is, I do not want to talk." But when she said in an awed voice, "India, it is the President himself," I relented and took the receiver. That dear man apologized for his military aide and old friend by saying, "India, you must forgive Harry. He is so bumbling sometimes that it irritates me greatly. The Boss and I both missed you today. We are very cross with Harry for being rude to you, for nobody deserves better treatment from us than you."

Very soon after the Republican victory in 1952, I began receiving telephone calls from friends in the media to tell me that Senator Joe McCarthy, then at the height of his power, was bragging whenever he was "in his cups" that the first person they were going to get rid of was India Edwards' husband. This did not turn out to be so easy. The Senator and his henchmen, Roy Cohn and David Schine, were not able to find any legitimate reason for getting rid of this particular civil servant. The Senator's influence was such, however, that he led the top men in the information division to understand that it would be better for them if they managed to force Herbert to resign, which they tried to do. For several months Herbert withstood their petty tricks, planned to humiliate him. When it came near time to appear before the Appropriations Committees, Herbert decided his presence would be a detriment to the program he had developed and also could jeopardize the loyal staff he had recruited. On April 15, 1953, he submitted his resignation.

A New York Times survey, done by foreign correspondents, cited the motion picture program as one of the most effective of all the government's overseas information activities. I think it was despicable for the Republican administration to punish my husband for my political activity. He was with the government when we were married, so my political work was not responsible for the post he held.

People who think all politicians are dishonest have asked me, "How could you bring yourself to support men you felt were unworthy?" The answer is that I never supported anyone I thought

would make a poor public servant. I may have campaigned for a local candidate about whom I knew nothing but what local leaders told
me. That candidate might not have been upright and capable, but it
was not for me to judge him if he had been selected by his fellow
Democrats.

As I remember, there were only two men running for national
office that I could not bring myself to urge audiences to elect:
"Jumping Joe" Ferguson, who was running against Robert A. Taft
for the latter's seat in the U.S. Senate, and George P. Mahoney, the
perennial Democratic Maryland candidate who ran unsuccessfully
for Statewide office twelve times. I was not active in the campaign in
which Spiro Agnew was Mahoney's opponent for the gubernatorial
race in 1968, but I fear I would not have spoken for Mahoney at that
time. Hindsight tells me that he would have been a better and more
honest governor than Agnew.

Many Democrats who could not stomach Mahoney supported Agnew in his bid for governor and they all ate crow. So did all the
Democrats I know who supported Nixon in his bid for reelection in
1972 with the exception of John Connally. Mahoney, who was a
contractor, spent his own money freely in campaigns but was unpopular with my kind of Democrat because he never faced up to issues and always based his appeal to voters on narrow, emotional
prejudice. He was constantly splitting the Democratic Party and en-
suring Republican victories, since the Democrats feared that if he
gained control of the statehouse he would use patronage jobs to
bring men of his own ilk into power. At the time Agnew ran against
Mahoney with the support of many Democrats, he was thought to be
a progressive Republican, because he had just come out in favor of
Nelson Rockefeller for President.

Joe Ferguson was not corrupt, but I agreed with those Ohio Democratic Party leaders who did not want or expect him to defeat Taft.
Taft was a statesman respected by Democrats as well as Republicans.

A letter I cherish arrived after the 1952 election from a young
woman who was a great admirer of Governor Stevenson and had
worked hard as a volunteer in his race for governor in 1948. When
he was our Presidential candidate four years later, he suggested that

I add her to my professional staff, which I was happy to do. I did need another courier. Early in 1952 I had appointed to my staff a small group of women experienced in political organization and speaking who could go, at the request of a local organization or club, to help in whatever way was needed. They put on campaign schools, they helped plan registration and "get out the vote" drives, they spoke from platforms or at tea parties in homes, and they appeared on radio and television shows. In short, they did whatever local leaders would have expected me to do if I had been there instead of the courier. The local organization paid their expenses except for their very moderate salaries from the National Committee. They did not replace volunteers, for we could always use volunteers, but it never seemed possible to have enough experienced speakers to meet the demand. A few Cabinet officers' wives always were willing to help and so was the pretty and attractive young Southerner, Dorothy Vredenburgh (later Bush) whom Bob Hannegan had selected as secretary of the committee in 1944 and who still is serving in that capacity.

Ironically, a community might have one of the best speakers in the country right there, or in a neighboring county, but they always wanted someone from Washington, preferably a person with a title. Since I could not be in more than one place at a time, I hit upon the idea of couriers. Judging from the way in which Democrats all over the country used them, I would say the couriers were a success. Venice Spraggs, who had left the staff of the Chicago *Defender* to be my special assistant in 1948, became the first courier in 1952. The others who served in this small group were Jane Schmidt of Illinois, Elsie Jensen of California, Kathryn Folger of North Carolina and Carolyn Moore of Kentucky.

Jane Schmidt returned to her husband and home in Rockford, Illinois, soon after that sad day in November when we knew Governor Stevenson was not to become President Stevenson. Here are excerpts from Jane's letter;

> I do want to tell you what a marvelous job you have been doing for the committee. Before coming to work for the committee I had a healthy respect for your work, based largely upon your reputation. But it was not until I joined the staff that I began to realize the tremen-

dous responsibilities which you carry, the ingenuity and energy you apply to them and above all the constant obstacles placed in your way. The latter would have killed a lesser person long ago, I'm sure!

As an idealistic one-worlder I frankly had a few qualms about the ethical and intellectual compromises which I suspected might be involved in full-time political work. Believing as I did in the Democratic Party and the stakes of a Democratic victory, I joined the staff, willing to swallow some of those scruples, and one of the things that made me happiest in working with the committee was that none of these fears materialized. I can honestly say that never once did you, or any part of the Women's Division, compromise with principle, and every time a decision along this line came up it seemed to me at least that you made the "right" choice—refusing to use questionable material, etc. Consequently I shall continue to raise my voice that politics need not be dirty—at least, not on India Edwards' staff.

I was once surprised and disgusted by several women—wives or widows of Army officers—who came to see me at my office in the Ring Building in Washington to offer to campaign against General Eisenhower because, as one of them said, "He is far from being Sir Galahad. He is the bull of the Army." Needless to say, we had no intention of allowing anyone to speak as a Democrat and campaign against Ike on such personal grounds.

I found it almost impossible to be polite to these would-be or cast-off mistresses of attractive Army officers. We had no need for their services.

Of all the campaigns in which I ever participated during my many years of working with and for Democrats, only one was filled with constant obstacles. In 1952 the chairman of the National Committee, Stephen A. Mitchell, seemed to look upon me and Wilson W. Wyatt, whom Stevenson had put in charge of his headquarters in Springfield, as the adversaries rather than the Republicans. I will not try to describe the ways in which Mitchell hampered Wyatt, since I really do not know about them, but I could fill pages with Mitchell's actions to keep me from being effective. I blame myself somewhat for his hostility. I should have been perceptive enough to have recognized him as the male supremacist he was the day he came to our headquarters, but I was so accustomed to dealing with men on an equal basis that it never occurred to me that I should become a feminine clinging-vine type and look to him for all wisdom. It did not take long, though, to discover that he knew nothing of politics. He obviously had no use for a woman politician who, in President Truman's words, "knows most of the answers" and "can be dealt with exactly as though she were a man." I did not realize until quite far along in the campaign that Steve was constantly putting obstacles in my way.

At the first and only meeting of the entire campaign committee in Springfield an action occurred that was utterly unlike anything I ever had encountered before. As we sat around a large table in a room at the Executive Mansion, a man from the Springfield staff that had been planning the campaign gave us a rundown on the plans. In turn each member of the committee expressed his views on the plans. The only woman in the group, I was the only one who expressed any doubts about the wisdom of the plans. I said it sounded as if we were running a cross between Franklin Roosevelt and Harry Truman while in reality we had a unique man, someone entirely different from either of them, great as they were, and that we did not seem to be taking advantage of his peculiar talents and charm.

"Governor," I addressed him as he sat at the head of the table, "how will you like whistle-stopping and speaking to crowds from the back platform of a train?" "Not at all," our candidate laughingly responded.

I went on, "And they will know it, too." I criticized the plan for spending the small amount of money we expected to have for television. I said that Adlai would enchant his listeners if he spoke to them tête-à-tête instead of from a platform and that it would be smarter to have a lot of short television spots instead of thirty-minute speeches at rallies. Most of the men agreed and Senator Clinton P. Anderson of New Mexico, vice chairman of the Senate Campaign Committee, said something to the effect that as usual India had hit the nail on the head.

At this Steve Mitchell, who had been about the first to speak and who was across the table from me, rose and announced, "I have to return to Washington," and out he went. All of us from Washington had come West together that morning and were planning to return East together the next day. I was greatly surprised at Steve's action. I followed him into the hall and asked what had happened to make him change his mind. "I'm not needed when you're here," he sullenly replied. He need not have worried. Although some thought my criticism of the plans warranted consideration, there were no changes made.

That Steve Mitchell's interference was not just my imagination was confirmed by a young committee employee who visited my office to say au revoir shortly after the election. He shut my door and said he wanted to apologize for all the trouble he had caused me. "Why, John," I exclaimed, "what troubles did you cause me? I never was aware of any." He confessed that part of the job the chairman had given him was to put every hurdle possible in my way. I stupidly had not realized this young man had anything to do with the obstacles I had encountered during the weeks of September and October and I was very much touched by his apparent sincerity.

Frank McKinney, who preceded Mitchell, was not the best chairman the DNC ever had (Truman thought he was great and was loyal to him through thick and thin), but he was far superior to Mitchell as a politician. It may not be nice or ladylike to write ill of the dead (both Mitchell and McKinney are gone) but if I am to "pull no punches," as my revered President Truman advised, I must state that both men had character faults that harmed our party. McKinney was an experienced politician from Indiana, a banker, financier and philanthropist. I always thought Matt Connelly persuaded Truman to name McKinney, who boasted that he "would serve without pay or any kind of compensation." Bill Boyle had been receiving $35,000 per year plus traveling expenses. In the opinion of the long-time comptroller, the budget officer and I, McKinney's expenses were amounting to much more than if he had been drawing even a larger salary than Boyle's. We all tried unsuccessfully to remonstrate with him about the expenses he and his three appointed assistant chairmen were spending. As I stressed on many occasions to many people on the committee, every penny was given for the purpose of electing Democrats and we owed it to the contributors to spend their money wisely.

In the middle of the Stevenson campaign I found I had a free morning in Columbus, Ohio. I had flown there the day before with the candidate for one of those ghastly big rallies. He was busy editing the manuscript of his speech until the moment before he was introduced. Half the time while he was giving it, the large audience in the armory and the larger one on television saw only his bald head as he bent, as usual, to read the lower half of each page. Also, as usual, he had not quite finished the speech when the television lights went off.

I was staying in Columbus for the night because I was flying on alone to Indianapolis the next afternoon to give a speech at a big labor meeting that night. None of the Columbus people knew I was not accompanying Stevenson and his party to the airport, so I was able to have the next morning alone, a blessed privilege during a campaign. Worrying about the way the campaign was going, that night I slept little. Early the next morning I called the manager's office to borrow a typewriter for a few hours. A machine and plenty of stationery came up with my breakfast, and I started writing to Adlai as I drank coffee and ate an English muffin. I poured out my heart and soul and told him how fearful I was that he was making so little headway that he could not possibly win. I outlined what I thought could be done to change the picture and ended with the words ". . . if only you had made Wilson chairman of the committee and kept Mitchell in Springfield where he would not be dealing with so many people. Perhaps it is not too late to make the switch."

I fully intended to mail the letter from Columbus, but when I read it I decided I'd better wait and reread it in Indianapolis. It was such a scathing indictment of Mitchell as chairman of the DNC. When I reached Indianapolis, I had no chance to reread the letter until midnight. I was tired, discouraged and asked myself, "How can I do this to Adlai when it perhaps is too late to make changes?" After reading the letter, I tore it into small pieces and threw it in the wastebasket. I wish I had mailed it in Columbus: it might not have done any good but it would have given me a clearer conscience.

Steve Mitchell was honest, there is no doubt about that, but that was almost his only virtue as far as I could see. One day in the spring of 1953, we were having an Executive Committee meeting and, as usual, he and I were sitting side by side at the table. Early in the meeting, when I was called upon to make a few remarks about women's activities, I had said, "I am going to start my informal remarks on coordinating women's activities with a preview of a statement we have ready for release after this session. The release reads, and I quote: 'The Executive Committee of the DNC unanimously passed a resolution this morning endorsing the new policy of integration of women into full party operations at all levels and recommending that henceforth national committeemen and women have equal authority and that there be two co-chairmen, a woman and a man, of every committee instead of a man chairman and a woman vice chairman, as is the custom now. The national committeemen and women and the co-chairmen of the committee will share policy-making, fund-raising and all other activities in which they engage as they perform their work of leading the Democratic Party to victory. The Executive Committee also recommended that the Democratic Party Manual be amended or rewritten to conform with this new policy of integration.' End quote. April Fool!''

Everyone laughed but Steve. He looked more sulky than ever. Having realized just before I began speaking that it was April 1, I thought I would add a little levity to the occasion, but it was not appreciated at all by the chairman.

After the 1952 election, I said to Steve that I realized how much he disliked me and how much he must wish I would leave, but that I was not going to resign until I was ready to do so. "But," I said, "I would be interested to know why you have disliked me so much from the very first day you came to the committee."

He gave me his reasons without even having to stop to think of them. "Well, first of all, it was apparent from the start that you wanted my job." I laughed at that and told him the President had offered me the job of chairman in October of 1951. Steve, smiling dubiously, evidently did not believe this and went on, "Then why did you send your three emissaries to me as soon as I was elected to suggest that you were capable of running the campaign?"

"I don't know what you are talking about," I said. "Please explain." He only continued to smile enigmatically.

"And you always get a better press than I."

"Yes, and I always will," I replied.

Then came the number one reason, I am sure. "You acted as if you were meeting me for the first time when I came to the committee."

I responded, "I'm sorry if I offended you by that. You know, I've met a lot of people in the last eight or ten years and I am afraid I don't remember them all. Did I meet you some place in Illinois?"

"No, you sat next to me at dinner once at Harriet and Jim Crowley's house and I thought I made quite an impression on you." That almost floored me, for the Crowleys had been away from Washington for several years and I must have met Steve at dinner in the late forties. It was unfortunate that I had not remembered him.

I did not find out the explanation for his statement about my three emissaries until some time in the sixties, when, as a former official of the DNC, I was attending a committee meeting. Calvin Rawlings, committeeman for Utah, said he thought that he himself, David Lawrence—committeeman for Pennsylvania and at that time either mayor of Pittsburgh or governor of Pennsylvania—and Jack Arvey—committeeman for Illinois—had done me a great disservice back in 1952 when they told the newly elected Chairman Mitchell that he was very lucky to have "such a damn smart politician" as his vice chairman. Steve had told the three men, the most powerful on the National Committee, that he hoped he could consult them by telephone whenever he needed help. They then said he had someone in a nearby office who could be of enormous help to him. Cal said Steve asked, "Do you mean India Edwards?" Whereupon they sung my praises until they realized Steve was not reacting very well to what they were saying. Cal finished by saying, "You see, India, we did not know him then."

Steve outwitted me when he decided to integrate the Women's Division into the committee. Theoretically it was a good idea, but I knew that actually it meant women would no longer be planning and activating the committee's educational work. It meant that the women would not have their own budget and not be able to make decisions about anything of importance. The magazine, *The Democratic Digest,* which had been edited by the Women's Division since 1922 and was of great value to both men and women of the party, was to be turned over to Clayton Fritchey and Philip Stern, who thought they could make it into a sort of political *New Yorker.* All the leaders of the Women's Division had fought valiantly to keep our magazine. Clayton and Phil were not the first p.r. men who wanted to edit and publish the magazine, but none had been successful until Steve proposed that women be integrated into the committee. If I had not been so tired and discouraged, I would have put up a fight, but it was just after a national defeat when I knew that we really were flat broke. Clayton and Phil were certain they could make the magazine pay for itself. Since they defied the Corrupt Practices Act by selling it for thirty-five cents an issue they took a chance!

I cannot remember how many hundreds of thousands of dollars their new style *Democratic Digest* cost the committee before it had to be buried, but I know our little magazine, which cost between thirty and forty thousand a year, was worth many times that to Democrats over the country. I always have blamed myself for not having fought to keep the *Digest* as it was, a sort of house organ for working Democrats.

After witnessing what Steve Mitchell did at a Southern regional conference, I decided I could not wait until we had sold "Arden," our lovely old place in Maryland, in order to leave the committee. Meeting in Birmingham, the representatives of the Southern States were to make reports on how they were reorganizing for 1954. The officers of the Committee sat at a table facing the small audience, most of them National Committee members or state chairmen and vice chairmen. Not one word about reorganization was spoken. Every speaker took the time allotted to him to damn ex-President Truman and to blame him for Stevenson's defeat. The chairman sat there smiling, while I was growing angrier by the minute. Finally, a Mississippian representing Governor Hugh White hit a new low in excoriating the former President and then began on Howard McGrath, who had been chairman in 1948. He told in thick, honeyed tones of how he and a group of other Southerners had sent word to Chairman McGrath in 1948 that they would like him to come to their suite in the Bellevue-Stratford Hotel. McGrath had sent back word that if they wanted to see him they would be welcome to come to his suite in the same hotel. The speaker continued, "But, of course we would not go to his suite, so we had to walk out of the convention the next day. I have a feeling we now have a chairman who would not act like McGrath. He would come to us and try to keep our party united."

"Yes, indeed," Steve replied; "you now have a chairman who would crawl on his bare knees across broken glass to reach you." My stomach turned and I really was afraid I was going to be ill right then and there. I should have left the room but instead I stood up and turned my chair so that I sat with my back towards Steve for the rest of the meeting, a childish gesture indeed.

The Mississippi Democrats loyal to Truman had sponsored a Democratic forum in '49 at which I spoke in spite of threats made to try to keep me away from Jackson. Tillie Clark (Mrs. John), the national committeewoman in Mississippi, was not in sympathy with the Dixiecrats. She urged me to come to the forum. The Dixiecrats on the State Committee said that no one who attended the forum would be allowed to vote in party matters in the future. The governor delivered a thirty-minute broadcast over a statewide hookup the night before the forum to decree that attendance would be noted down by monitors and would be considered a sin against Mississippi Democracy. Nevertheless five hundred Mississippians heard Assistant Attorney General Lamar Caudle, CIO-PAC Assistant Director Tilford Dudley and me preach the Fair Deal gospel, while photographers snapped pictures, not of the speakers, but of the audience. Poor Lamar, who was slow-talking and to me seemed slow-witted, was accused of tax fixing, was fired by Truman, and eventually landed in prison.

During the 1952 campaign in many places I visited with candidate Stevenson, it became apparent that most of his listeners did not realize that every President picks his own Cabinet. Even some well-educated people are surprisingly ignorant about the way in which their government operates. Secretary of State Dean Acheson was not popular. Very often after Stevenson spoke, someone would say to me, "But if I vote for him we still will have Acheson as Secretary of State, and I do not like him." I happened to think Dean Acheson was a great Secretary of State and often spoke enthusiastically about him and his achievements. To those who did not want to vote for Stevenson because they disliked Acheson, I would say that I liked Acheson but that the entire Cabinet resigns when a new President is inaugurated, so that there was little likelihood that Acheson would be Stevenson's Secretary of State.

The late Kay Armstrong, one of my writers, was the wife of Park Armstrong, a Department of State officer who worked very closely with Acheson. Once when the Armstrongs were at our house I told Park I wished Acheson would in some way make it clear in a speech that he naturally would resign along with the rest of the Truman Cabinet when and if Stevenson were elected. I explained to Park why I said this. Park promised to talk it over with Adrian (Butch) Fisher, one of the Secretary's assistants. Perhaps they could arrange for the Secretary to make such a statement in a speech. I never indicated, and I feel certain neither Park nor Butch intimated, that I had suggested that the Secretary announce he would not continue in public office in the event of a Democratic victory.

In his book *Present at the Creation,* Acheson wrote: "Mrs. India Edwards of the Democratic National Committee sent me a message through one of my colleagues, who should have had more sense than to deliver it. It was a request to announce that in the event of Democratic victory I would not continue in public office. This message I thought best to treat with intelligent neglect." In some way he had gotten my suggestion entirely wrong, which I regretted more for Truman's sake than Acheson's. I truly was astounded that a man of Acheson's mentality and cultivation could have remembered such a trivial thing and mentioned it in a book with such a grandiloquent title as *Present at the Creation.*

In the picture section of Secretary Acheson's book on his years in the State Department there is a picture of him wearing a typical Western hat with a six-shooter in his belt. His jacket is unfastened in a nontypical Acheson manner and he is not wearing a waistcoat. The caption is "A change of pace. In Dallas for a foreign policy speech, June 1950." Well do I remember that occasion, for it was I who persuaded the Secretary to go to Dallas to speak before the World Affairs Council. William H. Kittrell, a good Democrat if ever there was one, and an outstanding citizen of Dallas, called me on the telephone in the late spring of 1950 to ask if I knew Secretary Acheson well enough to call him and tell him how much it would mean to the Texas Democrats and the Truman Administration if the Secretary would accept the invitation of the group, which he had refused. I agreed to use what influence I had to try to get the Secretary to reconsider. When I explained to him how much Bill Kittrell said it would mean to have the Secretary of State talk about our foreign policy in Dallas, he said he would go on the date proposed. I always had good relations with Dean Acheson, whom I admired greatly, so that his unpleasant comment about me in his book was a great shock.

Bill reported that the luncheon meeting was one of the most successful in the history of the council. The perfectly groomed Secretary spoke interestingly and with authority and elicited polite applause. When the luncheon chairman asked for questions, there was none until Mr. Acheson left the head table platform and walked down to the floor. Wearing the hat that had been presented to him and unbuttoning his coat to show the revolver he had also been given, this Eastern gentleman bellowed, "Do you mean to say none of you so-and-sos wants to ask me a question?" It brought down the house. They kept the Secretary there answering questions until 5 o'clock.

In Phoenix, Arizona, on June 26, 1952, I was quoted in a speech as saying, "Secretary of State Acheson will go down in history as a great man. His fight is doubly hard for it takes such perseverance. The terrific responsibility he has is frustrating because the job cannot be done in a hurry. It takes patience. It takes thoughtfulness—it takes a long time."

That Phoenix speech was made at a dinner sponsored by the Maricopa County Democratic Women's Club. It occasioned more publicity, perhaps, than any other speech I ever made. The speech really did not cause the publicity. The interest was created by the press conference the Phoenix Press Club sprung on me about five minutes after I had arrived at the Westward Ho Hotel from the airport. The telephone rang just as I entered the suite reserved for me. Stephen W. Langmade, Democratic national committeeman, was calling to ask if I would be willing to come to the press club in the hotel for a conference right then. I said I would be guided by his advice. If he thought it a good idea, I was perfectly willing to hold an impromptu conference. I had not been at the club more than a few minutes when Robert A. Vogeler, recently released from imprisonment by the communist Hungarian government through the efforts of the Department of State, entered the room and came right to the platform. The press later claimed they did not know he was returning to the club, where he had held a press conference just before mine, but I must say it looked to me as if it were prearranged. The club president introduced Vogeler to me and said it would be interesting to hear both our views about the way in which the department had handled his case.

Vogeler, who was a vice president of ITT, was touring the country, campaigning for Robert A. Taft's nomination as the Republican candidate for President and damning Acheson everywhere he went. He claimed that his wife, acting as an individual, had obtained prom-

ises from the European countries to suspend trade relations with
Hungary "providing the U.S. State Department would lead the
way." Vogeler said, "Dean Acheson refused." He then went on to
claim that it was his wife who had obtained his release, not our Department of State.

I had not prepared myself for a debate of this sort and did not
know all the details of the Vogeler case, but I was sure no European
country would discuss the suspension of trade relations with an individual instead of with our State Department. I demanded that Vogeler give me a list of the countries. He claimed his wife had held
conversations with the Netherlands, Belgium, Switzerland, France
and the United Kingdom. I said I would get in touch with the department that night and see that a true report concerning Vogeler's release was given to the Phoenix press before I left the city the next
morning. Vogeler had been arrested by the Hungarian government
on charges of espionage and sentenced to serve seventeen months in
a communist prison. His release was gained only after strong pro-
tests and concessions from the U.S. government.

The fifteen-minute debate was hot and furious. I did not feel I covered myself with glory due to my ignorance of Vogeler's case, but
my anger was directed at the Phoenix press for finagling me into a
debate after inviting me to hold a press conference. The front page
space the *Arizona Republic* gave the debate the next morning and
the strong Republican bias shown by the members of the press the
afternoon before convinced me the entire affair was arranged. Stephen Langmade did not show very good judgment in advising me to
hold a press conference under such circumstances. He certainly
knew the mood of the local press. He also knew Vogeler was holding a press conference in the club just before I was asked to appear.

That night I called Howland H. Sargeant, then an Assistant Secretary of State, and told him about the claims Vogeler had made. I obtained clearance to lower the boom on Vogeler's untruthful statements at a press conference the next morning. Both the *Arizona
Republic* and the Phoenix *Gazette* covered it extensively. The conference was held in the press club, which the *Republic* found ironic
but which seemed suitable to me. Secretary Sargeant told me there
was nothing in the Vogeler file to support or refute Vogeler's claim.
Therefore, there never had been any conversation between Mrs.

Vogeler and the State Department, as Vogeler had claimed. The United Kingdom had suspended trade negotiations with Hungary—but that was because a British subject was picked up and imprisoned along with Vogeler. In June, 1952, that national still was in prison in Hungary.

Chapter 22

Herbert and I spent about ten months—from November, 1953, until September of the next year—in southern California. Still being vice chairman of the DNC, I was quite active in politics. Herb was uncertain whether he wanted to work in the documentary field of motion pictures in Hollywood or to return to New York, where he had lived and worked until he joined the State Department in early 1942. He decided he would prefer New York. We drove there, spent a few months in a hotel and finally took an attractive, fairly large apartment in an old brownstone on East Tenth Street. Part of the rent was paid by the New School for Social Research, for which I went to work as a development consultant to the board.

The New School was the first center for adult advanced education in the country. Under Alvin Johnson's advanced methods of teaching economics, sociology and politics, the school had become a center for the intelligentsia in the city. Like all schools, it was not self-supporting. The members of the board, some few noted scholars but most of them wealthy men and women who were passionately interested in the school, had to raise funds enough to cover each year's deficit. My job was to advise them, but since I never had been a fund-raiser, I was not very successful. I did, however, assist in planning some programs that may have been steps toward fund-raising. I persuaded some well-known journalists, including Eleanor Roosevelt, to lecture. I did not feel that I could ask the New School for a leave to accept Paul Butler's invitation to serve on the Democratic platform panel, but when asked a few months later to be co-chairman of the Harriman for President Committee, I said good-bye to the New School without a pang of regret.

Herbert now did free-lance work for several nonprofit organizations, including a survey of American public opinion about the United Nations. When he was asked to return to Washington at the end of 1956 to manage J.F. Begg's real estate office, I was very happy that he chose to accept the offer. We moved to an apartment in northwest Washington.

Paul Butler, then chairman of the DNC, had called me in New York in the early part of 1956 to ask if I could be part of a team that was to travel over the country and hold advance platform hearings, something that had not been done before. He said the others on the team would be a Representative and a Senator from Congress and Clayton Fritchey, who was a deputy chairman with the committee. Paul said it would require a knowledge of the issues and of good press relations to make a success of the undertaking. He, Clayton and Sam Brightman, who handled public relations for the committee, thought I could do the job. I shuddered to think of what Katie Louchheim would do if I were a member of the team but at that time, as I noted before, I did not feel that I could leave the New School.

In spite of the fact that Katie Louchheim and I disagreed about women's role in politics, I was angry for her sake at the way the Kennedys later treated her when Jack got the nomination in Los Angeles. She, as an officer of the DNC, had to be neutral officially during the time before the convention but she always was for Jack Kennedy. She supposed she would be kept on as director of women's activities and vice chairman of the DNC, for both Jack and Bobby Kennedy must have known that she was a JFK supporter.

I expected that Katie would not be replaced, all things considered. I told Walter Jenkins and Bobby Baker, LBJ's two closest aides, when they spoke to me the day it became known that "our man" had been asked by JFK to be the Vice Presidential candidate. "LBJ wants to know if you would consider going back to the committee if

Kennedy wants his advice about replacing Katie," they told me before the two men were to meet, apparently to talk over plans for the committee meeting the next morning.

"I would not," I replied, "and how silly can you be, thinking Kennedy would have me? What makes any of you think he will replace Katie? I feel sure he will keep her." The two said he was not going to keep her and asked whom would I recommend for LBJ to suggest if I did not want to have a rerun at the committee. "Well," I said without hesitation, "Margaret Price, the national committeewoman for Michigan, would be my first choice, and Geri Joseph, the National committeewoman from Minnesota, my second."

In her book *By the Political Sea,* Katie told of the brusque way in which Bobby had called her at midnight before the morning the national Committee would meet to elect its officers, chosen, of course by the candidate. "We're going to give your job to Margaret Price," he said. He expressed no apology, no explanation, no regret for this ruthless act against a woman who had every right to assume that she would continue to direct the activities of Democractic women.

Late that night in the cocktail lounge of the Biltmore Hotel, I was sitting with a group when Bobby Baker entered. As he passed the table where I was sitting, he stopped, attracted my attention, and made a circle with a thumb and forefinger. He smiled happily, so I took it to mean that JFK had asked for LBJ's advice and that Margaret Price would be tapped for vice chairman. I was pleased for Margaret and the committee, since I was sure she would do a splendid job for all Democrats, at the same time, I was upset about Katie. I hate seeing anyone, woman or man, treated so ruthlessly in politics. She was helpless, though, and accepted it with good grace, but she always seemed to hold it against Margaret rather than the Kennedys. Margaret was as surprised as Katie when Bobby Kennedy called her, although their surprised feelings were accompanied by very different emotions.

After moving back to Washington at the end of 1956, I wanted and needed a paying job. When a former New Yorker informed me that former Senator James Mead was retiring from the post of director of the Washington office of the New York State Department of Commerce and suggested that it would be an ideal post for me, I called President Truman asking if he thought it was the sort of work I could do. The President immediately wrote Governor Averell Harriman of

New York a letter suggesting that I would make a good replacement for Jim Mead. "India is a rough-and-tumble politician who knows a great many of the answers and did a wonderful job for the Democratic National Committee," the President wrote. When I read the copy of the letter that he sent me, I wondered whether Averell would consider that sentence the high recommendation that I knew the President meant it to be. Apparently the governor did, for he called me at once and asked me to accept the post.

I used to have to go to Albany about once a month for meetings with the commerce commissioner Ed Dickinson and with the governor and some of his top aides. Marie Harriman often invited me to stay at the Executive Mansion and on several occasions our mutual friend Jean Poletti, wife of former Lieutenant Governor Charles Poletti, was there at the same time. When we roomed together, a favorite topic of conversation was how to get Marie to do something about persuading Averell to wear a hearing aid. He was getting more and more hard of hearing. He seemed totally unaware of this disability. Meetings with him were something of a yelling match. Each of his aides who wanted the governor's attention would have to raise his voice. Finally I said, "Jean, you are his old friend, while I just work for the governor, so you must speak to Marie and tell her how embarrassing it is at times when the governor gives answers with no relevance to the questions." Jean agreed to do so, but she told me later that Marie pooh-poohed the idea, saying Averell had no trouble hearing her. He undoubtedly was so familiar with her voice that he did hear her, but he certainly did not hear many other people plainly.

Later he began wearing a hearing aid. They say at the Department of State that when he was ambassador-at-large in the Kennedy and Johnson administrations, he never hesitated to turn it off when the conversation became tiresome. This wonderful person, who has served in more important posts than any one else as the representative of Presidents Roosevelt, Truman, Kennedy, Johnson, and as adviser to Presidential candidate Jimmy Carter, was elected governor of New York in 1954. He would have been reelected four years later if any sort of effective campaign had been waged. I was appalled at the attitude of his Cabinet and the men running his reelection campaign. Not one of them seemed to think that there was any chance of Nelson Rockefeller's defeating Averell Harriman. Averell himself indicated that he was not in the least worried about Rockefeller. One of his closest assistants said to me when I voiced my anxiety, that "the Guv" would win by four hundred thousand. This same man had brought his prediction down to 250,000 about a month later, at which time I said that it was my opinion that our man would lose by at least 250,000. He lost by 573,034.

Upon my return to Washington from meeting with this group of men who seemed utterly devoid of any practical political ideas about how to publicize the splendid Harriman record, I sent the governor a letter which I rewrote at least a dozen times. I had to tone it down more and more each time. I started out being so frank that I was afraid he would be furious and not even read it. He might say to himself, "Who is this woman who thinks she can advise me more wisely than George Backer, Carmine DeSapio and the men who have worked with me for the last four years to build this record as a progressive but financially conservative governor of New York?" As far as I could tell, no plans at all had been made to publicize his record for every voter in the State to know it. The governor and his aides all seemed to have forgotten what had happened at the late-August State convention in Buffalo which the press had publicized as a crushing defeat of Harriman by DeSapio. Actually it was just that, so it had to harm Harriman with the reform Democrats, headed by Eleanor Roosevelt and Senator Herbert Lehman, and with independent voters, many of whom were members of the Liberal Party.

There was no valid reason why this should have happened. If the governor had a choice for the U.S. Senate candidate, he should have made it known before Carmine DeSapio—the Tammany Hall leader and Harriman's Secretary of State—announced his support for Frank S. Hogan, district attorney in New York County (Manhattan). The governor acted as if he were neutral and made several would-be candidates think he might support them at the convention. Actually, Harriman hoped to persuade Mayor Robert F. Wagner of New York City to run for the Senate, in spite of the fact that Bob Wagner had promised the voters that he would serve his full term as mayor when he was reelected in 1957.

In Buffalo, Harriman became convinced that Wagner would not be a candidate for the Senate. The governor then attempted to get Thomas K. Finletter, former Secretary of the Air Force, chosen. When that failed, he indicated he would support Thomas E. Murray, a former member of the Atomic Energy Commission. DeSapio stood firm in his support of Hogan and won. Governor Harriman, never a perspicacious politician in spite of the fact that he was a great diplomat, allowed himself to be pushed into a tug-of-war with DeSapio. The backroom bickering at endless closed meetings with leaders of the New York City boroughs in Harriman's and Wagner's suites in the Statler Hotel drew so many press to the police-patrolled corridor that it was almost impossible to push through the crowd. It was a ridiculous performance for experienced politicians. Finally Ted Tannenwald, treasurer of the Harriman for President group in 1956 and a great admirer of Harriman, asked if I would call President Truman and get him to tell Harriman that he was digging his political grave if he allowed DeSapio to win. Hogan was a good man, but by that time Harriman could not allow DeSapio's candidate to win the nomination.

Since I agreed wholeheartedly with Ted that Harriman must win, I called President Truman and started to tell him about the situation. He interrupted me, saying, "India, Averell has called me about this and I have told him what I think. He *must* be the boss. He cannot allow DeSapio to choose the candidate. But I cannot give him any more advice. He knows what I think and I hope he will make the right decision."

With this background, it seemed inconceivable to me that the governor and his campaign managers could be confident enough to conduct a listless and lackluster campaign. On September 21 I wrote:

> You will not welcome my thoughts since they are not exactly optimistic but—my loyalty and devotion make it imperative that I tell you some things that I think you should know and that you may not hear otherwise. . . . Your truly fine record as governor and the strong Democratic trend over the country should make it certain that you will be re-elected but to count on this would be displaying a fatal case of Deweyitis. . . . Frankly, I am worried because of the feeling prevalent among some Democrats and Independents since the State Convention. . . . I was upset to read in the New York *Times* last week that the opening of the Harriman headquarters in New York City was attended by about 100, most of them men. In the same issue there was a report that the opening of the Rockefeller headquarters in New York City attracted about 800, most of them women. This is a disturbing sign. . . . Most alarming to me is the fact that the Democratic National Committee has received many sustaining-member

pledge cards with no pledges but with such sentiments as "Not one cent for Tammany Hall," "Don't address me as Fellow Democrat for I'm not voting Democratic this year," etc. These come from New York voters who last year made annual pledges to the Committee. . . . More than just the determination not to vote Democratic is indicated when a person bothers to write such a sentiment. That type person talks and tries to influence others. I hope I am crying wolf when there is no wolf but I'd rather cry it unnecessarily than too late. Your great popularity and that of Marie; your splendid record as Governor, the general pro-Democratic trend and imaginative and dramatic use of television and radio will press home to the voters the advances your Administration has made in so many fields (particularly for the aging, the consumer and the small businessman). These can offset the unpleasant feeling engendered by the Buffalo convention. . . . Believe me to be among your most devoted and loyal supporters and well-wishers, albeit a worried one right now.

The day he received this letter Governor Harriman called me and said that if I felt so strongly about the way in which his campaign was being handled why didn't I come to New York and do something about it? I said I would if I were allowed to do anything constructive but that it would be ridiculous for me to be there with nothing to do, which is what I feared would happen. He assured me I would be given a free hand to do whatever I thought best, so to New York City I went. George Backer, in charge of the campaign headquarters, greeted me with a pitying smile and said, "Averell tells me you are very pessimistic about his reelection. Don't worry; he will be reelected with a huge majority. I think the best way in which you can help is to accompany Marie to meetings and make speeches. She is very popular and is invited to many luncheons and teas but she will not speak. You can do that."

So for seven or eight weeks I spoke mainly to women and men who were Democrats and already had decided to vote for Harriman. Except for keeping Marie company, I was useless. I thoroughly enjoyed the hours with her, for she was an enchanting conversationalist with a ripe sense of humor. I made suggestions to the men about many activities I thought would be helpful, but they made it plain to me that my suggestions were of no value. If I remember correctly I did take a busload of women on a tour of upstate places which seldom saw a Democratic politician. I have campaigned so many times in New York State that I forget whether I toured in a bus in 1958. I must have spoken in practically every city, town and village in the State, just as I have in all the forty-eight States that made up the United States during most of the years I was active in politics. I worked in Washington with Jack Burns, the Hawaiian delegate when the islands became the fiftieth State but I never have visited it or the forty-ninth, Alaska.

Hogan was not successful in defeating the Republican candidate for the Senate, Representative Kenneth B. Keating, who went on from the Senate to become a federal judge and then ambassador to India.

Resigning of course when Harriman was defeated, I agreed to stay on until the new governor had had a chance to name my successor to the position I held for New York State in Washington. I was pleased and touched to receive from Averell not only a formal letter of appreciation for my services in his administration but also another one which said, "I am sad to think you are leaving the State service. You have done such a splendid job, and I am most grateful to you. The Washington office had never amounted to much until you took hold. You represented the State of New York effectively both with the [Eisenhower] Administration and with the Congress. The information you supplied was of constant value."

A representative of the newly elected Governor Rockefeller came to Washington to ask me to stay on in the post. I told him it would be impossible for me to work for a Republican governor, even though nine-tenths of my work was nonpolitical. That other one-tenth was of a partisan political nature. I could not see myself, an ardent Democrat and former vice chairman of the National Committee, working for a Republican with strong Presidential ambitions.

Some of my friends felt I was making a wrong decision not to stay with the New York Department of Commerce as long as I could. Since I definitely was a political appointee, I felt it only fair that I resign when my governor was defeated, although I had worked as if I were a civil servant. Nelson Rockefeller undoubtedly would have been a pleasant, perhaps even inspiring, State chief executive under whom to work. Having occupied my position in the Democratic Party, I did not see how I could serve him, although his attitude during the campaign often made me admire him. For instance, he was reported to have said at a rally, "It was tragic to see a great governor rolled under by the party machine."

Averell took several months to forget his displeasure with me for not agreeing with his optimistic male supporters who had felt that he had nothing to fear from Rockefeller. I never felt sorrier for any two people than I did for the Harrimans on election night. His defeat was a stunning surprise to them. Many months later, when I was asking Averell for a contribution to Girls Clubs of America, he said it would have been better if he had listened to me in the campaign instead of the men around him, but who knows? Perhaps a changed campaign on his part would not have made any difference in the outcome. Also, his service as an adviser in international affairs to Presidents Kennedy and Johnson was of more value to the nation than anything he could have done in a second term as governor. His preference for the title governor rather than ambassador indicates, however, how much he valued the post he held as the chief executive of New York State. He is a man I am proud to have served.

I am glad Bob Wagner did not run for the Senate in 1958. He probably would not have won. In spite of the fact that he would have liked to sit in that august body of which his father Robert F. Wagner, Sr., was an outstanding member for many years, I think Bob's record as mayor of New York City is one of which he can be proud. I worked with the late Adele Levy in his campaign for the Senate in 1956, doing for Susan Wagner much the same sort of thing I did for Marie Harriman in '58.

When I think of the difference between what DeSapio and George Backer, the two leading strategists of the campaign to win the 1956 Presidential nomination for Harriman, told me in New York City and what I discovered to be true when I got to Chicago, I have to wonder whether these two men really were so naive that they believed they had as many promised delegates as they told me. They claimed delegates in States in which I could not find one who was not promised to Adlai Stevenson, who had been campaigning for the '56 nomination almost since the day he was defeated in '52. After I had been in Chicago a week, I knew Stevenson had the nomination in his pocket. I am sure Loyd Benefield, co-chairman with me, knew the same, but we and the others for Harriman continued to do our best to round up delegates for him. We hoped for a miracle of some sort, since we truly believed that Harriman would make a stronger candidate than Adlai that year. If he did not succeed in defeating the well-entrenched and popular President Eisenhower, Harriman would be a splendid titular head of our party.

Neither Backer, who had been publisher of the New York *Post*, nor DeSapio had any experience in national politics. I know De-Sapio realized this, because he said to me one evening in Chicago during the convention, "India, I am out of my depth on this national scene." George Backer, however, considered himself a skillful politician, but I never saw anything to justify his confidence either in '56 or '58. He was an attractive man, a quality that might have helped him as a candidate but did not help Averell Harriman.

I have enough letters from President Truman to paper a small room, since he was punctilious about acknowledging even a memorandum. His sense of humor came through in many of them. For instance on June 13, 1953, from his office in the Federal Reserve Bank building in Kansas City, he wrote, "I appreciated very much your good letter of the ninth. I know you will have an enjoyable time in Rome. I suppose you will be the guest of Mrs. Luce while you are there. You have no doubt heard about her interview with the Holy Father. I hope you will be careful and not upset any protocol when you call on His Holiness. He is one fine man. I am going to see your good friend Steve Mitchell this morning and discuss political matters. Mrs. Truman wants to be remembered to you and so does Rose."

President Truman was well aware of how I felt about Steve Mitchell and also Clare Boothe Luce and I know he felt the same as I did about them. I was the guest of Ambassador Luce for a very brief time while I was in Rome in 1953, and it was an amusing experience. I was traveling with a small group, including a former Republican Congressman from Indiana who made arrangements for the ambassador to receive our group. I tried to get out of going to the embassy, but the man who had arranged for our being received seemed to feel that it would be rude for me not to be in the group, so I went. When he presented us to Mrs. Luce, she greeted me as if we were old and good friends (I had met her casually at a couple of social affairs during the time she was in the Congress). When we were seated, she ignored the former Congressman and all the others and talked directly to me. She explained at length that she had not taken any part in the recent Italian elections, something for which she had been criticized in some of our press. President Eisenhower and Secretary of State Dulles said the criticism was unwarranted.

Why the lady was so anxious to impress me with her innocence I could not imagine. I, in no way, could come to her defense with anyone of importance. I was just an officer of the National Committee of the defeated political party, a nobody in the hierarchy of political Washington. There is no one so "out" as a member of the party that just has been defeated. I always believed the story that became known shortly after my visit to Rome about the ambassador's having been poisoned by arsenic in the flaking paint of her embassy bedroom. She looked like a very ill woman the afternoon she received us. She was and is a woman of great and delicate beauty, but she belied that description that afternoon.

When our group was received by Pope Pius XII, I again was singled out for special attention, because the official who presented us to His Holiness said that I was a good friend and supporter of President Truman. The Pope told me how much he admired the President and sent messages to him. When I saw the President after I returned from that trip abroad, I gave him not only the Pope's messages, but a Napoleonic gold coin I had bought in an antique shop in Paris. The coin was thin but in it had been inserted a tiny pair of scissors and a nail file. When I gave it to the President he noted the date on the coin and then spent ten or twelve minutes telling me about the Napoleonic wars and why that particular coin was minted. I was astonished time and time again by the knowledge the President had of so many things in addition to governmental and political matters.

On August 20, 1949, I had a letter from the President in reply to one of mine, suggesting that the term Dixiecrat was too good a name for those who deserted him the year before. He wrote:

> I am in agreement with you that Dixiecrat is too good a name for them and your suggestion of "Demicans" is all right but it sounds as if it might be a high sounding grade appellation for some scientific program which, of course, the Dixiecrats are not. It has been suggested Republicrats might do. You might leave the "r" out and make it "Republicats" but I don't think there is anything that will very well de-

scribe them except that good old fashioned word "bolter" and that is
the classification that will stay in my book. Just between you and me
and the gatepost I don't care what you call them—you can make it as
unprintable as you choose.

Bess Truman always wrote to me in her strong, characterful handwriting until arthritis made it necessary for her to dictate her letters.
Lady Bird always dictated letters to me, but usually added a heart-
warming sentence or two with a pen. Lyndon's letters were as
friendly as he always was with me. Typical of them is one dated August 31, 1965, in which he wrote, "Your letter cheered me and made
me grateful for loyal friends. No one has labored more persistently
than you in all those programs that are right and just for this Nation.
And no one has persevered with more warmth and fidelity as a
friend, counselor and worker-in-the-vineyard. Lady Bird and I send
you our undiminished affection."

Since I was not in LBJ's close circle, I was surprised and touched
at what a young woman who interviewed me in connection with her
Ph.D. dissertation at the LBJ school of Public Affairs at the University of Texas said to me when she told me why she had asked to see
me. "All I know is that in going through his papers I kept coming
across memoranda with the words 'check this with India Edwards'
written on them by him."

When Herbert accompanied me to Independence, Mrs. Truman
joined the President in showing us through the Truman Library. He
told us then that we should be greatly honored to have "the Boss"
as a guide, since she had not shown anyone else through the building. We were properly honored that day. The President did something we found greatly amusing.

After we had seen all the exhibits and the reproduction of his
office, he opened a door and asked us to follow him. We found ourselves on the stage of an auditorium filled with people. The President welcomed them and told them briefly what he hoped the library
would be and mean to all who visited it. When he concluded, a man
in the front row jumped up and said, "Mr. President, we are members of the Golden Age Club and we want you to become an honorary member of our club." Almost before he finished the President
snapped, "I will not. I am much too young!" The little man looked

flustered as well as disappointed, but President Truman cheerfully said, "Come again. Perhaps then I'll be old enough to join your club."

The letter, signed "Harry Truman" which I value the most was written on January 27, 1951, and sent to me while I was vacationing:

> Mrs. Truman handed me your letter from Vero Beach, Florida, and I read it with a lot of interest. I hope you will be patient and meet the situation as it develops because I am very anxious for you to be happy and stay in the position which you have so efficiently filled. Things are never just exactly like we want them and that is particularly the case with regard to the office which I hold. However, I do more than appreciate the efforts of those who are trying to help me do a good job and I've always considered you as one of them.

I have no copy of the letter I had written to Mrs. Truman, but I think I had said I was so tired of having to combat the deputy chairmen whom chairman Bill Boyle had appointed, that I was going to resign as vice chairman. Bill and I worked together amicably just as Howard McGrath and I had done. Neither of them always saw eye-to-eye with me, but I always felt I could rely on their word. They never seemed to carry a grudge if I won an argument or disagreement. Howard's deputy chairmen, Gael Sullivan and Creekmore Fath, were good working partners, but Bill made unfortunate choices, particularly because illness kept him away from the committee so much. I refused to have anything to do with them. Consequently my office was where almost all of the "visiting firemen" came—all but those seeking to make deals that would not bear scrutiny.

The American Christian Palestine Committee was an organization of Christian ministers and lay leaders interested in conditions in the Middle East and particularly in the experiment in Jewish nationhood in Israel. I was invited to join a travel party sponsored by this group in 1953. Our party was composed of Dr. Carl Herman Voss—a Unitarian minister and an officer of the ACPC—three newspaper people, the editor of a national church publication, two housewives, two free-lance writers, two professor-administrators from Howard University in Washington, D.C., the director of foreign language instruction in the New York City public schools, a Republican ex-

Congressman from South Bend, Indiana, and his wife, five ministers, two of their wives, and the foster mother of a third. The last
was the first woman to be elected an elder of the Presbyterian
Church and one of the most wonderful persons I ever have met.

Miss Sarah Dickson was in her seventies. When we started the
trip, I wondered how she would hold up. Looking at the schedule, I
saw that we were to be busy day and night. She looked as if even a
wisp of a wind could blow her away. She held up as well as anyone
and always was in a good humor. Twice on the two-week trip, hotel
space was limited, so I had to have a roommate. Once it was Miss
Sarah; the other time it was Alyce Walker, woman's editor of the
Birmingham *News*. From both I learned lessons which I hope have
stood me in good stead. Miss Sarah displayed none of the eccentricities of behavior that most old people (including myself I am sure)
have that make it difficult to room with them. Alyce Walker had had
polio, I think, in her youth, and only had one hand and arm that were
of use, but she managed as well with them as I did with two of each.

The night Alyce and I roomed together in Istanbul was the most
adventuresome of the trip. We had arrived at the airport from
Athens shortly before midnight and were driven in a two-decker bus
into the city. At that time the airport bus had no lights. The darkness
through which we raced was to me impenetrable, but the driver must
have had eyes like a cat's, for we killed no one as far as I know. By
the time we arrived at the Pera Palace Hotel, an old one which in its
heyday must have been the last word in luxury, Alyce and I were in
a state of near hysteria and the bellboy—what a way to describe the
brigand who led us through large public rooms and long corridors,
all carpeted in Turkish rugs which never had been desecrated by a
vacuum cleaner for clouds of dust arose with our every step—to a
large room in which there was an enormous brass bed. There were
no windows, only French doors at one end, so since the air was
stuffy, I indicated to our "brigand" that we would like the doors
opened. He did this, shaking his head but volunteering no reason
why. He did try to do business with us by offering more Turkish
money for our American dollars than we could get anywhere else, so
he said. We declined to deal with him, for which we were sorry later. If we had, perhaps he would have been more cooperative in helping us rid the room of the dozens of pigeons that flew in soon after
the doors were opened. The "brigand" had departed by that time.

Having peered out the doors and seen that we had a balcony overlooking a river, Alyce and I were ready for bed. We had decided we
would have our breakfast on the balcony the next morning. We did
not, for it had never been cleaned and the pigeons had roosted there
for years.

When the pigeons first started joining us, we tried to shoo them
out by ourselves. Seeing that we were waging a losing battle, I called
the desk and asked if someone would come up and help us get them
out of the room. The brigand came, but he was so slow it was a couple of hours before we could shut the doors and try to get a few
hours of sleep. Several times he said in a disgusted tone of voice,
"Why do the madames not like the pigeons? They are harmless."

Adlai Stevenson and I had exchanged itineraries before he had
left on a world tour on which he was writing articles for *Look* magazine. According to the schedule he had given me, he should have
been in Istanbul and left about a week before I arrived, but he had
been delayed, as I learned the morning after my arrival. American
consul general Robert B. Macatee awakened me early with a telephone call to invite me to a garden party he was giving that afternoon for Governor Stevenson and his small party. I said I would
love to accept, but that I was traveling with a group, most of them
great admirers of the governor, and I would feel funny about leaving
them. Unless I could bring them with me, I would have to decline
the invitation. He asked how many there were in the group. When I
said about twenty, he replied without hesitation, "Of course, bring
them all." I suppose diplomats have to become accustomed to such
things, although I really felt as if I were imposing on his hospitality.
But even the ex-Republican Congressman and his wife were thrilled
to meet Adlai.

At the garden party the consul general asked me to join Adlai and
a small group he was taking out on the Bosphorus the next day. I did
not feel it incumbent on me to include my traveling companions in
that invitation. When I returned to the hotel that night after dinner
and a night club, the brigand was at the service desk. He said, in his
quite good English, "Almost-President Stevenson, he telephoned
you and invite you to breakfast at 10 o'clock tomorrow morning at
the Park Place Hotel. I accept." It was evident that my standing had
risen considerably in the brigand's estimation and that there could
be no question as to whether I would accept the "Almost-Presi-

dent's'' invitation. Adlai had invited me himself at the garden party, but he asked me to come at 11 o'clock.

The next morning about a quarter to eleven I called the desk to order a cab. The brigand was on duty. Almost before I had finished speaking, he roared, "Madame Edwards, you were to be at Almost-President Stevenson's hotel at 10. You are very late." He paid no attention to my explanation that the hour had been changed and continued to scold me even as he put me in the cab. Everywhere I went—int he Middle East, in Paris and London—I found great admiration for Stevenson and astonishment that a military hero could have been preferred by the majority of Americans as their Chief Executive.

At breakfast that morning Adlai had asked me what I thought of Steve Mitchell and I had given him an expurgated opinion but made it clear that I thought he was not a good chairman. Adlai agreed that his appointment had been a mistake and said there would have to be a change made after he returned home. Then Adlai described himself as a philosopher, not a politician, a statement with which I agreed then, although I had felt differently the year before.

Chapter 23

Believing that he would be the most able President the voters could elect, I supported Lyndon Baines Johnson, Majority Leader of the Senate, for the Presidential nomination in 1960. Speaker of the House Sam Rayburn asked me to serve as co-chairman with Oscar Chapman of the Citizens for Johnson Committee. Before I accepted, I had a long talk with Johnson. I was struck by the feeling that it was Rayburn who wanted the Presidential nomination for the senior Senator from Texas more than Johnson himself. Nothing Johnson did during the preconvention campaign changed my opinion about this. In fact, I became convinced that Johnson did not expect the nomination.

I talked this over with Drew Pearson, who started out by saying I was crazy. After a while he came around to my way of thinking, but I am glad to say he never wrote about it. As far as I know, Drew and I were the only ones who suspected that Johnson was a halfhearted candidate, although I would think some of his closest associates must have guessed that it was only his deep affection for Mr. Sam that made him willing to go through the motions of being a candidate.

Oscar Chapman and I were supposed to round up citizen support for LBJ, but it was not easy to find men and women who knew Johnson outside the District of Columbia and Texas. The Majority Leader of the Congress was a big man in the nation's Capitol, but to the average citizen he was almost an unknown. Those who did know something about him thought he was a dyed-in-the-wool conservative. To attempt to change this image of him in a few weeks was impossible. If he had been willing to leave Washington and to make a real campaign for delegates, the result might have been different, but he did absolutely nothing to further his own candidacy. I went into some of the Northeastern and Middle Western states to talk to groups of delegates. I never felt I accomplished anything except for getting Lyndon Johnson's name in newspapers and on television and radio while I was in each city. In some places the delegates laughed when I said Johnson would make a President in the tradition of FDR and Harry Truman. When I was trying to speak about Johnson's voting record in Minnesota, there was so much laughter that one man got to his feet and said that they knew me well enough to know I would not support a man who was not liberal and they owed me the courtesy of at least listening to me. I doubt that LBJ or Sam Rayburn ever realized what an impossibility it was to expect LBJ to win the nomination in Los Angeles. I certainly did not, after I had visited New York, Michigan, Minnesota, Pennsylvania and a few other states.

Johnson wrote what I consider the truth about his own ambition when he quoted from a letter he had written to a constituent in the *Vantage Point:* "Frankly, I am not a candidate for the Presidency or for any job other than the one I now hold. I have gone further in life than anyone, except my mother, ever thought I would, and I have found my present responsibilities so very heavy that I could not possibly think of reaching for more." He then recalled his serious heart attack in 1955, from which he had recovered completely by 1960, and he concluded that paragraph with the words "I frankly did not think anyone from the South would be nominated, much less elected, in my lifetime."

Johnson did not want to be the Vice Presidential candidate. Some of his closest advisers agreed with him. Mr. Sam was against it until JFK talked to him. Then Mr. Sam urged LBJ to accept the Vice

Presidential candidacy. Oscar Chapman and I met one of LBJ's advisers, James Rowe, as we were approaching the LBJ floor in the Biltmore Hotel elevator. Jim told us about JFK's offer to LBJ. When both Oscar and I said, "LBJ *must* accept it," Jim said for us to hurry to tell him that ourselves. He was afraid LBJ would turn it down. By the time Oscar and I got around to the suite, LBJ was conferring privately. We told Walter Jenkins and Bobby Baker what we thought, with the request that they pass it on to LBJ for what it was worth (perhaps nothing). I said "Tell LBJ he never could look himself in the face when he shaved if he acted like a child who lost and then picked up his marbles and went home."

During the afternoon, word was circulated that all of us in the Johnson camp were to assemble at a certain time in the living room of the LBJ suite to hear his decision. When LBJ told us that he had decided to accept the Vice Presidential nomination, I was surprised at Lady Bird's reaction. She put her hands up to her face and said, "No, No." I was standing next to her in the rear of the room.

I believed then and still do that LBJ did not want the nomination. Only after becoming convinced by Jack Kennedy that he was needed to carry the South did the older man agree to go on the ticket. He was one of the proudest persons I have ever known. It must have galled him terribly to have taken a second place, which he knew from his many years in Congress was filled with humiliations and downright neglect. He knew the opinion of his fellow Texan, Jack Garner, FDR's first Vice President, who once observed that "the Vice Presidency wasn't worth a bucket of warm spit." Lyndon Johnson pocketed his pride when he ran with JFK. I for one feel certain that Kennedy would not have won without Johnson. None of the Johnson family wanted LBJ to accept the Vice Presidency, but being the kind of American and Democrat he was, LBJ had no choice but to accept the candidacy that JFK offered him.

Though LBJ never said a word to me, Oscar Chapman told me he was furious when I stated in a press conference in Los Angeles about a week before the convention opened that Jack Kennedy had Addison's disease, a chronic insufficiency of hormone production from the outer layer, or cortex, of the adrenal glands. I also said he took cortisone regularly to control the disease.

John Connally, executive director of the Johnson campaign, and I had discussed mentioning Kennedy's health if reporters brought up

Johnson's 1955 heart attack. I had volunteered to be the one to do it, since my career was nearing an end whereas John was a young man just starting up. If I had known then that he would become a Democrat for Nixon in 1972 and later a Republican, I am sure I would not have done anything to further his career.

I could not understand the immediate reactions of Bobby Kennedy and Pierre Salinger, JFK's chief press representative, to my statement. If they had not held a press conference to deny what I said, the revelation would have caused only a mild ripple and not stirred up the storm it did. Many doctors and laymen have written about JFK's health problems, and all have agreed that he had Addison's disease. Theodore C. Sorensen, JFK's alter ego during Senatorial and Presidential days, wrote in his book *Kennedy,* "Instead of the term Addison's disease, he [JFK] preferred to refer to the 'partial mild insufficiency' or 'malfunctioning' of the adrenal glands which had accompanied the malaria, water exposure, shock and stress he had undergone during his wartime ordeal."

Sorensen also wrote, "Two lieutenants of his chief rival for the nomination, Lyndon Johnson—Mrs. India Edwards and John Connally, later governor of Texas—chose to highlight a convention press conference with doubts about Kennedy's life expectancy based on the assertion that he had Addison's disease. Their subsequent explanation was that Kennedy's spirited defense of his youth and vigor on television that day [in reply to a Truman attack] had by implication cast doubt on the health of the other candidates, including heart patient Johnson. Johnson disowned the attack, and a subsequent explicit statement from Kennedy headquarters and a full exposition in the press put an end to all rumors and doubts."

Despite Mr. Sorensen's pat conclusion, there were rumors and doubts about JFK's health until the sad day when he was assassinated and they still abound.

Perhaps others, in addition to my friend Edmund G. (Pat) Brown, former governor of California, felt that I had made it sound as if Kennedy had syphilis. That certainly was not my intention. I had checked with several doctors who assured me that it was fairly common knowledge among their profession that Kennedy had Addison's disease which nearly killed him and necessitated his long convalescence after a back operation in the fall of 1954.

If I had it to do over again, I feel certain I would mention Kennedy's chronic ailment. I believe that the whole truth about the physical and mental health of every Presidential and Vice Presidential candidate should be made known to the public. It was tragic for George McGovern and Tom Eagleton and the Democratic Party when news of Eagleton's illnesses came out after he had been nominated for Vice President in 1972. It might have been even more tragic for the country if Eagleton ever had become President and could not pace himself in a crisis, as he said he had learned to do.

After the convention of 1960, I sent JFK a letter to his home. I wrote that, since he was the candidate, it might have been better if I had not mentioned his health and that he was showing a maturity I had not thought he had. Late in 1959 or early in 1960, David Lloyd, who had been one of President Truman's assistants, had come to me to say that Senator Kennedy wanted to know what he could do to get me on his team. I replied that nothing he ever had done as a Senator had made me think he was ready for the Presidency. I thought he was too immature and too much of a playboy to be our national leader. In light of my earlier judgment I stressed in my letter the new maturity I had observed to assure him of my 100 percent support of the Kennedy-Johnson ticket. I expected no reply nor did I receive one. When I was asked to be chairman of volunteers for the 1961 Inaugural Committee, I knew Jack was not angry with me. Bobby, however, never forgave me, and neither did some of Jack's "Irish Mafia."

Several months after JFK became President, I attended a meeting to plan a dinner to celebrate his birthday. When the President finished his brief remarks, the audience rose, applauded and remained standing to give JFK, his aides and the press a chance to rush away since it was apparent he was in a great hurry to depart.

As the President started to leave, I turned to Don and Dawson, who was on my left, made some casual remark, so I did not hear the rather peremptory "India," nor see the outstretched hand the President was extending to me over the vacant chairs in front of us. Herbert nudged me and said, "The President is trying to speak to you." Whereupon I turned and took Jack's outstretched hand.

He, in a characteristic way, pointed with his left forefinger at me and said, "India, I should have written you long ago to thank you for everything and to say I appreciated your letter and all you did in the campaign and for the Inaugural Committee. Keep up the good work.'' Rushing out, he ignored the many who wanted to shake his hand. His closest aides and many in the audience were astonished that he had singled me out as the only person, aside from the chairman, with whom to shake hands and speak a few words.

They thought, I suppose, that President Kennedy felt the same way Larry O'Brien did, when he told Helene Monberg that India Edwards was anathema around the White House as long as Jack Kennedy was in it. Helene had asked, "How can it be that a Commission on the status of women could be appointed and India Edwards, who has done more for women than any other living woman is not on the commission?" Helene, one of the hardest working and hardest hitting press women in Washington, has her own news service. I appreciated her asking why I was not on the commission and then telling me about it. Knowing full well how such things are handled, I was sure it was some of the "Irish Mafia" who put together the commission. Since there was no one at the DNC or in the White House who had any influence with them when it came to women's affairs, my being overlooked was understandable to me. How different from the days of President Truman's Administration, when the name of every woman proposed by anyone else for appointment by the President was submitted to me for an OK.

Incidentally, I never will forget the vehemence of a group of Democratic national committeewomen in describing a reception Jack and Jackie Kennedy gave for them before he received the nomination for President in 1960. All of the would-be candidates were wooing the members of the National Committee when they were attending a national conference that Katie Louchheim had planned. The most prized invitation was one from the young Kennedys to have cocktails at the Kennedy home in Georgetown. I, of course, no longer belonging to the committee was not invited, but I heard all about the affair in great detail from practically every committeewoman the next day. They all talked at once, so it was difficult for me to understand exactly what it was that they were so furious about. When dear old Maggie O'Riordan of Massachusetts said, "Indeed, it is not a custom of my State," I drew her aside and asked her to tell me what they were griping about. She was 100 percent for Kennedy but she said, "Well, the only solid refreshment that was served was a huge bowl of hard-boiled eggs on the dining table. Jack was warm and witty and wonderful and the drinks were good but—the only food was the eggs and a little salt. Can you imagine that?'' I suggested that it was a pre-Easter or post-Easter party, I forget which; that was all I could think of to account for such an unusual cocktail party ''dibby-dabby,'' as my husband calls cocktail party food.

Chapter 24

When I was asked to be chairman of the volunteer committee for the 1961 inaugural, I am not sure I would have accepted with such alacrity if I had known what a time-consuming job that was to be. I was told I could pick a co-chairman and we would have two paid assistants, both of whom already had been put on the inaugural staff. The co-chairman, Marjorie Lawson, a well-known black woman, was too busy with her law practice to spend much time at the inaugural headquarters. I knew one of the two staff persons because she had worked in various capacities for the National Committee, and I would not have chosen her, even though she was a hard worker. The other was a young, glamorous woman who had worked for a public relations firm before joining the Kennedy-Johnson campaign. These two women got along as well as two wild animals of different species would in a small cage. The older one spent long hours at the headquarters but ignored the system I kept trying to establish. Doing little work, the younger one came and went. We gathered over a thousand volunteers, whom we sent to the various subcommittees that needed them, so it was essential that we have an efficient method of keeping track of requests, assignments, etc. There was also need for a great deal of telephoning, since volunteers had to be called and told where and when they were to work. I developed what I thought would be an effective system, but it never had a trial until I persuaded my friend Ruth Blackshear to be volunteer executive director of the committee.

By that time the younger woman on the staff was gone for good, having charged some rather expensive items on the Garfinckel bill of a member of the Inaugural Committee. I had a long, serious talk with the young woman in which I said she seemed to be at a crossroads. "You are a bright young woman," I said, "and should go far if you stop this scummy behavior. But if you continue along this road, I hate to think of what the future holds for you." The last time I heard anything about her was when I read in the newspaper that she was employed by CREEP, the Committee to Re-Elect the President (Nixon), in 1972. Need more be written?

I was given two tickets for the inauguration and the parade by the National Committee with the information that buses to carry the National Committee members from the Capitol Plaza to the reviewing stands on Pennsylvania Avenue would be parked at a certain place and that box lunches would be provided on the buses. As a member of the Inaugural Committee I was given a walkie-talkie, but I never discovered what use I was to make of it. I suggested to Herbert that we not buy ball tickets, but when Lady Bird called me herself to invite us to sit with her and the Vice President in the President's box at the Armory, we decided we must accept this courtesy. A New York friend had invited us to the gala at the Armory on the night preceding the inauguration and we were invited to all the other receptions and parties planned for the festive few days. Since I was chairman of an inaugural committee, I was assigned a car and chauffeur (a young airman), which was a boon, indeed.

On the afternoon before inauguration day, I went to the beauty shop on Connecticut Avenue where Herbert and the chauffeur were to pick me up so that I could go home and change clothes for that afternoon's two receptions and the gala that evening. It started snowing while I was having my hair done. By the time I was finished the snow was so deep I knew Herbert would be late in picking me up. The snow was falling so heavily that traffic downtown was in a complete snarl. One inch of snow can completely demoralize traffic in Washington. On the afternoon of January 19, 1961, everything came to a standstill for hours.

I joined the ever-growing group of women awaiting their husbands or chauffeurs. Some few who had expected to use cabs were trying to "hitch" rides in every car that passed. Finally Herbert and my car arrived—about three hours late—so we forgot changes of clothes and the receptions and went directly to the Jefferson Hotel, where our New York friend was staying. We tried to dissuade her from attempting to go to the gala. Since she paid a hundred dollars a ticket, she wanted to go and to take her guests—us and another woman who, luckily, lived at the Jefferson. We grabbed a quick dinner at the hotel, forgoing an excellent dinner at the F Street Club. Then we began the long trek to the Armory, a trip that in ordinary circumstances would have taken at the most thirty minutes. It took us about four hours, so we saw only the last few acts of the gala entertainment. All the performers were in street clothes, since they did not dare leave the Armory after rehearsal to go to their hotels and change.

When we finally reached our home on Capitol Hill late that night, Herbert said he was getting a cold. He could not go to the inaugural ceremony the next morning, so I gave his ticket to my young airman and told him I would meet him there. Since we lived within walking distance of the Capitol, I was sure my feet would be the most dependable transportation for a short distance in that weather.

I was warmly dressed and carried a blanket. Regardless, I nearly froze to death during John Fitzgerald Kennedy's inspiring speech. I had fine seats in front of the platform, but unfortunately the television stand overshadowed us. The man beside me kept taking a flask of something—not cold black coffee—out of a pocket, and I kept wishing he would offer some to me. I had told the airman to meet me in the reviewing stand for the parade when the ceremony ended, so I made my way to the National Committee buses. There were a large number, which were all filled but unmoving. At length, there was not a single person left in the vast Plaza but still we sat. The drivers kept getting on and off with the doors open, so it was almost as cold in the buses as it was outside. Finally I asked our driver why we did not start. He said they had to wait for a dispatcher to give them the starting signal. In the distance I could see the floats being assembled for the parade, so I became the dispatcher. My seats for the parade were on the White House side of Pennsylvania Avenue next to the heated portion reserved for the President and his family, the Vice

President and his and a few VIPs. My airman had been there a long
time when I finally arrived.

That night was one of the most unpleasant of my life. Foolishly,
we went to a dinner party in Georgetown and then made a stop at a
dance in the Uline Arena for the service academies cadets who had
participated in the parade. Jiggs (F. Joseph) Donohue, chairman of
the Inaugural Parade Committee, had asked me if I could raise
enough money to pay for the music and the laying of a dance floor at
the old arena so that the cadets could be entertained that night,
something that never had been done before for the young men who
had come from the academies for previous inaugural parades. I persuaded two of Washington's most noted hostesses and philanthro-
pists, Mrs. Herbert May (Marjorie Meriwether Post Davies) and
Mrs. Morris Cafritz, to contribute the $5,000 Jiggs thought would be
needed. The Armed Services Hospitality Committee of the District
of Columbia, of which Jiggs was chairman and Gwen Cafritz a member, assumed the responsibility of providing partners for the cadets
(girls from boarding schools in and near the District). Jiggs made me
promise to look in on the dance on my way to the armory, but I
know he would not have blamed me if I had had the good sense to
break my promise. We had a dreadful time getting to the arena. And
I was to do nothing there but be introduced and wave to the young
men! The snow had turned to slush in many places. It was impossible to get near enough the entrance to avoid wading through slush so
deep that my slippers got wet in spite of galoshes. Many of the cadets were carrying their girls into the arena.

Later, when we entered the armory for the inaugural ball, Herbert
gave our tickets to an usher, who said, "You never will make the
Presidential box now. People have crowded into it who do not belong there and the Secret Service is wild. They are letting no one
near there. I advise you to stay in the VIP lounge where you will
leave your wraps and watch the ball on television. There is a bar and
a beautiful buffet there, so you can enjoy yourselves." We went to
the lounge to leave our wraps and then tried to get near the Presidential box in spite of the warning. It was right; I do not think a mouse
could have squeezed its way through the crowds outside. The box,
which should have accommodated about sixty, I should think, was
so jammed with bodies that I am surprised the Kennedys and John-

sons were not crushed. After one look at the mob we went back to the lounge.

The only other occupants of the lounge, watching the festivities downstairs on television, were the President's father, Joseph P. Kennedy, and Eunice Kennedy's husband, Sargent Shriver. The former ambassador to the Court of St. James's, who was kept out of sight in Los Angeles during the convention, still was "under wraps" and was not appearing publicly with his son, the President. Rose Kennedy was with the President and I presume Eunice Shriver was there also.

When the Presidential party started to come up to the lounge to get their wraps, we decided to leave also. My evening coat and fur scarf were folded on the chair on which I had put them, but there was no sign of Herbert's overcoat and high silk hat. An usher said, "Don't worry, whoever took them by mistake will discover it when he gets downstairs and will come back for his own things." No one came back and eventually there were no more wraps on the chairs. Fortunately, my fur scarf is large, so Herbert draped it over his head and shoulders. The next morning, I remembered having heard someone say he had come to get Speaker Rayburn's coat and hat before the influx of people picking up their own wraps started. I called Mr. Sam's administrative assistant and asked if by chance the Speaker had an extra coat and hat. "No," said the AA, "but Governor Stevenson has two. He sent someone to get the Speaker's, not knowing I had them. When the usher brought the coat and hat he thought were the Speaker's to the car that was to take them on to another ball, it was too late to send the extra garments back, so the governor took them with him."

I tried Adlai at the University Club in Washington, but he was not there, so I called Laura Magnuson (Mrs. Paul), an old friend of his from Lake Forest who had lived in Washington for many years, to ask her if she knew where Adlai was staying. "Right here," she said; "we are just having breakfast, so I will put him on the phone." He confirmed that he had a coat and silk hat that did not belong to him. I was amused when he asked me if Herbert's coat was made in London; it was. He was a cautious man!

The 1965 inaugural of Johnson and Humphrey must have been uneventful, for I remember little about it. Unfortunately, I had gained weight and could not wear the bright red evening gown I had bought for the 1961 ball. I have owned many different-sized wardrobes during my years in public life, for when I worked hard I would gain weight and not be able to wear anything I had recently acquired. I would have to buy some new clothes, and then under my doctor's direction I would lose twenty or thirty pounds and out would come the clothes I had put away several months before. Then pound by pound the ugly avoirdupois would come back and the new wardrobe would go into the storage closet and out would come the larger-sized garments. I really dislike even slight obesity, but apparently not as much as I should. I am still fighting "the battle of the bulge" to some extent and probably will continue to do so until I die.

I think Jacqueline Kennedy did a praiseworthy thing when she sought to furnish the White House with actual antiques or copies more suitable for that historic mansion than the modern furniture that she found in it. Although the structure had been rebuilt almost entirely when it was discovered in the late forties that it was literally falling to pieces, it still was and is the White House, the home of our Presidents, and it should be a house of which we all can be proud. Every First Lady has left her imprint on it. I hope it gives Patricia Nixon a happy satisfaction to know that Clement Conger, curator of the White House and the Department of State reception rooms, has said publicly that she did more to make it the authentic showplace it is today than any other First Lady. God knows the wife of Richard Nixon deserves to have what she accomplished when she lived in the White House acknowledged and appreciated.

I had an amusing experience one morning just after Jackie Kennedy had completed the main portion of her restoration of the White House when I accompanied a group of visitors on what is called a "private" tour. Private used to mean (I do not know what it means today) that certain persons were taken on a tour before the public was admitted. There might be thirty or sixty in the group, depending upon how many Congressmen had asked for private tour tickets for that day. This particular morning, the usher who accompanied our group was one I often used to see during the Truman Administration. After meticulously pointing out all the excellent changes made by Mrs. Kennedy, he drew me aside and said, "You know how hipped Mrs. Kennedy is on authentic antiques. Well, how do you suppose she could bring herself to paint the dark marble mantels in the East Room white? And how could she bring herself to gild the sterling silver chandelier and sconces in the dining room? And how could she make the Blue Room white with touches of blue? And how could she make the Red Room an ugly burgundy color?'' It was plain to see that he did not agree with the head usher, J. B. West, who served from 1941 to 1969, that everything Jackie Kennedy did was just right. I was glad when I read that Mrs. Nixon had returned the Blue Room to being blue and the Red Room to red.

Lady Bird's beautification project made Washington a much lovelier city than it had been. Her influence to make our outdoor surroundings more beautiful was felt all over the nation. She is a fine, strong woman. The LBJ Memorial Grove on the Potomac will provide another restful green place for residents and visitors to our nation's capital. The Grove is a fifteen-acre park of white pine trees. All of the two million dollars needed for the memorial is coming from donations by private citizens. A living memorial such as this seems to be very fitting for such a vital, nature-loving man as Lyndon Baines Johnson. To me, he seems to be a casualty of the Vietnam War just as much as any man in uniform who lost his life in that faraway and tragic land.

I was asked by Lady Bird Johnson to campaign with her and JFK's sister Eunice Shriver at the beginning of the 1960 campaign of JFK and LBJ, but unfortunately was unable to do so because of illness. I was ill during a great part of that campaign and consequently did very little. Late in the campaign I did make a trip to the West Coast with LBJ and his entourage. When Johnson ran for President in 1964 with Hubert Humphrey as his Vice Presidential candidate, I had a base from which to operate, for I had been named special consultant to the Secretary of Labor for Youth Employment. I made dozens of speeches—according to the speakers bureau of the committee the largest number by a woman in that campaign except for Lady Bird Johnson and Muriel Humphrey. Often in places where I was scheduled for one speech, I was called upon to give more. One day in Illinois I made seven speeches.

I always felt I owed Senator Barry M. Goldwater an apology for the scornful and sarcastic things I said about him publicly in the 1964 campaign. It seems to me that soon after his election LBJ started to do some of the things we Democrats criticized Goldwater for suggesting or even mentioning in connection with the war in Vietnam. I also felt guilty and sad when I remembered how enthusiastically I had described the "War on Poverty" which was just starting at the time of that campaign. The concept was one of the most exciting and noble of any political plan I ever have heard of. The actual outcome was such a dismal failure that I am afraid it accounts for some of the youthful violence we experienced in the late sixties and early seventies. The hopeful promises that were implicit in every phase of the program amounted to so little that it was heart-breaking to one like me naive enough to believe them. I did not consider them in the same category as some campaign promises. I really believed the War on Poverty could be a victorious one.

Knowing that statistics can prove or disprove anything, I have seen some figures which show there are fewer poor people in this country because of the War on Poverty. I doubt this very much. Some of the programs administered by the Office of Economic Opportunity, the agency created to wage the War on Poverty, still are functioning but they are now in other agencies as a result of the death blow given to the OEO by Nixon. I cannot say that I think Nixon's breaking up of the OEO was as heinous a crime as some Democrats maintained, for it had begun to fall apart even before he took office. Lydon Baines Johnson will be forever remembered for the glorious legislative victories he achieved in the fields of civil rights, health and education, but not, I fear, for his War on Poverty.

Sargent Shriver, who seemingly had been so successful in his direction of the Peace Corps, did not add to his reputation as the director of the OEO, mainly, I think, because he always talked in projections instead of actual plans or accomplishments. On the many occasions when I heard him speak, it was not possible to know whether he was projecting a goal or describing a functioning operation—and one functioning successfully. Usually I knew enough about the program to know that he was dealing in projections, a sort of numbers game, for which he could not be held entirely accountable. Too often, he was given data by his inexperienced young Ph.D's and p.r. men that were the results of their cerebrations. These might be translated into elaborate plans and monumental figures but were not concrete facts.

I had the opportunity to be somewhat involved in the plans for the

War on Poverty because of my work, lasting a year, on youth employment. The Neighborhood Youth Corps, one of the most successful of the many OEO programs, was planned and administered by the Department of Labor. Secretary Wirtz had assured me there was a job for me to do when President Johnson appointed me, but actually I never felt I had any work of importance at the department. The first day I was in my office—which had all the accoutrements to signify I was an executive—a rug, a lamp, a sofa, a coffee table, a water thermos jug—an administrative officer came in, introduced himself and asked if I had everything I needed. I said the office seemed to be well-equipped but that I would like a manual typewriter on a stand. "But you have a secretary in the next office," he said. I explained that I was accustomed to typing rough notes, for I seemed to think through my fingers. Before the man left, he asked how many assistants I would need and I laughed in his face, saying, "Assistants? I have no idea that I will need any. I do not know yet what I am going to do nor how I am going to keep a secretary busy."

If I had been a young woman wishing to build a small empire so that I would become a permanent fixture in Labor, I would have had a different attitude, but I knew I was there primarily in order to have a platform from which to step into the political melee whenever the President or the National Committee needed me. I did make a number of speeches for the department, in many different cities, most of them about the Neighborhood Youth Corps and other programs of the War on Poverty. I spoke at a number of universities. I also was asked to speak about the poverty program to a group of young Foreign Service officers who were about to leave for their first assignments. Thereafter I was invited to speak to every group of Foreign Service officers as it finished its training. When I was leaving I told Secretary Wirtz, an old friend of mine who had been a law partner of Adlai Stevenson, that I felt I had cheated the taxpayers. Although I had worked full-time I had not worked one-half as hard as I did on every other job. He said that if I had done nothing but advise him about the competent person to head the Neighborhood Youth Corps, I had earned whatever I had been paid.

I rather think that Larry O Brien's animosity toward me may have kept President Johnson from considering me as the director of the OEO. Gladys Tillett, who had been appointed to the United Nations by Presidents Kennedy and Johnson as our representative on the Commission on the Status of Women, decided when President Johnson first talked about starting the War on Poverty that I would be a good person to direct it. She talked and wrote to many Democratic leaders, women, governors, members of Congress, to ask them to write letters to the President endorsing me for this post if they felt I was qualified. Many of those she contacted wrote strong letters and sent her copies that she showed me. I had not known she was going to start this campaign for me, but when she told me, I felt it was something I might be able to do.

Some of those who wrote the President sent Gladys copies of the replies they had from the White House: perfunctory, short acknowledgements assuring them I would be given consideration for the post. All were signed by Lawrence O'Brien. When Gladys told me of her campaign, I called my old friend, Walter Jenkins, who at the time was LBJ's closest assistant. He said O'Brien had not shown one of the letters to him or to the President. I explained that I had not known of Gladys' activity until then, but that I would appreciate it if the President would consider me for the post. Walter left the White House staff not long after. I never heard anything more about Gladys' attempt to have me named to head the Office of Economic Opportunity. Nor did Gladys. So I often wondered whether LBJ ever saw any of the letters.

Chapter 25

I never expected to take any part in the preconvention activities of the DNC in 1968, but Margaret Price fell ill and could not be in her office to plan for the convention. John Bailey asked if I would take her place. I refused. When Margaret, who was in the Harkness Pavilion in New York, asked that I come to see her and begged me to step in, I had to say yes, for I loved her dearly. As I kissed her good-bye—and it was a final good-bye—she said, "India dear, I can sleep tonight for the first time in months without worrying about the committee."

I knew John Bailey must have been desperate to let me take over Margaret's duties. He had told some women in Kansas a few weeks earlier there was no doubt that I had the experience and know-how to fill in for Margaret, but that I had a mind of my own—which was something John's type of male politician could not abide. It must have galled him in 1974 when Ella Grasso of Connecticut decided to run for the governorship. Although she had been his successful protégée in earlier State races, she did not have his blessing when she sought to be the gubernatorial candidate until she defeated Attorney General Robert Killian in the delegate primary in his hometown of Hartford. Ella, who had served as Secretary of State in Connecticut

for three terms and had been in the U.S. House of Representatives
for two terms, was the first woman elected to head a State government who had not been preceded by her husband. The second such
instance was that of Dixy Lee Ray, elected governor of the State of
Washington in 1976.

There were three months in which to plan for the convention, and
that would have been enough if I had found an experienced staff—
even a small one—but there were only two women on the staff of the
office of women's activities—an administrative assistant and a
secretary. The committee had no printed material at all. At the conventions I had had anything to do with from 1944 to 1952, we always
had for distribution voting records of the leading Republicans and
something to show the differences between the two parties' ap-
proaches to the main issues. John Bailey asked me to make out a
budget of what I needed and it was a very modest one indeed. I said
we needed another secretary, a public relations person, and some
money for printing. I knew it was too late to assemble professionals
for research and writing, but fortunately I knew enough women who
would volunteer to do these jobs—and do them well, for they were
all ex-professionals. When John okayed the budget, I found a secretary and a p.r. woman, who gave up a job in the Department of
Commerce, although I explained to her that her appointment was
temporary and might not lead to anything else.

I persuaded my good friends Lillian Owen and Eleanor Israel to
work as volunteers. I had found enough volunteers to do all the writing I felt we needed: one-page flyers on a number of subjects com-
paring the Democratic and Republican Congressional achievements
from 1953 to 1968.

The subjects covered in eleven flyers were: conservation, consumer protection, education, civil rights, food, power, population
control, health and social sciences, housing and urban development
and safe communities, senior citizens, control of nuclear weapons
and international relations, rural America, labor. These flyers
showed the amazing contrast between the achievements of the two
parties during those fifteen years. I purposely used no names so all
the committee would have had to do was add the Presidential and
Vice Presidential names at the top. I asked the printer to hold the
plates so they would be available if they were wanted after the convention. He told me later that the DNC had ordered ten thousand of

each flyer printed, a number that was ridiculously and pathetically infinitesimal in a national campaign. We ordered that number of each flyer just for distribution at the convention!

I did not participate in the Humphrey-Muskie campaign, so I am not fully aware of how it was conducted. I do know that all the Humphrey people were aware for many months that he stood the best chance of being nominated. Yet they seemed to have made no preparation with that in mind. They acted as if he were a dark horse who managed to win the nomination to the surprise of everyone at the convention. I know they were short of money, but that does not explain their lack of planning. Poor Hubert never has managed to have really first-class people working for him, either as Senator, Vice President or Presidential candidate. He has the finest and quickest mind and the greatest knowledge of government of anyone I know in politics and is potentially a splendid President. Think of the agony the country would have been spared if he had been elected in 1968!

It had bothered me for years that there was no history of the Democratic Party, especially since many people had asked for one. I determined to have a history for distribution at the convention. Gail Owen Troutman volunteered to write it. Gail was very knowledgeable about things political. She had been a page for me at a couple of conventions and during the summer of 1962, after she was graduated from Radcliffe College, was chosen to handle a project that the Committee on Friendly Relations Among Foreign Students had agreed to do for the Department of State Cultural Exchange Division.

The history Gail wrote became a thirty-two-page booklet. Bess Furman, longtime reporter for the New York *Times* Washington bureau and one of those who wrote some of Molly Dewson's first flyers, covered the FDR Administration. I was very pleased with this little history.

It is wise and fruitful to remember what the Democratic Party has stood for since it was founded more than a century ago by Thomas Jefferson. The first page of our history reminds us, "The rights of man have been the cornerstone of the faith of the Democratic Party since its founding. Its strength has been derived from its responsiveness to the people of America, and from the participation of the people in the formation of Democratic policies.

"The Democratic Party has been a national party since its birth. It has not been dominated by one section of the country, nor been controlled by a lone interest group, nor served an exclusive power structure. Because of its unique strength it has changed as the needs of the country have changed. From this strength it has acquired the imagination and vision for new policies."

How I obtained the money for the printing is a story in itself. When I employed the two women, I wrote a memorandum to the treasurer asking that they be put on the payroll. Two weeks passed and they received no checks. During the short time I had been occupying Margaret's office, I had learned from various sources in the committee that the chairman's OK meant nothing, that the treasurer was the "top banana," and that practically even the purchase of postage stamps had to be okayed by him. I called his secretary and asked for an appointment. It took several days to get one. He did not keep it and his secretary did not cancel it. Furious, I called again and this time talked to him. He said he would see me at 9 the next morning, so I was there in his office at that time. I had learned early in my political life that if one was insistent on such silly things as who went to whose office, it could take a long time to accomplish anything. When I wanted to see anyone I went to his/her office, no matter whether he/she was over or under me in the organization chart. After waiting for John Criswell for about twenty minutes, I told his secretary I would go to my office to work and she could let me know when he came in. I never heard from her all day, so I had to presume he either did not come in or he did not want to see me.

Late that afternoon, I sent President Johnson a note saying that since he had taken himself out of politics perhaps I should not bother him with anything political, but I did not know where to turn, if not to him, and I would like very much to have an off-the-record appointment at his convenience. I would not have been surprised if he had not acknowledged the note for some time. Early the next morning Jim Jones, his appointments secretary, called to say the President would see me at 5:30.

I went in the side door opposite the executive office building and was taken up to the Cabinet room by a route where I was not seen by any press. I chatted with various members of the Cabinet who came in until young Jones took me into the Oval Office. I did not wait very long. As he led me into the office Jones said, "As you saw, the President has others waiting to see him." I replied that I got the picture and would not stay long. As usual, I was greeted with a Johnson bear hug and a kiss. I was aware that a photographer was there then, but as far as I could see, he left when the President took me over and put me into a corner of a sofa. He drew up a big rocking chair, sat in it, and put his feet up on a hassock. At that moment it dawned on me that it might be difficult to guide the conversation to the point where I literally was going to say, "The treasurer you have appointed for the National Committee is a so-and-so." I need not have worried. After telling me how glad they all were to have me taking over for Margaret he asked, "How are things going for you?"

"They aren't going, which is why I am here," I replied.

He said John Bailey had told him he had okayed everything I wanted, whereupon I laid my hand on his arm (lèse majesté) and said, "Don't you think we have known each other too long for you to give me apple sauce like that? You know perfectly well that John Bailey's O.K. does not mean a thing."

"Whose does?" he asked.

"The treasurer's."

He said in a surprised tone, "But you surely are not having trouble with him?"

I responded, "Indeed I am. I have never met the man. He makes appointments with me and doesn't keep them. I am working as a volunteer in this job because I love Margaret and am concerned with our party, but I do not have to put up with such treatment and what's more, I won't. I have better things to do with my time than to sit in back of a desk in a handsome office and do nothing, and nothing is all I can do if I have no staff nor any money for printing. I thought I owed it to you to tell you this, for just as there was publicity when I came, there will be publicity if I leave."

The President then told me John Criswell was a strange young man. The President had been trying to get him to accept an appointment on a commission, but Criswell seemed to want to stay at the DNC. "But he cannot interfere with you," he said. He proceeded to ask me what my plans were, and we had a long conversation about the whole political situation. For the first time, I became convinced that he was for HHH, but that he would do nothing before the convention to help him. Several times I started to leave, but each time he would say, "Don't go." So on we went with our political conversation. I truly do not remember all that was said—nothing of earth-shaking import. He agreed wholeheartedly when I said I thought we should have a flyer enumerating his striking achievements in the way of domestic legislation to distribute at the convention. I figured ten thousand dollars would take care of that printing. I said something about the shabby way I thought women had been treated at the committee in the last eight years, and went on, "You know, I never would have stood for such treatment. I never have been a doormat and I am not about to become one in my old age."

He laughed and said, "No, no one ever has treated you like a doormat and I do not think any man would try to do so."

Finally, I got up to leave. This time he escorted me to the door and said to Jim Jones, "Jim, tell Arthur Krim (chairman of the Finance Committee), John Bailey and John Criswell that India Edwards is to have whatever she feels she needs and that's an order."

The next morning when I called Criswell for an appointment, his secretary said to come right in. He was examining the mail as I entered his office. He neither looked up nor indicated in any way that I was there. I pulled up a chair, sat down, and said, "John Criswell, you and I are going to have to work together for the next ten weeks, so let's be as friendly as we can. I don't blame you for being furious that I went to the President about you, but you forced me to do so. You are the rudest, most gauche man I ever have encountered in all my years, but I'm willing to forget that and start anew if you can be at least halfway decent from now on. How about it?"

He had put aside the mail as I talked and then he said he did not know in what way he had been rude. I replied that it must be ignorance that kept him from knowing, so I repeated, "Let's forget what is past and go on from here." I started telling him that I wanted the two new employees put on the payroll as of two weeks ago and that I would need his OK on contracts that I was ready to sign with the Blackstone and Hilton hotels in Chicago.

"You are to have anything you want," he said in a peevish voice, "so you do not need my OK on anything."

"Now you are being childish," I said. "As treasurer, I need your OK on any contract I sign and you know that. Please be reasonable. You will find me a very easy person to get on with if you will drop the chip that is on your shoulder." Well, he dropped it to the extent that he put no hurdles in my way, but neither did he help to remove any that were there. Our relationship was not the pleasant one I had had with previous treasurers: George Killion, Joe Blythe and Sidney Salomon, but it was not intolerable.

The next Monday after seeing the President I found a large envelope from the White House on my desk. It contained the most amusing set of candid pictures, taken in the Oval Office when I thought the photographer was not present. Two pictures (one in color) showed the whole office with the President and me with our heads together in serious conversation, and five others showed my face and the back of the President's head. I could not imagine what he had said to account for my expressions except in one picture: that surely was when he had okayed the ten thousand dollars I had said I needed for printing.

Yoichi Okamoto, the favorite of LBJ's photographers, told me later that the President roared with laughter when he saw the pictures and said, "Make up a set for India." Yoichi said, "Not those candid shots, surely. No woman would like those of herself." The President replied, "Yes, those, too. India will love 'em." And love 'em I do.

I showed them once to a close associate of LBJ and he said, "They all are wonderful, particularly the one that shows Lyndon listening. That is unique."

Since there had been a telephone strike in Chicago for weeks, we knew we would be handicapped at convention time, but when a bus strike hit us too, we really were in hot water. At every other convention there had been a telephone in my room connected with the hotel switchboard, several that went through our own special switchboard installed for the duration of the convention and a private line which went through no switchboard. In 1968 I had nothing but the hotel lines and it often was impossible to receive or make calls on them because the operators were so busy. It was maddening. I had a suite in the Blackstone and an office in the Hilton. When I wanted to talk to someone in the office I would have to send a page across the street to carry the message.

"Scooter" Miller, Liz Carpenter and Bess Abell all were helpful at the 1968 convention in planning the women's programs, which consisted of three Food for Thought luncheons at the Blackstone Hotel and a Salute to Women of Action luncheon in the largest ballroom of the Hilton Hotel on the fourth day. Awards were given to

Women Doers, chosen by regions, a contest planned by Margaret Price and carried on under the direction of Peggy Mann (Mrs. James), a prominent Montgomery County, Maryland, Democratic leader and a former president of the Women's National Democratic Club in Washington. Following the awards, which we hoped up until almost the last minute would be presented by Lady Bird Johnson, and the luncheon, the "pièce de résistance" of our programs was given. It was a historical fashion show entitled "Alexis, We Love You," written by Addie Yates, wife of Congressman Sidney A. Yates from Chicago, and Mary Anderson, who ran his Chicago office. The show was clever and entertaining, and the women who participated in it were pictures in their gowns from the early eighteen hundreds to the present. Polly Shackleton (Mrs. Robert), now an elected member of the D.C. Council, gave so vivid a portrayal of Eleanor Roosevelt that it was almost as if that great lady were with us. We had a member of every candidate's family in the show. Those who walked down the runway neither spoke nor sang. The master of ceremonies was Addie herself. Three professionals sang Addie's and Mary's jaunty lyrics. The show was such a success that it was repeated a number of times later as a fund-raiser in various places, including Washington, where the Woman's National Democratic Club sponsored the performance.

The Alexis we loved was Alexis de Toqueville, that perspicacious Frenchman who wrote in *Democracy in America* in 1835 after a prolonged visit to this country, "If I were asked . . . to what the singular prosperity and growing strength of that people ought mainly to be attributed, I should reply: To the superiority of their women."

Memories of the 1968 convention stir a sick feeling inside me. I was so disgusted with the way the young hippies who thronged Grant Park across from the Hilton behaved and were treated by the Chicago police and the National Guard that I felt as if we were throwing away the election right there in Chicago. In my opinion there was no excuse for the use of "people pushers" (Jeeps encased in barbed wire). To look out the tenth-floor windows of my suite in the Blackstone and see solid rows of policemen with clubs and of soldiers with drawn bayonets and in front the people pushers, made me wonder whether we were in the United States or in a country run by a dictator. If we had been smart enough to have held the convention elsewhere, there could not have been this confrontation. It was only because Grant Park offered a great expanse of open ground that it was possible for those thousands of foolish young people to gather there. What they hoped to accomplish I never knew, but if it was the nomination of Eugene McCarthy I can think of no better way in which to make certain that he was not the nominee than the way they chose.

I saw some of the advertisements in Eastern papers urging young people to go to Chicago by bus (the fare was ridiculously low, far below normal) and promising bed and board there. I doubt there was bed and board for the many who took advantage of the offer, because most seemed to sleep in Grant Park in what they were wearing, whether or not they had blankets. The nights were very cold, down in the forties.

I had urged that the convention site be changed, because after a couple of preconvention visits to Chicago I feared there would be trouble, but I was told that HHH needed the Illinois delegation. He had the majority of the Illinois delegates with him, 112 of the 118 voting for him on the first ballot. McCarthy and McGovern each got only three votes. It was Illinois that moved to make Humphrey's nomination unanimous. In the general election he lost the State to Nixon by a tiny percentage. Nationwide, Nixon won 43.4 percent, 31,783,783 votes, and Humphrey 43 percent, 31,271,839 votes. Wallace carried the other 13.6 percent.

Courage like Harry Truman's is a rare commodity in politics; perhaps after Watergate it will not be so rare. Doing the right thing is best in politics. Surprisingly, the right thing often turns out to be the best for garnering votes for the candidate. I truly believe that almost everyone knows the difference between right and wrong if he/she thinks about it.

The convention that year was a horrendous experience. I kept feeling I would awaken to find it was not happening. The shame of it is something that, as a Democrat, I cannot forget nor can I forgive those responsible. It is a miracle that there was no bloodshed, only some battered young people, some of whom I saw as they were being picked up by police just for sauntering along Michigan Avenue. One afternoon I had come out of the main entrance of the Hilton to walk to the corner to cross to the Blackstone. A long-haired young lad was walking slowly in the same direction. A bluecoat told him to "move on," which the lad did but no faster than before. Whereupon the police clubbed him and dragged him to a Black Maria at the curb.

I know there were nasty incidents in which some hippies behaved in a way to warrant arrest, but I also know there were hundreds of youngsters taken to jail for no good reason. The men in charge seemed to have lost all sense of balance, of rational behavior. For instance, I could see no reason in the world why my little black purse was turned out and examined every time I entered the convention hall, for I wore badges to indicate that I was a former vice chairman of the DNC and a distinguished guest and I had box seats. I know little about firearms but I do not think there is a pistol made that would have fit into my small bag. I was insulted every time the guard insisted upon going through my purse and I grow angry now when I remember the incident.

I did persuade John Bailey to put two women on the program: Katherine G. Peden of Kentucky, who was running for the U.S. Senate, and Betty Furness, special assistant to the President for Consumer Affairs. Senator Philip A. Hart of Michigan gave a tribute to Margaret Bayne Price, who had died July 23. I had written a long and glowing obituary that was used in its entirety in many metropolitan papers, something I hoped would have pleased Margaret. She was a lovely person and deserved better treatment by the two Presidents whom she served than she received. When I went to see President Johnson when I was filling in for Margaret the two women on her staff were absolutely amazed. They said that never had Margaret had a private interview with either JFK or LBJ, that she had seen them only in groups and never had any private conversation with either. How could a director of women's activities function properly if she never had any contact with the leader of the party? Remember, she was an elected official of the committee, just as the chairman was, not one of the hired help.

She had told me after the 1960 campaign, when she traveled extensively with the Presidential candidate, that she had paid all her own expenses and that she received little recognition in the places they visited. Jacqueline Kennedy did not travel with her husband since she was expecting a baby, but occasionally a Kennedy woman was in the party and she was accorded more courtesy than the vice chairman of the committee. Of course, Margaret was not known around the country. Without advance notice from the candidate's staff, it was not surprising that she was treated by the local leaders as if she were a secretary. I urged her to assert herself more, but I do not think she ever did.

Dear Margaret, she never knew the finagling Carrie Davis, wife of veteran Congressman Clifford Davis of Tennessee, and I practiced to get President Kennedy to receive the women attending the first of the national conferences Margaret sponsored every other year. Katie had started these conferences and they had grown enormously. In Katie's time there was no expectation of going to the White House because the Eisenhowers were there, but for the first conference Margaret planned, the women would expect to be received at the White House. Carrie and I were on the large committee working with Margaret. Every time we would meet we would ask when the President would receive the women. Margaret would say each time she had not had a response to her letter to him. As the time drew near for the program to be printed, Carrie and I got together and decided to do something about the problem. She said she would talk to the Vice President on Monday and ask him to speak to the President at the regular Tuesday morning Congressional leaders' breakfast at the White House about the importance of his receiving the women. My job was to write JFK a letter stating in plain language how much it would hurt him politically if he ignored several thousand Democratic women who had worked hard for him and had come to Washington. I knew if my letter went through Kenny O'Donnell, the President probably never would see it, so I had it delivered to his personal secretary, Evelyn Lincoln, late on Monday with the request that she put it on his desk Tuesday morning.

Our strategy worked. When we went to the DNC for a meeting Tuesday afternoon, Margaret beamingly said Kenny O'Donnell just had called to say the President would receive the women. It was not certain that the First Lady would be there, but that was comparatively unimportant. Carrie and I had agreed that we would tell no one of the part we played in this little episode, so Margaret never knew about it.

In my opinion Eugene McCarthy did more to defeat Humphrey in the Presidential campaign of 1968 than the Republicans. If McCarthy had been a good enough sport to have supported Humphrey wholeheartedly from the day he won the nomination in Chicago, it is entirely probable that Humphrey instead of Nixon would have won the close election.

McCarthy had the right to take his courageous stand of opposing the Vietnamese war and to validate his opposition to President Johnson by running in the New Hampshire and later primaries in 1968, but his behavior just before, during and after the convention was unsportsmanlike and unforgivable in my judgment. I was in the middle of that convention, so I know a great deal about it. One of the things that made me admire George McGovern was the way in which he accepted defeat when HHH was nominated.

Despite my retirement to California, two of the leading Democratic contenders in the 1972 primaries (not McGovern), asked me to work for them, but I did no political work until after the convention. Then, after much persuasion by Esther Murray, who, with Ann Taylor, proposed to raise funds so that Eleanor McGovern could continue to campaign for her husband, I accepted the chairmanship of the Friends of Eleanor McGovern. I was happy with George as the Presidential candidate, for I regarded him highly and thought he had a chance to defeat Nixon, but I did not see how I could be of much use in his campaign if I stayed in California, which I was determined to do. With this understanding, I agreed to be chairman of their committee, if it were cleared with the McGovern leaders.

I asked my friend Anna Roosevelt Halsted if she would be co-chairman. Luckily, she was also enthusiastic about McGovern and was willing to assist in raising money for Eleanor's traveling expenses. Anna lived in Hillsdale, New York, so we decided we must have a Washington coordinator. Neither Esther nor Ann wanted the job. I persuaded one of the best executives I know, Peggy (Mrs. James H.) Mann, to take on the job. I also undertook to get the wives of all those who had sought the nomination before the convention to serve on the committee. Most of them responded enthusiastically. Everyone agreed with the Florida reporter who wrote, "She's George McGovern's greatest asset. Honesty and beauty are the first things that come to mind when one talked with Eleanor McGovern."

Peggy, Esther and Ann enlisted volunteers, and Anna and I wrote to many of our friends to ask them to join in the project. We wanted each friend to send twenty-five dollars to the committee and to write to five prospective friends to do the same, etc. The committee hoped there would be thousands of friends. The idea was a good one, especially for women who were not particularly keen about George but were willing to help Eleanor. I must admit that after thinking George would make a good President, I lost much of my enthusiasm for him during the time he was vacillating about his Vice President. Whatever chance George had before, he certainly lost when he said he was 1,000 percent for Tom Eagleton and then began backing away.

Chapter 26

Many persons who are unacquainted with politicians think the great majority are almost illiterate, inclined to be foul-mouthed and to enjoy a racy joke, but this is far from true, especially in the case of the old-fashioned political bosses. They usually were well-educated, although some (particularly Southerners) chose to speak in the vernacular when they were with constituents who had not had much formal education. In the presence of women they eschewed the mildest oaths and frowned upon double entendre or smutty jokes. When Hugo Rogers, the head of Tammany Hall before Carmine DeSapio, invited me to speak at a dinner his club was having in New York City, I had to regret because of a previous engagement to speak in Texas that night. The chairman, Howard McGrath, was very much upset. He asked if I could not rearrange my schedule to take in both places. "To my knowledge," he said, "this is the first time Tammany ever has invited a woman to speak."

This was impossible for me to do, so I offered to send a new Congresswoman from Utah to speak to the New Yorkers. Mr. Rogers was hesitant but finally agreed after I told him she was a stunning woman, a former judge and a brilliant speaker. "She will be much better than I," I promised. Imagine my dismay when Mr. Rogers called Howard the day after she had spoken and said they all were shocked that a lady would tell an off-color story and that he was surprised I had recommended her as a speaker. Mr. Rogers indicated that they would have no more women speakers. I asked the Congresswoman what story she had told at the dinner. It was so innocuous that it was practically a shaggy dog story with no double entendre whatsoever.

My first encounter with James Aloysius Curley, whom Massachusetts Democrats elected mayor of Boston and also governor of the State (one victorious election was when he was in jail) came early in my political career when I was seated next to him at a National Committee luncheon in Washington. I had not heard his name when we were introduced and I could not see his place card. His conversation—and his appearance—made me think of a Shakespearean actor. Nothing he said gave me an inkling of who he was or where he came from. As soon as we left the table, I asked one of the staff who that amazing old man was. I was surprised to hear that he was the Curley of Boston about whom I had heard for years.

The next time I saw the Irish "pol" at close quarters was during the Stevenson campaign in 1952 when I went to Boston with the candidate and his entourage. The women had dinner together while the men dined in state with Mayor Curley. Later, when we got into sports cars with the tops down to drive to the hall where Stevenson was to speak, I was placed in a car with Curley. The first car was filled with Secret Service men, the second occupied by Massachusetts Governor Paul Dever and Stevenson, and the third by the mayor and I. The vast crowds that lined the streets through which we passed paid no attention to the man who was running for the Presidency and their governor, but when they saw his Honor, the mayor, they swarmed into the roadway to touch the slow-moving car and kiss the hand of their beloved mayor as he extended it in much the same way the Pope does. I sank lower and lower into the seat and soon was almost sitting on the floor. I never suffered more embarrassment than during that drive.

That afternoon I had accompanied the mother and sisters of the Senatorial candidate, John F. Kennedy, to about five tea parties which were utterly unlike any other political affairs I ever attended. No one spoke—there were no reasons given why the handsome young Representative should be elevated to the Senate. The thousands of females in the five towns near Boston that we visited were content to come to the party, shake hands with Mrs. Joseph Kennedy, some of the sisters and me, whom they did not know at all, then have a cup of tea and a cookie. Jack Kennedy did not appear that afternoon and I doubt that he attended many of these tea parties that were given all over the State during the campaign. It was apparently a successful way of campaigning in Massachusetts, but it surely was unique. Neither Mrs. Kennedy nor any sister would speak, except to individuals in the receiving line. "Don't you want me to speak for a few minutes?" I asked. I was assured there was no need to bother with talking about issues.

Though I knew Steve Mitchell wanted me out of the committee in 1953, I timed my departure to suit my convenience since I felt I owed him nothing. I had the right and the obligation to the women leaders who had preceded me at the committee to be sure my successor was a qualified woman, and he agreed that I could pick her. It was not easy to find anyone willing to work with him. I asked Martha Ragland first but, even if she had felt that she could work with Steve, her husband Tom would not hear of her taking a post that would keep her away from their home in Nashville a great part of the time nor would he agree to move to Washington even though he was retired. I could not argue with the Raglands on this point. A happy marriage is worth more than success in politics or in anything else.

Then I talked to Eugenie Anderson, Katharine White and Georgia Neese Clark Gray (she had been married to Andrew Gray before resigning as Treasurer of the United States), but none of them would consider the post as long as Steve was chairman. They all had husbands who could have lived in Washington. Steve suggested Katie Louchheim, who with her husband Walter lived in Washington. Steve said, "She has a lovely house in Georgetown, entertains beautifully and has a wealthy husband."

"But does she have political know-how?" I asked. Steve often complained that the Democratic Party lacked snob appeal and he thought Katie agreed with that philosophy. She is an attractive woman who writes delightful poetry, but her approach to women in politics was very different from that of her predecessors. Katie seemed to think that women were more interested in raising money for the benefit of the party than in the issues that Franklin Roosevelt and Harry Truman had believed to be of interest to them. "Don't talk about issues," she cautioned me often in later years when the women assisting her in planning regional meetings would want me as a speaker. I paid no attention to this admonition when I would find that organizational matters were on the agenda but that no one was scheduled to talk about issues. Good organization is a must in successful campaigns, but women who see that all potential Democratic voters are registered and that they go to the polls must know enough about the issues of the day to discuss them intelligently.

Since Steve wanted Katie, I decided it would be good for him to have her. I felt, however, that I would be letting down all the women leaders who had preceded me if I did not insist upon having a more professional female politician at the committee also. I suggested to Steve since Katie would work as a volunteer that Genevieve Blatt of Pennsylvania be employed as associate director. I would resign not only as director of women's activities but also as vice chairman, so Katie could enjoy whatever kudos accompanied that post.

Genevieve was an attorney who had been active in the Young Democrats before becoming the strong right arm in politics of David Lawrence, mayor of Pittsburgh from 1946 to 1959. She was one of the most capable politicians with whom I had dealt, so I was happy Steve agreed that she would be a strong backup for Katie and even happier when Gen said she would love to come to Washington after the mayoralty campaign. It was early October when I told her Steve would talk to her after Mayor Lawrence's reelection in November. I was authorized to tell her that the salary would be ten thousand, which in 1953 was good.

Gen was keen to live in Washington for a while. She had a sister in Bethesda and she welcomed the opportunity to engage in politics on a national level. I left Washington feeling entirely content about the situation at the committee, but Gen never heard from Steve. I was not in Washington for a year and not in close touch with anyone at the committee, so I did not realize that Gen was not there until much too late to do anything about it. There probably was not much I could have done, actually, and perhaps when she was elected secretary of internal affairs for the Commonwealth of Pennsylvania in 1954, she was glad that she had not gone to Washington. She was reelected to that office in 1958 and again in 1962. In 1962 she almost defeated Senator Hugh Scott for his seat in the United States Senate, receiving 49 percent of the vote. Of that campaign she said, "I could have played up my 'femininity' but I wanted to stick to the issues. I could have urged women in particular to come out and vote—I just didn't want it to be that kind of campaign—I don't know, maybe I didn't do it right." She did it right from my point of view, even though she did not win. For a woman to appeal for votes because she is a woman is utterly disgusting. Gen would have made a splendid Senator. She has served well in everything she has done. In January, 1972, when she was in private law practice in Harrisburg, Governor Milton Shapp appointed her to fill a vacancy on the Commonwealth Court of Pennyslvania. The next year she was elected to a ten-year term.

Since Steve never called her in 1953 as he had told me he would, she probably had no occasion to discuss moving to Washington with Dave Lawrence, who moved from being mayor of Pittsburgh in 1959 to the governor's office. In 1963 he joined the Kennedy Administration in Washington; he died there in 1966. He was the national committeeman for his state for many years. He and I worked together amicably with respect for each other, but I am sure he would have objected to Gen's taking the job with the National Committee, judging by an experience I had with him. President Truman said he would consider a woman for an impending vacancy on the federal bench if I could find one qualified in the district concerned. Having watched Ann Alpern, city solicitor for Pittsburgh for some time, I admired her ability and hoped a judgeship in that district would be available for her.

I consulted the necessary legal and political powers-that-be about Mrs. Alpern's qualifications and was assured she was an outstanding attorney and a worthy Democrat. Mayor Lawrence agreed with this estimate of her, but said he would like to talk to me about her. He came by appointment to my office from Pittsburgh the next afternoon. Leaning over my desk and talking to me as if he were a school principal and I an unruly student, he asked, "Why should she have a lifetime appointment as a federal judge that pays $15,000 a year, which would mean that she would be making more than her husband does? She now makes $7,500 as city solicitor and I think that is enough for any woman to be paid. I do not approve of women making more than their husbands. So, I will not endorse her. That is final." And final it was. There was no use in trying to persuade President Truman to bypass Dave Lawrence. Lawrence was a fine man and a wise politician, but a generation or two behind in his thinking about women in politics. This may be said of many male politicians, although most are not as frank as Dave Lawrence.

I wonder how he would have felt if he had been alive when Judge Blatt was given the annual St. Thomas More Society award by the diocese's Catholic lawyers in November, 1974. She was the second woman to have received the award in the fifteen years it has been given. In accepting the award, Judge Blatt reminded her mostly male audience of attorneys and judges of a statement by the English saint that "God did not give minds to women to be wasted," and she recalled that Thomas More insisted his daughters receive the type of education that in those days was reserved only for noble-born men.

With the distaff side of the DNC settled (so I thought) and "Arden" sold, Herbert and I made plans to motor to California. I resigned as director of women's activities and intended to resign as vice chairman as soon as Gen started to work, so Katie could be elected to that post. We were going to store just enough to furnish a small abode for ourselves, wherever it might be, and send a vanload of furniture, china, silver, glassware, etc. to Cissy in California, but there still remained so many belongings that we held a sale.

As we drove west we stopped in Cincinnati, Chicago, St. Louis and Oklahoma City for me to keep speaking engagements I had made months before. In Oklahoma City I looked at a map and said to Herbert, "Darling, we're only a hop, skip and jump from Mexico, so why don't we run down there before going to California?" Herbert thought my geography queer but agreed. We drove south and entered Mexico by way of Laredo. Spending some weeks there, we saw a great part of the country and were entertained delightfully in Mexico City by our many friends in the embassy.

I know there are many persons who think there is no difference between the two major parties, but I am not one of them. The basic philosophies of both parties differ so greatly I can tell whether a person is a Republican or a Democrat after talking to him or her about the local, State or federal government. I might have trouble recognizing an independent, who thinks the man or woman is more important than the party. I disagree with that opinion, for every executive officeholder needs the backing and support of an organized political party if he/she is to accomplish his/her goals.

It is difficult to describe the differences in the parties in a few words. Since the end of the Civil War, the Republican Party has been allied with big business, rejecting group after group of the American electorate, mainly farmers and labor, for the sake of corporate interests. I was not personally concerned with politics until the thirties, but I have studied political history rather carefully. I firmly believe that the Democratic Party is more concerned with the welfare of the ordinary citizen and especially those who belong to minority groups than the Republican Party. I would not claim that there are not progressive Republicans who put the good of the many ahead of that of the privileged few, but they are the ones who often vote with the Democrats in legislative bodies. I don't claim that *all* Democrats put the interests of the many ahead of self-interest, but on the whole I think my characterization is valid. I have many Republican friends, but so far I never have voted for a member of that party!

Our President has great power but he does not "run" the government alone. Congress shares the responsibility, and unless the President's party has control of both the House of Representatives and the Senate, a President is hard-pressed to achieve even a small part of his program. When Lyndon B. Johnson was Majority Leader in the Senate during most of the Eisenhower Administration, he played the role of the leader of "the loyal opposition" so well that President Eisenhower was able to accomplish a creditable record in spite of the fact that in the opinion of many, he actually was a "do-nothing" President. Johnson's cooperation with President Eisenhower did not please some of his own party, but I always was convinced that LBJ put the good of the country ahead of that of his party or himself. He gave Eisenhower support because of this belief.

LBJ's campaign manager in the preconvention days of 1960 carried this spirit of cooperation to an extent that horrified me when I saw the dummy of a rather large booklet that was to be distributed to all Democratic convention delegates and alternates on LBJ's behalf. It was expensive-looking campaign material and might have been suitable for campaigning if LBJ had won the nomination, but it certainly would not help him win votes in a Democratic convention. The dummy had so many pictures of President Eisenhower and the

Majority Leader that one would have supposed they were of the same political faith. The captions also suggested that the two men belonged to the same party. I refused to okay it, much to John Connally's annoyance, I suppose, and perhaps even of the would-be candidate and some of his other advisers. I never discussed it with anyone but the advertising man who presented it to me for approval. I told him in no uncertain terms how ridiculous it was to send out such a brochure to Democrats who were to choose the Presidential nominee in Los Angeles that summer. "If our man wins the nomination then we can woo Republicans and independents by showing how closely LBJ worked with Ike, but this will be no recommendation with the partisan men and women at the Democratic convention."

The President should be a good judge of men and women and be able to pick capable administrators to direct the work of the executive departments. No one person possibly can have the knowledge or the experience to handle the myriad details of the federal government, but he should make an effort to understand the workings of every department. I remember a veteran civil servant telling me how impressed he was when President Truman asked him to return to the White House that evening to go over his report presented to the President for signature. "I dislike asking you to work overtime, but I must understand this report before I sign it," said the President, "and in the thirty minutes allotted to us this morning you cannot possibly answer all my questions." My friend, who was below Cabinet rank, said he was delighted to work overtime and wished President Eisenhower had asked him to do so when he first presented his annual report for Ike's signature. Instead the five-star general who had been elected President indicated that he did not understand the report and that it was too long for him to read. Anyway, it was the civil servant's responsibility to be certain it was correct. If it were not, his head would roll. Perhaps this illustrates the difference between a military and a civilian approach to the Presidency.

Franklin Roosevelt's New Deal saved us, I think, from a revolution, but the concepts of that philosophy will not solve the problems of today. As one who was an ardent New Dealer and also admired and supported Truman's Fair Deal policies, I must admit I think Johnson's Great Society promised too much. The federal government has a limit to its responsibility, its capability, and its resources.

Politicians who do not recognize these limitations and tell the citizens the truth should not be entrusted with the leadership of the nation. Anyone who wants to be President is going to have to face cold, hard facts and to explain them to the voters so that they will not be expecting him to bring about the millennium soon after he is inaugurated.

Leadership and inspiration are the two qualities that must emanate from the White House if we are to make the changes that every student of government knows must be made in the federal structure, which has grown obese in its two hundred years of seeking to provide the good life for most of our citizens. Now we must trim away the fat, the excess, and get down to the business of meeting the crises brought about by expanding populations, shrinking horizons, depleting natural resources, and polluting of the air and water and even the ground in which we grow our food. Every generation of Americans has wanted more material wealth, more luxury for the next generation. In my opinion the time has come when we must hope our children and their children ad infinitum will want from life more than material success. They must have enough of that to ensure a roof, clothing, food and some recreation, but, if we are to survive for another two hundred years, we must change our way of life. The inspiration must come from the White House. "Business as usual" is not good enough, nor even "business as it was in the 'Good Old Days.'" We must tailor our governments—federal, State and local—to present-day conditions and future probabilities, and that will take the combined effort of every man, woman and child in this nation with inspiration and guidelines from a man (or a woman) in the White House.

The Chief Executive sets the tone for his administration. A President who has integrity does not long tolerate dishonest men in his official family. When a President himself lacks the ability or the will to differentiate between right and wrong, such a tragic affair as Watergate can happen. I would judge from all I have read and heard about that unique segment of our political and governmental history that it was the character of the man at the top that made it possible for over forty men to be involved in activities that were criminal in nature. Whether they were basically honest or dishonest, they thought what they did was right because they knew their chief would approve of their actions. "I'm not a crook," the President of the

United States—undoubtedly the most powerful man in the world—told all who listened on television as this tragic man sought to allay the steadily growing qualms of all but his few devoted admirers that he was indeed just what he was proclaiming that he was not—a crook.

The so-called Watergate period was the saddest time for all citizens of this nation, in my estimation. It gave the country a sense of the dangers inherent in a Presidential administration completely lacking in understanding of the freedom, humaneness and liberty promised in our Constitution. The fact that the man who headed this corrupt administration was elected to the highest office in the land should bring a flush of shame to everyone who voted for him. If sovereign citizens in a democracy can be so misled that they choose as their leader a man like Richard M. Nixon, what might become of this country?

It has been said and written too often that what Nixon did was no different than what was done by preceding Presidents, that the only difference was that Nixon was caught. One would have to be biased indeed to say that one of our major political parties was more honest and decent than the other. There have been wrongdoers in both parties, even as high as the President. From my thirty years in Washington, all but the first two deeply involved in Democratic politics, I must admit that there were times when I was ashamed of a fellow Democrat who was a public servant but they were few and far between. The great majority of men—and all the women—whom I have known in both the Democratic and the Republican parties have been persons of integrity and high moral purpose. I admit to bias when I write that Harry Truman heads the list. I knew him better than any other President and was well acquainted with his administration.

I never was in the employ of the federal government except for the year I spent as special consultant on youth to Secretary of Labor Willard Wirtz. Working for the Democratic or Republican National Committee is not being an employee of the government. The DNC paid my salary for services in the Women's Division, not for being the elected vice chairman of the committee. Some men and women work as volunteers, as I did in 1944 and later in 1968, but it is my opinion that quality work is done by professionals. On a volunteer basis the size of one's own income (or that of one's spouse) determines whether or not a man or woman can be the head of a national political organization, rather than actual qualification for the job to be done.

During my years with the DNC I was active in the Woman's National Democratic Club, which is the leading forum for Democratic, Independent and many foreign diplomatic speakers as well as popular members of the media. No fee is given, not even for expenses, but the club never has trouble providing two and sometimes three outstanding programs each week during nine or ten months of the year. It was established in 1922 with Mrs. J. Borden Harriman (the popular Daisy) as a founder-member. She was active in club affairs until her death in her nineties. Emily Newell Blair, also a founding member and the third club president, was vice chairman of the Democratic National Committee in 1922. She wrote that "the club was to make it a place of tolerance, where minds may meet, where we may sometimes listen to things in which we do not believe, a place where we may learn to iron out our difficulties and hit the middle of the road." When Mrs. Harriman sought President Wilson's endorsement to found the club, his reply was firm. "You will have my blessing if its purpose is political and educational, but not if it is to be merely social." Over the years the club always has been an effective working partner of the women working in the National Committee headquarters. Some years ago I was made an honorary vice president of the club.

I joined the Women's National Press Club shortly after moving to Washington and am still a member. The club has become the Washington Press Club, and numbers among its members most of the leading male journalists of the city. It seems to me that more women's organizations have let down their bars to admit men as members than vice versa. For instance, the National Press Club still has no women members and neither does the White House Correspondents' Club.

The Women's Medical College of Pennsylvania, for which I have been a national board member and strong supporter since 1953, had to change its name in 1969 to The Medical College of Pennsylvania in order to qualify for federal and state grants. This unique college was founded in 1850 by a group of courageous young women determined to become doctors and a small group of equally courageous male doctors, largely Quakers, with headquarters in two rented rooms in Philadelphia. The men of the Philadelphia County Medical Society had pronounced women as "unfit for the profession due to their delicate organizations and predominance of the nervous system," and medical men and schools all over the country agreed with that point of view. One woman, Elizabeth Blackwell, who was to become the first American woman physician, was refused admittance to a Philadelphia medical school but eventually was admitted to Geneva Medical College in New York State (now Hobart and William Smith Colleges), where she graduated at the head of her class in 1849. But no other woman was able to follow in her footsteps at Geneva or in any other medical college.

In 1861 the Female Medical College of Pennsylvania, which was the original name of the college in which I became interested so many years later, obtained a charter for a hospital for women and children and for the first hospital-sponsored school of nursing in the United States. In 1895 the hospital became a general one, admitting men, women and children as patients. Today the college owns and operates a general teaching hospital with 329 adult beds and 40 bassinets. Out of five thousand applications for approximately 100 places each year, over two thousand come from women. My interest in this splendid college has continued. I try in every way I can to help the college secure the funds necessary to carry on its important work. The three major sources of income to cover the costs of education for the medical school are federal capitation grants, State capitation grants, and tuition. These sources provide about $10,400 per student. Because the current yearly cost of education in medical school is $14,000, it is essential that voluntary donations be made. There are many public-spirited women all over the country who help in this important endeavor.

A national organization of which I became a board member in the early fifties and in which I still retain a keen interest is the Girls Clubs of America. It was President Hoover who suggested to some of his friends on the board that I be invited to join. He was a strong supporter of boys' clubs and was helpful in advising GCA in how to become a national organization. There were about sixty-five clubs at the time in which I became interested in the organization. Today there are well over two hundred in thirty-two States, each doing a good job "to help girls of all backgrounds to grow and work together in a climate of freedom and harmony; to help girls find their own identity, develop their potential and achieve a sense of responsibility to self, family, community, country and world; to help girls of all racial, religious, and economic backgrounds to live and develop creatively in a democratic society in a continuously changing world.'' During the years I served as committee chairwoman and then as president I was a good fund-raiser (this is the main task of every board member of every organization, as far as I know). Through the efforts of two New York women whom I brought into the organization, Alberta Jacoby and Martha Cogan, and I, The Reader's Digest Foundation became interested in GCA. The latest contribution of Lila and DeWitt Wallace through their foundation was one million dollars, but I can claim no part in obtaining that generous gift.

In Washington my nonpolitical volunteer efforts were with the D.C. Health and Welfare Board and Friendship House, the oldest settlement house in the District of Columbia. I found my greatest satisfaction, however, in pursuing an old-fashioned form of personal philanthropy: giving school clothes and many hours of recreation to two large families who lived in our neighborhood in the northeast section of Washington.

My political activities now are confined to making what contributions we can afford to certain candidates. In some cases, I try to get other contributors for those candidates. Money, money, money! Everyone running for office is dependent upon it. The Congress has taken a first step in trying to regulate Presidential fund-raising by providing matching funds to amounts raised by preconvention candidates, but they are far from a solution to the problem of how to ensure that only ''clean money'' is used in every political campaign for office from the Presidency to dogcatcher.

I always felt that the Women's Division of the DNC should be able to raise at least part of its budget. In my time, we were feminists, but not militant enough to insist upon being financially independent. We were delighted to be ''kept'' women, dependent upon the chairman and treasurer, but we demanded the right to spend the money allocated to us in the way in which we thought most effective.

There are so many women with whom I have worked in politics whom I would like to eulogize in this book—some who are well-known and some who are known only to their intimate co-workers, but I cannot possibly list them all. So I will content myself by writing something I truly believe—that most men go into politics to make money, directly or indirectly, whereas women go in to fight for causes and for men and women in whom they believe. As I said once in a speech which Eleanor Roosevelt and Lorena Hickok quoted in their book *Ladies of Courage,* "If I didn't have the crusading spirit, I'd get the hell out and go home".

Twenty or more years ago, when Steve Mitchell did away with the Women's Division and integrated women into the DNC, there were many of us, including Eleanor Roosevelt, who feared that integration might mean interment. In spite of the progress women have made in the elective field, it often has seemed to us oldtimers that women in the Democratic National Committee are not as much full partners as Molly Dewson and I were in the Roosevelt and Truman administrations. Mrs. Roosevelt wrote in her column after the policy of integration of women had been announced by Mitchell, "This habit that men sometimes have of making decisions and then announcing them to women is one that will require a little watchfulness on the part of the men. It is perfectly natural for men to forget women; they have been in the habit of doing that for a long time, and women have let themselves be forgotten." She hailed the new policy if it was to be carried out, not just announced.

Women have made enormous strides in the last decade, but they still do not seem to understand what a power they could be if they took more interest in government on all levels. If they realized how much government affected their lives and those of their children, they could not resist having a stronger voice in the affairs of the nation, the states and their home communities. We are not a minority but we still are treated as though we were one, and a small one at that.

I did not enjoy fighting men during my politically active years, but I am sorry to say that I had to do a lot of it. I doubt that it is very different today in spite of the advances women have made in practically every field. Adoption of the Equal Rights Amendment to the U.S. Constitution will do more than remove the remaining discriminatory and unfair laws against females. It will take time to change the thinking of men who consider women inferior beings and women who enjoy being considered in that insulting manner.

There were so many pictures of me in publications during the years I was active in politics that I seldom noticed them. I really did not care whether they were flattering, nor did I mind particularly what was written about me. All I wanted was for Democratic women to be in evidence, for it to appear that my party valued that great body of women who make up over half of the electorate. I wanted it to appear as if I were treated with the same consideration that the men leaders were. Nothing infuriated me more than for women always to be expected to be subservient to men, even when both were elected and were supposed to have equal status in the party. I fought for equality for all women, not just for myself, and I think the women and men of the Democratic Party knew this. As I reflected on what I had accomplished during the years President Truman was in office to bring Democratic women a larger share of the political pie, I realized I had not given them an unmitigated blessing. Many men resented the growing influence of women and made their lot harder than ever. These men resented President Truman's treatment of me and that he gave evidence of considering women persons. Even a man as enlightened as Blair Moody, then one of Michigan's Senators, said to me once (this was before he recommended that the President make me chairman of the DNC) that it did not seem right for a woman to be the strongest person at the committee and the most influential at the White House. I told Blair he should be ashamed to voice such an opinion. I could have accomplished nothing without the president, the committee chairman and Don Dawson.

Epilogue

"Firsts for Women" seem as worthy of consideration by present-day men and women as they are memories worth treasuring to my generation. Therefore, I close this book of memoirs with "Women Firsts" under the Roosevelt and Truman administrations and with notes on later Presidential appointments of women.

ADMINISTRATION OF FRANKLIN D. ROOSEVELT 1933–1945

Member of Cabinet, Secretary of Labor, Frances Perkins
U.S. Minister to Denmark, Ruth Bryan Owen
U.S. Minister to Norway, Mrs. J. Borden Harriman
Director of U.S. Mint, Nellie Tayloe Ross
Assistant Secretary of U.S. Treasury, Josephine Roche
Assistant U.S. Treasurer, Mrs. Blair Banister
U.S. Circuit Court of Appeals judge, Florence Allen
Member of Social Security Board, Mary W. Dewson
Chairman, Consumer's Advisory Board, NRA, Emily Newell Blair
Only woman member of National Defense Advisory Commission,
    first defense agency set up by the President in 1940, Harriet Elliot
Judge of Circuit Court, Hawaii, Carrick M. Buck

271

Member of U.S. Employees' Compensation Commission,
Mrs. Jewell W. Swofford

Chairman of the Women's Advisory Committee, War Manpower
Commission, Margaret Hickey

U.N. conference, served as delegate to Conference on Food and
Agriculture, Josephine Schain

U.S. delegation to U.N. Conference on Relief and Rehabilitation,
Mrs. Elizabeth Conkey and Mrs. Ellen Woodward

U.S. Delegate to Conference of Allied Ministers,
Dean C. Mildred Thompson

Member of U.S. delegation to U.N. Conference on International
Organization, Dr. Virginia C. Gildersleeve

ADMINISTRATION OF HARRY S. TRUMAN 1945–1953

U.S. representative to U.N. General Assembly, first and second
parts of first session, Mrs. Franklin D. Roosevelt

U.S. representative, U.N. Human Rights Commission, Economic
and Social Council, first six sessions, Mrs. Roosevelt

Municipal Court Judge, District of Columbia, Nadine Gallagher

Alternate U.S. representative to first session, second part, U.N.
General Assembly, Helen Gahagan Douglas

Representative on the Preparatory Commission of UNESCO, Dr.
Esther Caukin Brunauer

U.S. representative to U.N. Commission on Status of Women,
Judge Dorothy Kenyon

Member of Federal Communications Commission, Frieda Hennock

Member of War Claims Commission, Georgia L. Lusk

Treasurer of the U.S., Georgia Neese Clark (now Gray)

Judge, U.S. District Court of District of Columbia,
Burnita Shelton Matthews

U.S. Minister to Luxembourg, Perle Mesta

Ambassador to Denmark, Eugenie Anderson

Assistant Secretary of Defense, Anna M. Rosenberg

Member, International Development Board, Margaret Hickey

Member, Board of Foreign Scholarships, Department of State,
Dr. Margaret Clapp

Members, Civil Defense Advisory Council, Mary McLeod Bethune
and Dr. Lillian M. Gilbreth

Members, National Science Board, National Science Foundation,
Dr. Gerti Theresa Cori and Dr. Sophie D. Aberle
Member, Subversive Activities Control Board, Dr. Kathryn
McHale
Superintendent of the Mint of the United States, Gladys Morelock
Controller of Customs, Margaret Daly Campbell

Mrs. Owen was married to a Danish national, Bror Rohde, while
serving as minister, so she had to resign. Later President Truman
appointed her as an alternate to the U.N. General Assembly. President Truman appointed Miss Perkins to the U.S. Civil Service Commission and reappointed Mrs. Ross and Mrs. Banister.

President Eisenhower appointed a woman, Oveta Culp Hobby of
Texas (a Democrat until the general ran for office) to a Cabinet post,
Secretary of Health, Education and Welfare. Eisenhower appointed
Clare Boothe Luce Ambassador to Italy, and a career diplomat,
Frances Willis, Ambassador to Switzerland. He named Ivy Baker
Priest to succeed Georgia Clark as Treasurer of the United States
and Congresswoman Frances P. Bolton and Mary Pillsbury Lord to
the United Nations Assembly and the U.N. Human Rights Commission respectively. He also made quite a number of other women appointments to high-ranking positions in the federal government.

There is a long list of women appointees by President Kennedy,
but most were to commissions that met annually or were temporary.
He did make Esther Peterson Assistant Secretary of Labor and also
appointed her Executive Vice Chairman of the President's Commission on the Status of Women, which he established in December,
1961. Mrs. Roosevelt was the chairman of that commission. Kennedy was the first President to have a female physician. Dr. Janet
Travell, as the White House resident doctor. He sent Eugenie Anderson to represent him in Bulgaria and appointed women to most of
the posts to which President Truman had appointed "firsts."

President Johnson appointed many more women to office than any
previous President. After his death, in reply to my letter of condolence to Lady Bird, she wrote, "Lyndon was devoted to you, and I
am sure that his eagerness to open up more and better opportunities
for women was in large measure due to his admiration and respect
for you."

President Johnson's precedent-breaking appointments of women

included scientific and business fields. Among these firsts were Dr.
Mary I. Bunting to the Atomic Energy Commission; Mrs. Elizabeth
S. May to the Board of Directors of the Export-Import Bank; Mrs.
Virginia Mae Brown to the Interstate Commerce Commission; Mrs.
Dorothy Jacobson to be Assistant Secretary of Agriculture; and
Esther Peterson to be Special Assistant to the President for Con-
sumer Affairs as well as Assistant Secretary of Labor. President
Johnson also appointed four women ambassadors: Katherine Elkus
White to Denmark, Margaret Tibbits to Norway, Patricia Harris to
Luxembourg, and Eugenie Anderson to the United Nations.

President Ford was the first Republican President to recognize
women's worth and he has done extremely well in that line. With a
wife like Betty Ford, he could not be anything but keenly aware of
the power of women and their capabilities. President Ford appointed Carla Hills of California to his cabinet as Secretary of Housing
and Urban Development. He appointed quite a number of women,
including the chairman of the Republican National Committee,
Mary Louise Smith of Iowa. So, women are making progress although it is slow and not very satisfactory to those who feel that by
now a female's appointment or election to a responsible government
post should be a matter of course, not an extraordinary occurrence.

The leading Democratic feminists got assurances from Jimmy
Carter as Presidential nominee and President-elect that he would
appoint a woman to the Supreme Court, if a vacancy occurred, and
also to his Cabinet. He pledged that he would see that a feminist division at the Democratic National Committee will not be subservient
to the chairman and that the Women's Division will be adequately
financed and staffed to promote feminist objectives. He also agreed
with the goal of having State parties have an equal number of wom-
en delegates at the 1978 midterm conference as well as at the next
convention in 1980.

As of this writing (President-Elect Carter has just announced his
entire Cabinet and some "Little Cabinet" members) it seems that he
is living up to his promise to consider women for policy-making
posts and not just as window-dressing for his new administration. I
do not know Juanita Morris Kreps, the nominee for Secretary of
Commerce, but her background in economics and administration is
impressive. I have known Patricia Roberts Harris ever since she
started teaching law at Howard University. Although she has had no
specific training for the post which Carter has given her, the Secre-

tary of Housing and Urban Development, I do not doubt that she will be as successful in it as she has been in every other job she has undertaken.

Jimmy Carter has made no appointment that has given me more hope than that of Lucy Wilson Benson (formerly president of the National League of Women Voters) as Undersecretary of State for Security Assistance. One of her duties will be to set United States policy on overseas arms sales and to work on the nonproliferation of nuclear weapons. This post puts her in line to become the highest-ranking woman in Department of State history and to be one of the architects of a world of which most civilized people dream: one in which war will be outlawed.

President Carter's appointment of Margaret Constanza as an assistant in the White House is a record-breaking one which is long overdue. I had persuaded President Truman that a female assistant would be of great help in his administration, and he was agreeable to naming the one I had recommended, Catherine E. Falvey. She had been a major in the Women's Army Corps during World War II, and before entering the service had been a member of the Massachusetts State Legislature. She was an attorney, a brilliant speaker and a very attractive young woman—just the right sort of person in my judgment to assist the President in dealing with women's organizations. However, "the boys" vetoed the idea.

Ms. Constanza—Midge to everyone who knows her—was running for a seat in the Rochester, N.Y., City Council when Jimmy Carter met her and they became friends. As the highest vote-getter in the council she was entitled to be the mayor of the city but she agreed to become vice mayor instead so that a man could be mayor. She was one of Carter's most loyal and hardworking supporters during his long campaign for the Democratic Presidential nomination, so she was one of his first appointments to his White House staff.

Good luck to all the women who will be working with men to give us the sort of clean, open government President Carter has promised. I wish I were young enough to be one of them!

Edwards, I

ulling no